Ma Barker

Ma Barker

America's Most Wanted Mother

Howard Kazanjian and Chris Enss

TWODOT®

GUILFORD, CONNECTICUT
HELENA, MONTANA

A · TWODOT® · BOOK

An imprint and registered trademark of Rowman & Littlefield

Distributed by NATIONAL BOOK NETWORK

British Library Cataloguing-in-Publication Information available

Library of Congress Cataloging-in-Publication Data available

ISBN 978-0-7627-9631-1 (pbk.)
ISBN 978-1-4930-2586-2 (e-book)

∞™ The paper used in this publication meets the minimum requirements of American National Standard for Information Sciences—Permanence of Paper for Printed Library Materials, ANSI/NISO Z39.48-1992.

For Mr. Hoover & his G–Men

CONTENTS

Foreword

THE ONE-WAY STREET IS THE ONLY ROUTE THE GANGSTER TAKES, AS readers will be reminded in Howard Kazanjian and Chris Enss's compelling new book about one of the most notorious criminal families of the gangster era, the Barkers.

Ma Barker and her brood terrorized cities from Chicago to Reno, perpetrating crimes and running from the law until it all ended for them in a brutal gun battle at a two-story house in Ocklawaha, Florida. The Ma Barker house and the Albright family, of which I am a proud member, seem to have a mutual attraction for each other. This "attraction" started on January 16, 1935, when more than a dozen FBI agents descended on the quiet little town of Ocklawaha, Florida, on Lake Weir, hot on the trail of the Barker-Karpis Gang. My grandfather, then twenty-seven-year-old George J. Albright Sr., was getting his mail on the other side of Lake Weir, in the equally small town of Weirsdale. The post office was abuzz with word that "all hell was breaking loose" in Ocklawaha.

My grandfather, always the inquisitive one, immediately hopped in his car and made the five-mile drive from Weirsdale to Ocklawaha. Once there he found the roads blocked, so he parked and went on foot toward the middle of the town, to the Carson Bradford House, lying directly on the lake. The property was surrounded by FBI agents, so he and the other townspeople settled in behind ancient oak trees to watch the longest gun battle in FBI history! My granddad recalled many times that a spray of machine-gun bullets from the Barkers came his way; he was forced to jump behind an oak tree to avoid being hit, and in the process split his pants from top to bottom. Being the gentleman he was, he walked down to the local hardware store and bought a new pair of pants, then went back to continue watching the melee between the good guys and the bad guys!

Fast-forward to the early 1950s, when my father, George J. Albright Jr., was at the University of Florida. Dad had been three years old at the date of the gun battle. My father was quite involved in student politics and became friends with Betty Bradford, whose family owned the Ma Barker house, and her future husband, Morton Good. This friendship lasted for decades, with my father buying a lake house for our family in 1966 directly next door to the Ma Barker house.

I was ten years old at the time, and the Good family hired me to mow the grass and be the general caretaker for the Ma Barker house, as the family resided in Miami and generally came to the house only in the summer. It was a job I relished, as I thought the whole gun-battle thing was totally cool (and I enjoyed making some spending money).

Fast-forward again to 2016, when my dad is now eighty-four, and I just turned sixty. Dad and I, along with the current family owners of the house and their representative, Carson Good, with whom I grew up, have been working to preserve the property and place it into public hands. In 2015 the FBI visited the house several times. Carson, Dad, and I were there in September of last year, when an FBI agent walked into the house for the very first time since 1935!

As of this date there is no firm plan in place to transfer the property into public hands. However, I am pleased to report that the people who own the house are very committed to historic preservation, and we feel certain the Ma Barker house will be saved for future generations to visit and enjoy.

In the meantime Kazanjian and Enss's engrossing book about Ma and her boys will more than suffice. Step back in time to an era of roadsters and revolvers, of back-alley boarding houses, Model Ts, and Prohibition, and read how far we've come in both crime and punishment.

—*GEORGE J. ALBRIGHT III, ESQ.*
FORMER REPRESENTATIVE IN THE
HOUSE OF REPRESENTATIVES
OF THE STATE OF FLORIDA

ACKNOWLEDGMENTS

THE PREPARATION OF THIS BOOK HAS INCURRED MANY DEBTS TO historical society members, librarians, and archivists. The following organizations and individuals were very helpful at the onset of this work and provided valuable information and expertise until its completion.

Steve Weldon, Jasper County Archivist at the Jasper County Records Center in Carthage, Missouri

Jenny McElroy, Reference Librarian at the Minnesota Historical Society in St. Paul, Minnesota

Ian Swart, Archivist and Curator of Collections at the Tulsa Historical Society and Museum in Tulsa, Oklahoma

Stephanie Sneed, Office Manager at the Sedalia Public Library in Sedalia, Missouri

Liz Moore, Archivist at the Nevada State Library and Archives in Carson City, Nevada

Barry Williams, Fact Check Editor in Phoenix, Arizona

The archivists at the Lansing State Prison in Lansing, Kansas, and the Leavenworth Federal Prison in Leavenworth, Kansas

George Albright, Former Member of the House of Representatives and Current Tax Collector and Barker Family Historian in Marion County, Florida

Erin Turner, Editorial Director at TwoDot Books in Helena, Montana, and the talented, hard-working individuals at Rowman & Littlefield in Guilford, Connecticut

To all of you, a grateful thank you.

INTRODUCTION

IN A TIME WHEN NOTORIOUS DEPRESSION-ERA CRIMINALS WERE terrorizing the country, the Barker-Karpis Gang stole more money than mobsters John Dillinger, Vern Miller, and Bonnie and Clyde combined. Five of the most wanted thieves, murderers, and kidnappers by the Federal Bureau of Investigation (FBI) in the 1930s were from the same family. Authorities believed the woman behind the band of violent hoodlums that ravaged the Midwest was their mother, Kate "Ma" Barker.

Ma Barker is unique in criminal history. Although she was involved in numerous illegal activities for more than twenty years, she was never arrested, fingerprinted, or photographed perpetrating a crime. There was never any physical evidence linking her directly to a specific crime. Yet Ma controlled two dozen gang members who jumped at her behest. FBI director J. Edgar Hoover called her a "domineering, clever woman who coldly and methodically planned the abduction of two of the nation's most wealthy men."

Ma's misdeeds were well plotted, schemed, and equipped. "The most important part of a job is done weeks ahead," she is rumored to have told her boys. She is remembered early on as a woman who took her four sons, Herman, Lloyd, Arthur, and Fred, to church every Sunday and to every revival meeting that came along. She was also known as a woman who never admitted her sons were capable of wrongdoing. She ruled the family roost, defending her brood against irate neighbors whose windows had been shattered by the boys and later against the police when the boys began their lives of crime in earnest. At a young age they were involved in everything from petty theft to murder.

Ma Barker, in light of later developments, was and is thought by law enforcement officers not only to have condoned but to have encouraged her boys' criminal activity. FBI records indicate that she conducted what amounted to an academy of crime, not only spurring

Herman, Lloyd, Arthur, and Fred on but proselytizing other boys, one of whom was a former Topeka marbles champion, Alvin Karpis.

The Barker-Karpis organization was tied to not only a seemingly endless string of bank robberies but also the robberies of jewelry stores and the theft of automobiles and business payrolls.

Herman Barker never made the big leagues of crime, nor did Lloyd. Herman was slain in an encounter with Wichita police officers, and Lloyd drew a long prison term for robbing the US mails. Fred and Arthur Barker did make the top criminal echelon, along with their mother, who once told a police chief, "All these boys would be good if you cops would just let them alone."

The heat generated by the kidnapping of bank president Edward Bremer—which resulted in $200,000 in ransom being paid after the wealthy man was released on January 7, 1934—chased the Barkers, or what was left of them, into hiding. Those who stayed in the Chicago area adopted easy disguises. Alvin Karpis and Fred Barker felt it necessary to take more drastic measures as they were too well known to the FBI. In mid-March 1934 Karpis—nicknamed "Old Creepy" because of his expressionless eyes—and Fred Barker went to the secluded office of Doctor Joseph Moran to have their fingerprints altered and faces changed.

Doctor Moran had a respectable practice until he started drinking heavily, became an abortionist, and was eventually sent to the Joliet prison. When paroled, Moran was hired as a physician for the Chicago Chauffeurs, Teamsters and Helpers Union and set up practice in a hotel, where he led a double life, treating gangsters as well as ordinary patients.

The night he operated on Alvin and Fred he was a physical ruin. His fumbling fingers did little more than butcher his two patients, who were injected with morphine and sent off to recuperate.

Ma Barker gave them medical attention. Though Alvin was stoical, Fred often screamed from the pain and had to be restrained forcefully. In addition to nursing duties, Ma was completing arrangements with gangster Adelard Cunin, a survivor of the North Side mob in Chicago, to launder the $100,000 the Barker-Karpis Gang received as a ransom for kidnapping William J. Hamm Jr., the president of Hamm's Brewery in St. Paul, Minnesota. Adelard had agreed to handle the ransom money from the Bremer kidnapping job as well.

The Chicago branch of the FBI was made the busiest field office in FBI history by the depredations of numerous well-known gangs, the perpetrators of the Kansas City massacre, and the normal flow of investigations. Melvin Purvis, the special agent in charge, was the nominal chief. However, that spring of 1934 the office on the nineteenth floor of the Bangers Building was also the headquarters of a special squad that the director of the FBI, J. Edgar Hoover, supervised personally.

Hoover's dogged concentration on Midwest crime prompted Ma Barker to advise her sons and their outlaw companions to leave the city. She decided it was too dangerous for any member of the Barker-Karpis Gang, disguised or not, to remain in Chicago. Most of the gang scattered. By January 1935 FBI agents had disposed of Pretty Boy Floyd and John Dillinger's gangs. Ma's son Arthur had also been seized by authorities.

A postmark on a postcard is said to have been the tip-off to where Ma and Fred were hiding. It was found at the time Arthur Barker fell into the hands of the law. Arthur's only remark was, "This is a helluva time to be caught without a gun." Arthur was sentenced to Alcatraz and was killed four years later in a desperate bid to escape from prison.

It was shortly after dawn on January 16, 1935, when more than a dozen FBI agents converged on Ocklawaha, Florida, and surrounded a two-story vacation home where Ma and Fred were hiding. The feds ordered the home's occupants—known to neighbors as the Blackburns—to surrender. Soon gunfire rang out from the house, and the agents returned it.

The machine-gun blasts lasted more than four hours. When it was over, FBI agents had pumped nearly two thousand bullets into the house, and the mother and son inside the dwelling were dead.

The Barker-Karpis Gang is credited with killing more than ten people and with the theft of more than $3 million. Less than half the money the outlaws took was ever recovered. Convicted felons like Alvin Karpis insisted that Ma Barker never participated in or planned any of the group's illegal undertakings. "She could barely organize breakfast," he joked in his autobiography. The government disagreed with his characterization of the matriarch of the gang. Ma Barker used more than five aliases during the time of the mob's reign. She had storage units in Chicago and Minnesota where she kept many household items, jewels, and furs her boys had stolen and given to her. At best she was an accessory after the fact and guilty of harboring fugitives. Ma Barker prospered as a result of the violence her boys wrought on the public.

The Barker-Karpis Gang was the last of the deadly gangster era. They represent a chilling testament to unbridled juvenile delinquency. Ma Barker let her sons get away with murder. In fact her boys counted on her to see them through whatever ruthless act they executed—proving that even murderous gangsters need their mother.

CHAPTER ONE

Brains of the Operation

It was a raw, gusty day in mid-January 1934 when bank president Edward G. Bremer dropped off his nine-year-old daughter, Betty, at Summit School in St. Paul, Minnesota. Parents and children dressed in heavy overcoats and wearing woolen hats hurried across the street and passed in front of Edward's black Lincoln sedan on their way to the building. A light snow began to fall as he pulled away from the elementary school and headed toward his office. Edward was the president of the Commercial State Bank and traveled the same route to work every day. Each morning he waved good-bye to his little girl at 8:25 and proceeded to his job. He traveled along Lexington Avenue for a half hour, stopping at all the traffic signs along the way.[1]

The car Edward drove was comfortable and warm, and cheerful music spilled from the radio as he contemplated the paperwork waiting for him on his desk. He cast a glance in his rearview mirror every so often but noticed nothing out of the ordinary. It wasn't until Edward stopped at a stop sign and Alvin Karpis, a tall, slim man in a blue shirt streaked with mud, hurried to the driver's side window holding a gun that he considered anything was wrong. Edward was stunned and didn't move as the armed man flung the driver's side door open and shoved the weapon into his side. "Move over or I'll kill you," Alvin barked at him.[2]

Before Edward had a chance to comply, the passenger's side door of his car was jerked open, and Arthur "Doc" Barker leaned inside the vehicle. Arthur struck Edward on the head several times with the butt

Scene of the Bremer kidnapping, Lexington and Goodrich, St. Paul, Minnesota
COURTESY OF THE MINNESOTA HISTORICAL SOCIETY

end of a .45 caliber automatic revolver. Blood from the gash sprayed the dashboard. Edward slumped in his seat, unconscious, and Alvin pushed him onto the floor. Arthur jumped inside the car and closed the passenger's side door.[3]

Drivers honked at the thugs as they sped by the action. They were unaware that anything criminal was going on, simply annoyed that the stopped vehicle was interfering with the morning commute. Arthur quickly shoved a pair of goggles on Edward's face and secured them to his head with adhesive tape. The tape covered every part of the goggles, prohibiting Edward from seeing at all. A gag was shoved in his mouth and secured in place with a piece of rope. Arthur jumped out of the vehicle and hurried to the car stopped directly behind the action. Alvin slid into the driver's seat and put the car in gear. Both cars hurried away from the scene.[4]

Alvin smiled to himself as he eyed the stupefied victim lying on the frontseat floorboard. He quickly placed Edward's hat on his head, removed a newspaper clipping from his suit pocket, and tossed it on the seat beside him. A photograph of Edward was front and center. The story under the picture noted that "New Bank President Edward George Bremer is a member of the Bremer family and one of the wealthiest and most prominent families in St. Paul. He is the son of Adolf [*sic*] Bremer, part owner of the Schmidt Beer Brewing

Company, and the nephew of Otto Bremer, Chairman of the American National Bank. Edward Bremer is married and has one daughter."[5]

Fred Barker, an impetuous, quick-tempered brute, drove the vehicle following the Lincoln sedan. His brother, Arthur, sat beside him in the passenger's seat. Arthur's hands and the butt end of the gun he was carrying were dotted with blood from Edward Bremer's head. The beating he'd given the kidnapped victim was indicative of the treatment most received from Arthur. His partners in crime considered him to be exceptionally ruthless.[6]

Edward George Bremer COURTESY OF THE MINNESOTA HISTORICAL SOCIETY

Trailing close behind the Barker brothers in a stolen Buick were Harry Campbell and William Weaver. Both men were career criminals, bootleggers, and ex–car thieves. Their car was parked across the intersection of Goodrich and Lexington when Edward Bremer was snatched. They took their cue from Alvin, the gunman driving Edward's vehicle. Alvin had coal-black hair and a sinister look that had earned him the name "Creepy."[7] He was initially against the idea of kidnapping Edward. He preferred robbing banks. Alvin believed the chance of getting caught wasn't as great when robbing a bank. Few in the gang he ran with felt the same way. Since the kidnapping of millionaire aviator Charles Lindbergh's infant son in 1932, abduction of the wealthy had increased. The culprits in that incident made off with $50,000, and more than half of the money was never recovered. Bruno Richard Hauptmann, a thirty-five-year-old carpenter, was arrested for the kidnapping in 1934. The Lindbergh baby was discovered dead six weeks after he was taken from his nursery.[8] The risks were substantial in a kidnapping, but like some of those who belonged to the notorious Barker-Karpis Gang, lawbreakers considered the rewards to outweigh the dangers. If successful, the band of thieves would collect a $200,000 ransom for Edward.[9]

The line of three cars proceeded out of town without incident and assembled at a prearranged location in the country, twenty minutes south of St. Paul. Arthur jerked Edward out of the vehicle and slammed the six-foot three-inch, two-hundred-pound man against the hood of the sedan. According to gangster Alvin Karpis, "Bremer was bleeding like a stuck pig where Arthur had slugged him when we grabbed him." The culprits needed Edward to sign three ransom notes addressed to his father. His blindfold was partially removed and a pen shoved into his hand. Edward objected at first, but Arthur managed to persuade him to scrawl his signature at the bottom of the typed message. Once the deed was done and the blindfold secured again, Edward was forced into Fred's car. Arthur rapped the victim on the head again in an effort to get him to resume his position on the floor of the frontseat. Edward complied without saying a word. The kidnappers piled into their two vehicles and drove away from the scene, leaving Edward's car behind.[10]

According to the January 19, 1934, edition of the *Albert Lea Evening Tribune*, "Bloodstains on both front and rear seats of Edward Bremer's automobile inspired fear for the safety of the thirty-seven-year-old bank president held for ransom by kidnappers who have threatened to kill him." Edward's car was found by police shortly after 10:00 on the morning he was kidnapped. The authorities told the press that it was obvious from the amount of blood found in and on the vehicle that he was seriously wounded. "Meanwhile, the kidnappers were reported to have made no effort to communicate with the family," the *Albert Lea Evening Tribune* article continued. "A shroud of secrecy has hedged the movement of friends and relatives to bring about the release of Edward G. Bremer. It is known only that members of his family are eager to establish contact with the kidnappers, are willing to pay the ransom demanded, and are desirous of acting independently of the police, lest harm befall the captive man.

"It was known that they [the Bremer family] had taken the first step toward achieving a contact with the abductors, by following the demands of the kidnappers as outlined in the note that informed them of the kidnapping of young Bremer. That step consisted of a two-line advertisement placed in the personal column of the Thursday morning edition of the *Minneapolis Tribune*. It read tersely, 'We are ready.' It was signed 'Alice.' The 'Alice' of the signature is believed to be Walter Magee, St. Paul contractor and friend of the Bremer family, who first received news from the kidnappers that Edward Bremer had been abducted. Adolf [*sic*] Bremer, father of the kidnapped youth, urged that authorities step aside, at least for the time being. 'Wait,' Mr. Bremer beseeched. 'Don't make a move that will endanger Eddie's safety.'"[11]

Edward Bremer was transported to a hideout in Bensenville, Illinois. The room where the banker was stored was unpretentious. The furnishings consisted of a bed and a cane-backed chair. The windows were boarded up. A single lightbulb hung down from a ceiling stained by an overabundance of rain and snow. Edward was tied to the chair with a thick rope. The kidnappers had bandaged his head but had done little else to provide for his care.[12]

"He was a pain in the ass," Alvin offered in his autobiography. "We no sooner stopped him from bleeding than he started demanding a drink," he recalled. "I didn't have any booze for him. I got him coffee. He asked how much ransom we wanted. I told him $200 thousand and he let out a yell. 'You're crazy,' he said. 'My father wouldn't pay that much for me.'"[13]

Edward struggled against anyone who tried to take any of his personal belongings from him. He wore a gold watch studded with rubies he insisted was given to him as a gift from his mother. The keepsake was something he didn't want to part with, and he repeatedly asked his captors to leave it alone. He made a similar request about an item in his wallet. It was a train receipt that indicated two people had occupied a drawing room on a recent trip from St. Paul to Chicago. Edward didn't want the receipt used as a way to identify him. His wife had thought he'd made the trip alone. "Keeping that kind of confidence is going to cost extra," Alvin informed him. "It won't do you any good," the victim responded.[14]

Edward's account of the events noted in the FBI files report that he pressed the men holding him hostage to tell him who was in charge of their operation. The Barker-Karpis Gang had as many as twenty-eight individuals working for them at one time or another since their humble beginnings in southeast Missouri in the mid-1920s. There were nine involved with the Bremer kidnapping, and that didn't include the women who kept company with the outlaws and delivered the occasional message from one criminal in the organization to another.[15]

Harry Sawyer and Fred Goetz, aka "Shotgun" George Ziegler, were the first to suggest Edward as the target. Both men had participated in armed robberies and murders for hire with underworld figures in Chicago. Harry disliked bankers. He believed they were all thieves. After spending time at a St. Paul bowling alley with Ziegler, Harry suggested that banker Edward Bremer be taken and held for ransom. He had read that Edward was a member of one of the wealthiest families in the country. He had also read that Edward's father had contributed more than $350,000 to Franklin Delano Roosevelt's presidential campaign in 1932. In Harry's estimation Edward was a big name, and kidnapping Edward would yield a small fortune. Ziegler didn't disagree.[16]

Arthur Barker's good friend Volney Everett "Curly" Davis thought the idea was sound. Volney was a convicted bank robber and an associate of John Dillinger. He and Arthur had worked together often, and he seldom questioned the course the Barker-Karpis Gang wanted to travel. Volney's girlfriend, Edna Murray, explained in an article she penned for *Startling Detective Adventures* magazine in October 1936 that her paramour, as well as the other men in the group, "always did as ringleader Ma Barker told them to."

According to author and reporter Courtney Ryley Cooper, Arizona (also known as Kate) "Ma" Barker was a strange figure of the underworld. "Short, hard-featured, her red hair always carefully groomed, her brown eyes brilliant and remorseless, yet withal queerly able to present the appearance of a mild, even tempered lady. This woman had made a weird success of rearing criminal spawn."[17] Numerous historical records, including files kept by the FBI and its director J. Edgar Hoover, agree that Ma was the brains of the outfit. Her violent sons and their equally ruthless associates, most notably Alvin Karpis, made their opinions known, but Ma had the final say.[18] "She had a vision," Courtney Ryley Cooper wrote of the femme fatale in 1936. "She wanted more for her boys than a string of petty crimes to call their own where danger was assured and financial independence was always in question."[19]

When the suggestion to kidnap Edward Bremer was presented to Ma, she ordered her crew to meet and discuss the proposal. In the summer of 1933, the Barker-Karpis Gang had kidnapped William Hamm Jr., the president of Hamm's Brewing Company. The caper was successful, yielding the gang $100,000 in cash for the return of the millionaire. News of the kidnapping was reported throughout the country. "Money or death was the ultimatum laid down by the culprits that absconded with Hamm's Brewing Company executive," the June 17, 1933, edition of the *Albert Lea Evening Tribune* read.

William had been captive near the same location in Bensenville, Illinois, where Edward Bremer was secured away. The police had withdrawn from the case at the request of the family. They were frightened of what might happen to William if law enforcement interfered. The ransom note from the abductors warned the Hamms that William would be shot and killed if the police were allowed any involvement. A note sent to William's father instructed him to deliver the ransom money in "$5, $10, and $20 bills." Payment of the ransom for the release of William, the kidnappers directed, was to be made using one of the company's beer trucks. Not only did the Barker-Karpis Gang get the full amount they were asking in ransom, but when the authorities did begin investigating the kidnapping, a rival gang was arrested for the crime.[20]

"J. Edgar Hoover himself announced from Washington that his men had put together a solid case against the Touhy gang," Alvin

Karpis wrote in his memoirs. "The scientific evidence left no doubt at all," Hoover said, "that the Touhys were behind the kidnapping of William Hamm."[21]

The ease with which the Barker-Karpis Gang was able to get away with taking William and collecting the ransom was an argument for kidnapping Edward Bremer. In late December 1933 Ma's boys convened at William Weaver's apartment in St. Paul to talk through the details of the abduction. Who would trail Edward to learn about his habits, routine, friends, and work associates; who would write the ransom notes; who would deliver those notes to what contact; and when the job would be done were all determined. With the exception of Arthur, who Ma suggested might have been a little too rough with the victim, everyone performed his duties as planned.[22]

When the police found Edward's abandoned vehicle with bloodstains on the dash, seats, and floor, it prompted the press, also at the scene, to conclude that Edward had been murdered. On the off chance Edward was buried in the area, a variety of agencies in the city, including the American Legion, the Boy Scouts, and fire department, began digging in the location where Edward's car had been found.[23]

In addition to the first ransom note, delivered to Edward's friend contractor Walter Magee on January 17 at 10:40 in the morning, there were a number of bogus notes sent to the Bremer family from opportunists claiming to be in on the kidnapping. The federal authorities had rendezvoused in St. Paul and were reporting information of evidence and notes to Hoover in Washington, including a message mailed to the postmaster in Minneapolis, Minnesota. "Was by accident [he] was bumped off. Body near Anoka, Minnesota. Will not be found until after snow goes. Contact off. Please forgive us. All a mistake by one of our gang [sp] been drunk. Please tell Walter Magee—St. Paul. One of the gang." The fake information in the note sent a flood of officers to Anoka, Minnesota, to dig around for Edward.[24]

According to FBI File No. 7-30, several calls were made to the Federal Bureau of Investigation from unnamed individuals who suggested that Edward Bremer had not really been kidnapped but was merely hiding until a personal matter was settled. The authorities explored the possibility that Edward could be faking his disappearance and looked into his finances for evidence of misconduct or hardship. They discovered nothing out of the ordinary.[25]

On January 20, 1934, two members of the Barker-Karpis Gang placed a note into a bottle and tossed it through the plateglass door of the home of Dr. H. T. Nipper in St. Paul at 6:00 in the morning. Dr. Nipper was a longtime friend of the Bremers as well as the family physician. It was determined by the police that the bottle was thrown into the doctor's home as a sign that he had been selected as a second contact man by the kidnappers. On January 22, 1934, two sealed envelopes were slid under Dr. Nipper's front door. One envelope was addressed to Mrs. Edward Bremer and the other to Walter Magee.[26] The note read as follows:

> *You are hearby declared in on a very desperate undertaking. Don't try to cross us. Your future and E's are the important issue. Follow these instructions to the letter. Police have never helped in such a spot and won't this time either. You better take care of the payoff first and let them do the detecting later. Because the police usually butt in, your friend isn't none too comfortable now, so don't delay the payment. Place the money in two, large suit box cartons big enough to hold the full amount and tie with heavy cord. No contact will be made until you notify us that you are ready to pay as we direct.[27]*
>
> *You place an ad in the Minneapolis Tribune as soon as you have the money ready. Under the personal column (We are ready, Alice). You will then receive your final instructions. Be prepared to leave at a minute's notice to make the payoff. Don't attempt to stall or outsmart us. Don't try to bargain. Don't plead poverty. We know how much they have in their banks. Don't try to communicate with us. We'll do the directing. Threats aren't necessary. You just do your part, we guarantee to do ours.[28]*

The line in the ransom note that read "your friend isn't none too comfortable now" proved to be an understatement. Edward was made to write a portion of the ransom notes, but before his arms were untied so he could pen the instructions, Arthur smashed his fist into Edward's face and gut. He wanted to make sure he had the victim's attention. Arthur shoved a pen into Edward's hand, and he slowly but surely copied down the message laid out before him. "Mr. Chas. Magee, I have named you as a payoff man," Edward scrawled on the paper. "You are responsible for my safety. I am responsible for the full amount of the money."[29]

Immediately after Edward signed his name at the bottom of the note, Arthur yanked the pen from him and shoved him back in the seat. Alvin fashioned a rope around Edward's arms, pulling them tightly as he went. "No matter what we did . . . Bremer hardly ever let up," Alvin recalled in his memoirs. "At one point he told me we had kidnapped the wrong man. He said that he knew a man in St. Paul who had put aside a quarter of a million dollars in a safety deposit box to be used by the guy's wife in cash he should ever be kidnapped. Bremer told me that we should have grabbed that guy instead."[30]

According to Alvin, Edward made several statements that led him and Arthur to believe that not all of the banker's business dealings had exclusively been with reputable clientele. He wanted the gang to promise to contact him after his father had paid the ransom so they could collaborate on some "lucrative deals." He told Arthur and Alvin that he was a good friend of Harry Sawyer. The information took the men aback. Harry Sawyer was a member of the gang who ran an underworld tavern in St. Paul. His name hadn't been mentioned in full by the kidnappers. Ultimately, Edward's comment was dismissed as being merely talk. The situation was remedied by placing another gag in his bloody mouth.[31]

On one of the notes, the authorities matched a pair of fingerprints to Edward Bremer. Edward's fingerprints had been obtained from the military; he had served in the navy for a time. There were no sets of prints on the message belonging to anyone connected with

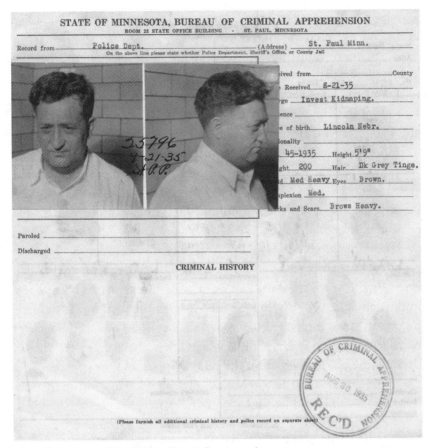

STATE OF MINNESOTA, BUREAU OF CRIMINAL APPREHENSION
ROOM 22 STATE OFFICE BUILDING - ST. PAUL, MINNESOTA

Record from ____ Police Dept. ____ (Address) ____ St. Paul Minn.
On the above line please state whether Police Department, Sheriff's Office, or County Jail

........ived from_____County

.... Received __8-21-35__

.......ge __Invest Kidnaping.__

.....ence _____

.....e of birth __Lincoln Nebr.__

....ionality _____

........45-1935___Height_5'9"

....ght___200___Hair___Dk Grey Tinge.

....d Med Heavy Eyes___Brown.

....plexion _Med.

....ks and Scars___Brows Heavy.

Paroled _____

Discharged _____

CRIMINAL HISTORY

(Please furnish all additional criminal history and police record on separate sheet)

Harry Sawyer, one of the Barker-Karpis Gang members COURTESY OF THE MINNESOTA
HISTORICAL SOCIETY

any previous crimes. The FBI and law enforcement in St. Paul were working around the clock to determine who had kidnapped Edward. Reporters at the *Washington Post* and the *New York Times* pressed authorities for answers, or at the very least speculation, on who they believed was responsible.[32] Outlaw Verne Sankey's name was mentioned in relation to the crime. Sankey had been a suspect in the Lindbergh baby kidnapping and had perpetrated the same type of crime in 1932 when he took St. Paul business executive Haskell Bohn's son and held him for ransom. Sankey, along with his partner Gordon Alcorn and their gang, collected $22,000, and Sankey and Alcorn became two of the most wanted men in America.[33]

There were numerous similarities between the Edward Bremer kidnapping and that of Haskell Bohn's son, from the method used to apprehend the victim to the various contacts used to deliver the ransom notes. The focus of the police and FBI agents was on Sankey and Alcorn, and the press was quick to make that information public as well. News about where and to whom ransom notes were sent was announced. The authorities vehemently denied the reports were accurate. Having been told by Ma not to involve the "coppers," the police were quick to dismiss any notion that they were conspiring with the ransom notes' contacts.[34]

The January 23, 1934, edition of the *Harrisonburg Daily News* reported that authorities confirmed the Department of Justice had cast a dragnet over the Twin Cities to bring in underworld characters in the hope that they would have information about Edward's kidnapping, but they emphatically denied the idea that two ransom notes had been delivered to Dr. Nipper. When asked about the notes thrown through the glass on his front door, Dr. Nipper told the *Harrisonburg Daily News* that "a bottle was hurled through the glass, but there were not notes in it nor did he find any on the porch."

Adolph Bremer, Edward's father, was worried about the news coverage the kidnapping was getting and the scores of detectives that were working on the case. He appealed to his good friend President Franklin Roosevelt to intercede and order law enforcement agencies to cease their efforts to free his son. Adolph believed his son would not be returned alive if the actions of the police continued. "I am sorry the impression has been spread that information has been given to the police," Adolph announced from his home and which was later publicized in the January 23, 1934, edition of the St. Paul *Pioneer Press*. "Whatever information has been passed out has been given against my will and has created a false impression. Chief of Police Thomas Dahill has been fine in offering every help he can give us, and we all appreciate it, but we do not want the police, or the state, or federal authorities to do anything about it now. We want to get Eddie back home safe."[35]

On February 6, 1934, twenty-one days after Edward Bremer had been kidnapped, $200,000 in ransom money was delivered to a designated spot in Farmington, Minnesota. The following evening Edward was released. The banker was driven to Rochester, Minnesota, and instructed to get out of the car in the middle of the street and to stand with his back toward the direction in which the vehicle was headed. According to the FBI files, he was then told to count slowly to fifteen, after which the goggles and tape over his eyes could be removed.[36] The FBI report continued:

After Mr. Bremer had returned safely to his home, Special Agents were free to pursue the investigation of the kidnapping vigorously. Mr. Bremer, although having been injured at the time he was kidnapped and had been blindfolded with taped goggles, was able to hear various sounds en route to the hideout where he was held. The gang did not keep him blindfolded at all times at the hideout and he was able to observe things which were later to be of assistance in identifying the place where he was held captive. Mr. Bremer was able to furnish the investigators with information that, upon his arrival at the place where he was held, he heard two dogs barking, and these dogs appeared to be very close to the house, and they barked on frequent occasions. Mr. Bremer also heard a group of children playing in close proximity from four to eight years of age. Mr. Bremer also heard children passing through the area adjoining the hideout house. After the first few days of Mr. Bremer's confinement, the goggles which had been placed over his eyes at the time of his abduction were removed and he was permitted to sit in his room without any obstruction over his face and this afforded him an opportunity to observe the furnishings of the bedroom in which he was held. He made a mental picture of the wallpaper and was able to describe it in such detail that similar wallpaper was traced by Special Agents and found to have been sold by a large mail-order house. A specimen of this wallpaper was obtained, and Mr. Bremer was able to positively identify it as being similar to that which was on the walls in the bedroom.

Although blindfolded, Mr. Bremer was able to furnish certain information concerning the toilet room in which he was taken from time to time. He learned that the lever for flushing the toilet consisted of what appeared to be a metal screw. The enamel which had covered the screw had either been removed or broken. He observed a crack in the wall of the bedroom. Overhead Mr. Bremer heard a small child crying and estimated the age of the child to be about one year, and he also heard another child approximately four years of age playing on the floor above him. Mr. Bremer was convinced that there was a coal stove adjacent to the room in which he was held, as he heard sounds indicating that coal was being shoveled from a bin into a scuttle and the sound indicated that the coal was being kept in a position near the kitchen. Mr. Bremer was further able to describe the sounds of traffic, which traffic apparently was in close proximity to the hide-out house. He could hear the brakes being applied to either buses or trucks, which gave him the impression that he was near a stop sign on a main highway. Sounds of trains could also be heard, Mr. Bremer being of the opinion that these trains were probably inter-urban in character as they passed most frequently in the mornings and in the afternoons.

The men who held him captive spoke with various accents: French, German, Italian. At one point he heard the voice of an older woman praising the criminals holding him hostage saying, "Now, you're thinking, boys. Now you're thinking." Mr. Bremer assessed it was the voice of Ma Barker.

Mr. Bremer was unable to state definitely the number of hours he was transported after being kidnapped at St. Paul, but after traveling several hours they arrived at the hideout and his abductors dressed his wounded head, which wounds had been inflicted upon him at the time he was kidnapped. Mr. Bremer was of the opinion that they traveled through a city of medium size en route to the hideout, inasmuch as he heard streetcars. Mr. Bremer also was able to furnish the Special Agents with information concerning his return trip to Rochester, Minnesota. He stated that upon leaving the hideout sometime during the morning of February 7, 1934, he was placed in what appeared to be a one-seated automobile by his abductors; that after riding a short distance he was transferred to another car and that this second car was a sedan. He was forced to enter the sedan and sit on the floor immediately behind the driver with his back against the left rear door. At this time his hand touched the butt of what appeared to be either a shotgun or rifle on the floor. He also was able to ascertain that there was a tin can immediately on his left side on which he could comfortably rest his left elbow; that this can appeared to be an ordinary five gallon tin can which contained gasoline, as he could smell the strong odor of the fuel.

Mr. Bremer estimated that after approximately one-half of the distance had been covered between the hideout house and Rochester, Minnesota, the car in which he was riding turned off from the paved road and after ten or fifteen minutes the car pulled to the side of the road and the two men who were in the frontseat of the car and the one in the rear seat guarding him got out and took out of the car at least two tin cans containing gasoline. He heard his abductors pour gasoline into the tank of the car in which he was riding, after which the journey was resumed. He recalled that his abductors at the time the tank of the automobile was refueled turned off the paved highway, because he heard gravel striking the windows of the car.[37]

Once Edward was home safely, the federal authorities wasted no time in pursuing the kidnappers. They used all the information provided by Edward to try to narrow down where he might have been held and the exact location of his release. While law enforcement was busy dissecting the crime and retracing the route Walter Magee used to deliver the ransom, Ma and her boys were waiting for the day when the money they'd acquired would be evenly distributed among them. Members of the Barker-Karpis Gang scattered once Edward was released. With the exception of Ma Barker and Shotgun George Ziegler, all were living in various apartments or rented houses in the Twin Cities. Ziegler lived outside the town of Wilmington, Illinois. Ma had a place on South Shore Drive in Chicago. Before anyone collected the ill-gotten gain, the gang all converged in the Chicago area.[38]

The ransom money the Barker-Karpis Gang had acquired was stashed at Mrs. Ziegler's uncle's home in Wilmington. Ma gave instructions to her cohorts to use their time wisely while waiting for the money to be divided. New license plates for the gang's automobiles needed to be secured, alibis needed to be refined, and new identities needed to be created. Not everyone was content to do the jobs they were given and keep quiet about their accomplishments. Ziegler was a man who liked to talk and at times said too much. He let it be known to his associates in Chicago that he might have been involved with the Bremer kidnapping. Ma sent a warning through Volney Davis for him to shut up, but Ziegler continued to babble.[39]

On March 20, 1934, Shotgun George Ziegler's voice was permanently silenced when he was shot and killed outside a restaurant called the Minerva near Cicero, Illinois. The May 8, 1938, edition of the *San Antonio Light* reported that Ziegler received a call at his apartment on the evening of March 20, 1934, and was summoned to the eatery. He arrived at the scene unaware there was anything wrong. He met friends at the location and was "loquacious as always," the article read. As he exited the building after visiting and having a bite to eat, he was gunned down.[40]

"There were four booming explosions from sawed-off shotguns," the *San Antonio Light* article noted. "Horribly mutilated, the bleeding form of Ziegler sank to the pavement." The bullet-punctured body of the criminal was found lying in a gutter. It wasn't until the morning of March 21, 1934, that his remains were identified by police.[41]

Federal authorities investigating the crime suspected the murder was committed by Arthur Barker at the behest of his mother. Alvin

Karpis wrote in his autobiography that he wasn't certain who killed Ziegler, but he believed it was a "syndicate job, a deliberate rubout to keep Ziegler from talking." When the FBI searched Ziegler's body, they found considerable evidence that he had been engaged in illegal activities. Among his possessions was money that was eventually linked to the Bremer kidnapping. Agents later surmised that Ziegler had taken some of the ransom money and stashed it at his place for himself before the funds were officially divided between the gangsters.[42]

After the assassination of Ziegler, Ma and the other members of the gang decided it was advisable to move the ransom money from its location in Wilmington, Illinois. On March 23, 1934, Ma Barker, Ziegler's widow, Irene Dorsey, and Volney Davis transferred the money to Fred's apartment. Shortly thereafter Ma began making plans for getting the money received from the Bremers to be replaced with cash from legitimate sources.[43]

Fred and Alvin had been of little use to Ma from mid-March to the time the money was moved. Both men had undergone painful operations on their fingers, and Alvin had plastic surgery. It was an unsuccessful attempt to alter their looks to keep from being recognized or identified. An ex-convict named Dr. Joseph P. Moran was in charge of the procedure, which involved looping elastic bands tightly around the gangsters' fingertips at the first joint and injecting cocaine into each of their fingers and thumbs. Using a scalpel, the doctor would then scrape the skin completely off the digits. The work Dr. Moran did to remove the scars on Alvin's face was equally as barbaric and unpleasant. In the end the extreme discomfort proved to be a waste of time and money. According to the FBI report dated November 19, 1936, Fred Barker was a "raving maniac" due to the pain.[44]

Dr. Moran performed other services for the gang, such as laundering some of the kidnap money through his Chicago practice. Dr. Moran suffered from the same problem of running his mouth that Ziegler had. He drank too much, which made him especially talkative. He bragged to a couple of prostitutes in his company that he was a big doctor from Chicago who could erase fingerprints and change

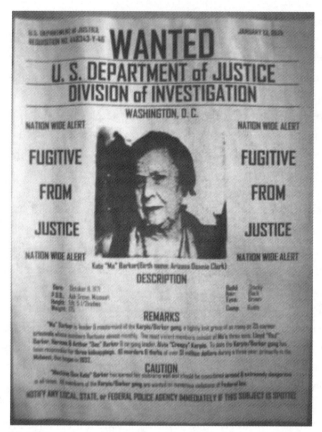

Ma Barker's wanted poster, issued by the Department of Justice

people's appearances. His actions weren't tolerated for long by the Barker-Karpis Gang. He was warned to be quiet, but he defied orders by stating, "I have you guys in the palm of my hand."[45]

By the summer of July 1934, Alvin and Arthur were tasked with handling the situation. "Doc and I shot the son-of-a-bitch," Alvin recalled years later. "Anybody who talks to whores is too dangerous to live. We dug a hole in Michigan and dropped him in and covered the hole with lye. I don't think anybody is ever going to come across Dr. Moran again."[46]

On February 8, 1934, the FBI found four flashlights equipped with red-film lenses where the ransom money for Edward Bremer was delivered. They traced the flashlights to a store in St. Paul, Minnesota, that dealt exclusively with the model and make of the item. An employee at the store identified a photograph of Alvin Karpis as having purchased the flashlights prior to the kidnapping of Bremer. Gasoline cans and a tin funnel found by a farmer near Portage, Wisconsin, on February 10, 1934, were examined for fingerprints. Edward remembers his kidnappers stopping somewhere to refuel when they escorted him to the spot where he was to be released. The fingerprints on the gas cans matched Arthur Barker's. From that moment, the hunt was on for Arthur Barker, Alvin Karpis, and anyone else in the Barker-Karpis Gang who had played a part in the Bremer kidnapping.[47]

The search for the guilty parties would lead authorities to the woman J. Edgar Hoover deemed the "brains of the gang's operations" and the "most dangerous woman in America." Ma Barker and her boys became the scourge of the police from coast to coast.[48]

CHAPTER TWO

Ruthless and Daring

KATE BARKER MARCHED HER FIFTEEN-YEAR-OLD SON, HERMAN, through the remains of a cornfield outside Webb City, Missouri. Using the collar of her boy's shirt as a lead, she steered him past bent and weathered stalks of corn. It was a hot, humid September afternoon, all white light and glare. Herman chanced a look back at his mother, hoping the scowl on her face had softened. Kate wore a gray sweater embellished with rhinestone buttons and a blue-and-white plaid rayon dress with a sashed belt and bow collar. Her hair was nicely coiffed with spit curls on each temple in the style of the times. Although she had been born and raised in the rural Ozark Mountains and married a miner from a nearby town, she was no house Frau. She carried her plump, five-foot four-inch frame with a confidence generally relegated to those with a wealthy, sophisticated background.[1]

Herman was dressed in jeans and an old shirt two sizes too big for him. He was barefoot and occasionally grimaced when his toe connected with a jagged rock on the ground. His mother was furious with him and disinterested in how uncomfortable their fast-paced walk made him. Herman had been caught with a few wallets he'd stolen from the deacons of the local Presbyterian church. The preacher had graciously contacted Kate about the matter after he had informed the police. Mother and son now had an appointment with the Jasper County judge, and Kate was determined not to be late. Herman stumbled a time or two, but his mother jerked the boy to his feet and urged him on.[2]

Webb City in 1910 was a rough and wild mining community with a population of more than eleven thousand. The majority of the people living there were excavators who worked in the numerous galena ore mining companies in the area. Galena is the chief ore of lead. Wages were low but steady. There was nothing opulent about the businesses and homes in Webb City. They were modest in design, dusty, and uninspired. Among the enterprises that flourished in town were the mercantile businesses, courthouse, and numerous taverns that lined the main thoroughfare. Railroad tracks cut through the center of town, and trains announced their passing with loud blasts from their horns.[3]

A train was making its presence known as Ma and Herman reached the courthouse. Without saying a word, she pulled open the door of the building and escorted her son inside. She led Herman to a pair of empty chairs in the courtroom, and the two sat down to wait for the judge.[4]

The March 29, 1936, edition of the *Kansas City Star* and the July 22, 1939, edition of the *Joplin Globe* reported that Ma vehemently defended her son to authorities. She insisted that all four of her boys were law abiding. Ma admitted they were "high-strung and mischievous" but not at all the renegades some people had made them out to be. In fact she believed her boys were persecuted by the police. Ma accused the authorities of targeting her children and setting them up to take the fall for every unfortunate incident that occurred. When it became clear that the court was unwilling to accept any responsibility regarding her children's misconduct, Kate changed her tone from accusatory to pitiful. She pleaded with the magistrate to spare her son from being arrested and to let her take Herman home and deal with the situation herself. Moved by her tears and dedication to her boy, the judge granted her request and let the mother and son go with a warning.

Years later FBI director J. Edgar Hoover reflected on Ma Barker's ability to convince judges in courts from Webb City, Missouri, to Tulsa, Oklahoma, to excuse her boys' criminal behaviors as tragic. He referred to it as a "lurid lesson" for American parents. "Were I to list what I believe to be one of the greatest present-day contributors to our growing crime annals," Hoover told reporters in the summer of 1935, "I am afraid that I should be forced to lay blame squarely at the door of parental overindulgence."[5]

Herman received a severe tongue-lashing from his mother on their way home. The cause of Kate's aggravation wasn't that her son had committed a crime but that he allowed himself to get caught. She reminded Herman that confession to anyone other than God was always a sign of weakness and then reiterated a lesson she had shared with her boys numerous times: Family kept their secrets and took whatever punishment was due them in silence.[6]

Arizona Donnie "Kate" Clark was born on October 8, 1873, in Greene County, Missouri, eighteen miles from Springfield. She was one of four children born to John and Emeline Clark, a Scotch Irish couple who worked a small farm and did odd jobs. Kate, a handle she selected on her own because she didn't care for the name Arizona, idolized her father. John died when she was seven, and her mother remarried shortly after his passing. Reuben J. Reynolds moved Emeline and her children to Tulsa, Oklahoma, and it was there that the couple had two children of their own. According to author and historian Ronald L. Trekell in a report titled *A History of the Tulsa Police Department*, Kate's stepfather served as a law enforcement officer on and off from 1906 to 1920.[7]

Historical records indicate that Kate did not get along well with Reuben. She was of the opinion that he favored the two children he had with her mother over the four Emeline had with John. The relationship became even more strained when Kate married George Elias Barker on September 14, 1892. Her mother and Reuben were concerned about the ten-year age difference between George and Kate. Kate didn't mind that he was older. She wanted more for herself than a life in rural Oklahoma and believed George had the potential to provide her with the start for which she hoped.[8]

George was a farm laborer from Lebanon, Missouri. He was short and had a dark complexion, a long face, and deep-set blue eyes. He also was shy, mild mannered, and honest. Kate's dominating personality overwhelmed him. Shortly after the two wed, Kate tried to persuade George that they should move to Kansas City, where the opportunity for him to find a job working in the corporate world was better. Kate discovered too late that he was an uneducated man and content to be so. The Barkers stayed in Aurora, Missouri, where George was employed planting and harvesting corn and beans. Kate grew tired of barely making ends meet and eventually approached her stepfather about loaning them money to improve their condition. Reuben turned her down. Kate was insulted and refused to ever speak to him again.[9]

Reluctantly, Kate resigned herself to a simple life of domesticity. She attended church on a regular basis and was seldom seen around town without a Bible and a hymnal in her hand. Behind closed doors she was preoccupied with newspaper and magazine articles about outlaws such as the Dalton Gang, three brothers and a handful of their friends who robbed banks. The gang was finally caught on October 5, 1892, and news of their violent end made headlines everywhere. The Daltons were from Jackson County, Missouri, not far from where Jesse James and his brother Frank, along with the Younger brothers, began their criminal pursuits. The Daltons and the James boys were raised by strong, defiant mothers who made sure they knew how to use a weapon and fight for what they wanted. The influence the women had on their families and the devotion their sons felt toward their mothers struck a chord with Kate. She aspired to have it in her own life.[10]

An article in the March 29, 1936, edition of the *Kansas City Star* described Kate's upbringing, subsequent marriage, and early life with George as "typical." "Her life had been that of an ordinary Missouri farm girl—church, Sunday school, picnics, hayrides, candy pulls, and a little red school house," the article read. "Somewhere she acquired a need for riches and personal power. She hoped to obtain gold and glory by way of her husband but eventually learned it could only be realized by her sons."

On October 30, 1894, Kate and George welcomed their first son, Herman, into the world. On March 16, 1896, a second son, Lloyd, was born. Their third son, Arthur, joined his brothers on June 4, 1899. A few months before Arthur was born, the Barkers managed to scrape enough money together to purchase a place of their own in Missouri. The home itself was nothing more than a dilapidated miner's shack. Kate disliked the tumbledown structure and expressed her unhappiness to George. He assured her that in time he could transform the sad homestead into a place of which she could be proud. In the meantime he planted a few crops to help feed his family. On December 12, 1903, the couple had their fourth son, Fred.[11]

Although George worked extra hours at the mine and on his small farm, he was barely able to provide for his wife and sons. Kate's disposition didn't improve. She pushed George to find a job that paid better, but he was not interested. When George wasn't working, he was spending time with his children. He taught his boys how to hunt and fish. All four Barker boys were exceptional shots, something of which both George and Kate were proud.[12]

Kate, or Ma, as she was now called, concentrated on being a good homemaker. She was known as an exceptional cook, and she made sure her sons knew how to cook as well. Any discipline the Barker boys needed was handled by Ma. George tried unsuccessfully to correct his four children when they did something wrong, but Ma always interceded. She would not allow him to touch the boys and loudly argued her point if George made an attempt to punish them. He eventually gave in to Ma's demand and left her solely in charge of that part of the boys' upbringing.[13]

Ma insisted the children attend church with her every Sunday. Fidgeting in their seats or refusing to sing along with the organist resulted in a smack on the back of the head. An article in the March 29, 1936, edition of the *Kansas City Star* described the scene this way:

She [Ma] attended church regularly dragging her brood after her. George, her husband, went as well. He was a mild, ineffective, quiet man who seemed somewhat bewildered by his domineering wife. This was especially true when he attempted to assume the guidance of the growing boys. There was a feline intensity about Kate's determination that no one but herself should be their mentor, and in her eyes they could do no wrong.

Ma Barker socialized with very few people. She was cordial when spoken to but rarely initiated a conversation. Neighbor and fellow churchgoer Gertrude Farmer was the only woman with whom she spent time. Gertrude and Ma were described by Webb City residents as odd and unapproachable. The two had a great deal in common: They were both poor, were roughly the same age, were unhappy in their marriages, and were mothers. Gertrude's husband, William, occasionally worked as a miner, but his main field of endeavor was crime. He was a con man who would trick people out of their money using a variety of nefarious tricks such as the coin-matching game. The coin-matching game involves two operators who cheat a victim during a game where coins are matched. One operator begins the game with the victim, and then the second joins in. When the second operator leaves for a brief moment, the first colludes with the victim to cheat the second operator. After rejoining the game the second operator, angry at losing, threatens to call the police. The first operator then convinces the victim to pitch in hush money, which the two operators later split. Not unlike Ma, Gertrude hoped her husband would aspire to do more with his life.[14]

The Farmers' son, Herbert, and the Barker boys were enamored with William. He shared stories with them about outlaws and their conquests. He was more than happy to teach the children the various con games he'd mastered. Ma and George Barker's time in Webb City was peppered with complaints from residents and authorities about their four sons. It seems the tales they heard at the feet of William Farmer about gun-wielding desperados had significant influence. Herman, Lloyd, Arthur, and Fred were frequently in trouble for vandalizing property, fighting, and petty pilfering. In a desperate attempt to get his family away from the location where they were in danger of being lost to lawless acts, George moved his wife and kids to Tulsa,

Oklahoma. It was 1910, and Tulsa was an oil boomtown and, for the most part, quite violent. The environment only served to fuel the Barker boys' illicit behaviors.[15]

The Barkers' new home was a two-room clapboard house near the Santa Fe railroad. The floor was composed of bare boards laid on the ground. The bathroom was a fly-infested lean-to behind the house. Broken glass covered the majority of the windows on the rundown structure, and there were no screens. Flies continually congregated in Ma's kitchen. The condition of the home, the town to which George had transplanted his family, and his inability to improve their circumstances frustrated Ma. George left mining and took a job with the local water company, but his income did not change; once again Ma made her dissatisfaction clear. Her appetite for finer things had not waned. George took her criticism and complaints without saying much in return. The Barker boys fled the scene to get away from the bickering and lost themselves in a string of misdemeanors.[16]

The FBI records note that the names of all four Barker boys were on the police blotter for some infraction of the law between the summer of 1910 and the fall of 1911. "The boys were known as the town toughs before they were out of school," the July 22, 1939, edition of the *Joplin Globe* noted. "Their home became a meeting place for ne'er-do-wells, a crime school so successful that many of those that congregated there graduated to try it on a bigger scale, under a variety of assumed names."[17]

When Ma's boys and their associates were not at the Barker home, they assembled at Central Park in Tulsa. Authorities referred to them as the Central Park Gang. The park and the Barker house became a well-known community center of sorts for aspiring outlaws and convicts just out of prison. The July 22, 1939, edition of the *Joplin Globe* reported: "Partnerships in crime were engineered in both locations by Ma who sometimes charged a fee for thieves to use being in her presence as an alibi when a crime was perpetrated. Sometimes she conspired with lawbreakers for the sheer warped joy of it."

Ma embraced the lifestyle once she got a sample of the spoils from various crimes her boys committed. She reveled in the fur coats, jewelry, and silverware. Ma not only encouraged her sons to continue what they were doing, but she also provided them with the names and addresses of people she believed had more than they deserved and could afford to part with some of their possessions.[18]

Ma's oldest son, Herman

Herman was the first of the Barker boys to be arrested. According to the November 16, 1915, edition of the *Joplin Globe*, he was taken in on suspicion of attempted theft. Authorities found Herman in the basement of a drugstore. "Herman Barker, alias Harry Davis, was held in circuit court after waiving a preliminary hearing before Judge E. G. Morrison yesterday," the *Joplin Globe* noted. "He was arrested on November 4th by Patrolman Kelley and a charge of having burglar tools in his possession was preferred against him.

"Barker was detected in the basement of the Jackson Drug Company's store on the night of his arrest. It is said he went into the store basement and hid shortly before closing time. He was discovered by a clerk. A set of burglar tools was found in his possession."[19]

Ma's tearstained appeals for Herman and her other sons were successful initially. "Ma ruled the roost with an iron hand and took nothing off of nobody," Tulsa police officer Harry Stege told reporters for the March 22, 1949, edition of the *Tulsa Tribune*. "Her boys were slippery, young hoodlums," he added. "She adored her children, but apart from Fred, didn't consider them to be especially clever." The boys regularly skipped school, and their poor reading and spelling skills reflected their disdain for higher education. Apart from being a thief, the only aptitude Herman had was for cooking. Shortly after his experience at the Jackson Drug Company's store, he took a job as a cook. From there he drifted to Springfield, Missouri, where he was arrested for assaulting a man and taking his property. The farther away Herman drifted from his mother, the more trouble he got into.[20]

Ma's influence with the authorities stretched only so far. After Herman's encounter with police in Springfield, Ma convinced her son to return to the Barker home in Tulsa. Herman traveled back to Oklahoma, but his time spent there was short. By July 1916 he had made his way back to Springfield and immediately began robbing businesses. In the latter part of July and early August 1916, Herman burglarized the Hawkins and Miller Jewelry Store. He stole rings, watches, stickpins, and buckles. One of the owners of the establishment discovered the merchandise was missing at 11:00 in the morning on August 6, 1916. Detectives were summoned to the scene, and the investigation revealed that two people were involved in the crime.[21]

A set of fingerprints found on a window high above the front door indicated that someone of small stature had pushed the glass open and crawled through the frame and down the other side. The second thief had lifted his accomplice to the window. The accomplice then opened the front door and let his partner inside. The pair left through the same door once they had secured the jewels in their bags. The search for suspects led police to a rooming house in town where Herman was living. Herman was now twenty-two years old and fit the description of the smaller burglar. He was 5'5" tall and weighed 122 pounds. The police found several items stolen from the jewelry store in Herman's possession. He was promptly arrested and taken to jail. He pled not guilty to charges of burglary and larceny.[22]

The August 13, 1916, edition of the *Springfield Missouri Republican* reported that Herman was convicted by a jury and sentenced to four years in prison. While waiting to be transferred to the state penitentiary where he would be serving time, Herman met another prisoner named Ed Conn. The two men made plans to escape. The August 22, 1916, edition of the *Springfield Missouri Republican* explained how the felons managed to break out of the Green County, Missouri, jail:

All prisoners are allowed the freedom of the bullpen during the day. Entrance into the bullpen is gained by passing through a small cage about five feet square. The inside door of the cage is manipulated by a lever, which may be worked from either side.

Yesterday morning was cleanup day at the jail, and Jailer William Bishop had placed a tub at the disposal of the prisoners in which to place their trash. During the early part of the afternoon, frequent calls had been made to him that the trash was ready, and he decided to get it.

Barker and Conn, both of whom are below the average stature, had concealed themselves in the small cage and were laying on the floor. Owing to the fact that it was dark there and no notice would be taken of them, Jailer Bishop did not know of their presence until he opened the door of the cage.

Jailer Bishop exhibited remarkable bravery, and but for this fact the delivery probably would have been general. He refused to enter the cage and backed up the corridor leading to the stairway to the second floor of the building. Conn, armed with a razor, followed, but when Barker left him to go to the jailer's office he turned and retreated from Mr. Bishop.

In the office the two prisoners immediately made for the jailer's desk and obtained three revolvers from a drawer. Then they dashed from the door leading into the cell room, hoping to force Jailer Bishop into the cage at the point of a pistol. Showing great presence of mind, Bishop closed the door in their faces and held it with his shoulder.

Realizing their chances for a clean delivery were gone, the two men dashed from the jail. Conn ran out of the side door, cut around the courthouse and was last seen near Boonville and Center streets.

Barker, passing through the door into the basement, made his way from the jail by a door on the north side and ran in a northwesterly direction. Neither was seen again.

Herman hurried back to Tulsa and to Ma. Knowing the law would be looking for her runaway son, Ma encouraged him to take refuge at the Farmers' place near Joplin, Missouri. She promised the family would join Herman there once the police had paid her the expected visit and she was sure they were searching elsewhere for her boy. Among the fugitives harbored at the Farmers' home were bank robbers Al Spencer, Frank Nash, and Ray Terrill and train robbers Earl Thayer, Francis Keating, and Thomas Holding. These accomplished lawbreakers and a number of other wrongdoers would eventually use the Barkers' tiny Tulsa home as a safe house in addition to the Farmers' homestead. Ma charged the men a modest fee to hide out at her place, where she kept the fugitives fed and steered authorities in a different direction if they came nosing around.[23]

Herman grew restless waiting for the law to catch up to him at the Farmers' place. After a quick good-bye to Ma, he traveled west. By October 1916 Herman was residing in Billings, Montana, and planning to break into an apparel shop with fellow thief George White. Herman and George's crime spree included stealing from a jewelry store and a pool hall as well as Bowen's Clothing Store. The pair was apprehended in Columbus, Montana, two days after they perpetrated the crimes. Herman told police his name was Bert Lavender. More than a month passed before officials discovered they were holding an escaped criminal. Although several attempts were made by the sheriff in Springfield to extradite Herman to Missouri, the Montana courts would not agree. Herman was made to pay for crimes committed in Billings and sentenced to a six- to twelve-year term at the Montana State Prison.[24]

Back in Tulsa, Ma lamented over the imprisonment of her oldest son. She didn't challenge Herman's involvement in the crimes but believed he had been set up to take the fall for George White. George's sentence was less than half what Herman was given. Ma was convinced George bribed authorities to be lenient with him. His family included wealthy business owners in the East. Ma speculated they could afford to pay for favors and shared that speculation with her boys. According to the March 29, 1936, edition of the *Kansas City Star*, "Without realizing it, she [Ma] taught herself and her sons that trouble was something only to be gotten out of and that justice could be bought and sold. The lesson made her the most ruthless and daring criminal leader of her time. Not once, apparently, did it enter her head to punish her boys for wrongdoing. Laws counted little against her belief that they could do no wrong."

From 1917 to 1920 word passed from crook to crook that there was a place in Tulsa where a criminal could get not only protection but shrewd advice on the best gangster to team with to do a job and which politicians and police officers could be influenced with a gratuity. "Criminals from a dozen penitentiaries sought out Ma Barker," the March 29, 1936, *Kansas City Star* article reported. "Only two things were lacking at Ma's, liquor and women. 'A man was a fool to drink,' she said. 'Likewise, he was a fool to run around with women; sooner or later they'd put the law on him.'"

George Barker was overwhelmed by the scandalous activity in his home. Any comment about the questionable paths on which his sons were going met with an indignant response from Ma. She accused him of siding with all those who wanted to see their boys behind bars. The disagreement between him and Ma would escalate quickly, with Ma accusing George of being too weak to defend their children against law enforcement agencies specifically targeting the Barkers. George assured Ma his intentions were only to see the boys had a chance for a prosperous future. She consistently challenged his motives, and he eventually learned to say nothing at all about the boys' upbringing. Occasionally a neighbor or business owner would confront him about his children's behavior, but he would simply refer the matter to his wife. "You'll have to talk to their mother," George would say, shrugging his shoulders. "She handles the boys."[25]

Ma found it difficult to be faithful to a passive husband. She began spending time with the older, seasoned hoodlums who frequented the Barker home. She readily accepted the gifts they gave her—clothing, jewelry, trinkets for her home—and she would accompany them to the movies or nightclubs. George wasn't unaware of what his wife was doing, but he lacked the intestinal fortitude to object.[26]

By the mid-1920s George decided he'd had enough. He left Ma and Tulsa and moved to Joplin, Missouri, where he operated a small filling station. Ma was indifferent about the separation. Her main interest was in her boys, the lucrative prospects for the Central Park Gang since Prohibition had passed, and on an up-and-coming law enforcement agent in a new division with the government called the Bureau of Investigation.[27]

The Bureau of Investigation was a well-disciplined organization composed of experts in accounting, fingerprinting, handwriting, and ballistics. The bureau's main objective was to stop violent crimes executed by gangs like those of the Barker boys. J. Edgar Hoover was the head of the bureau. Hoover, a lawyer from Washington, DC, joined the Department of Justice in early 1916 and began his career tracking deadly weapons (machine guns, missiles) smuggled into America from the world's battlefront by GIs and officers. Somehow the weapons had found their way into the hands of criminal elements and were being used to rob armored trucks carrying money to banks. Four years later Hoover was made a special assistant to the attorney general and placed in charge of radical activities.[28]

According to the February 18, 1920, edition of the *Saturday Spectator*, members of the House Un-American Activities Committee tasked Hoover with tracking the growth of communism in the country and ferreting out those who opposed the American way of life. In November 1921 Hoover was named the director of the Bureau of Investigation. In the 1930s Hoover became so consumed with apprehending Ma Barker and her villainous boys that he appealed to the public for help in the matter. "The eyes of Arizona Clark Barker . . . always fascinated me," Hoover is quoted as saying in May 1935. "They were queerly direct, penetrating, with some strongly smoldering flame, yet withal as hypnotically cold as a muzzle of a gun."[29]

Hoover's dogged pursuit of the Barkers would prompt the Bureau of Investigation to employ every method available to locate the group

J. Edgar Hoover, head of the G-Men, demonstrates how to use a machine gun to Mickey Cochrane, manager of the Detroit Tigers, Department of Justice, Washington, DC LIBRARY OF CONGRESS, LC-USZ62-123126

and hold them accountable for their dastardly deeds, especially those of Ma Barker.

CHAPTER THREE

The Firstborn

MA BARKER REMOVED A TATTERED HANDKERCHIEF FROM THE NAVY-blue pocketbook cradled in her lap and dabbed away a fake tear. The guards on duty at the Oklahoma prison were disinterested in her supposed grief. Their job was to make sure the inmates at the facility moved efficiently from the visitors' area back to their cells. Ma watched a pale-faced, stupefied guard escort her son Arthur out of the room. It was mid-February 1920, and mother and son had concluded a short visit. A thick, long glass separated the convicts from the civilized world. Here communication was done using plain black phones minus a dial wheel, wired from one side of the glass to the other. Arthur and Ma each had their own receiver to talk through, as did several other families and friends visiting their loved ones through the glass partition.[1]

The iron-barred doors clanged shut as the last prisoner was ushered out of the room. Ma sat stock-still until she heard the guard lock the door behind the inmates. As she turned to get up from her assigned seat, a heavyset guard approached her and with flinty eyes looked her up and down. She looked more frumpy than menacing. The coat she wore was big and bulky, frayed in spots, and a few buttons were missing. The tan, bell-shaped hat on her head had seen better days, and her hair underneath it was pinned back in a haphazard fashion. "My boys would be all right if the law would leave them alone," she told the guard. He had no response and simply led her to the exit of the room, and she shuffled along as little old ladies do.[2]

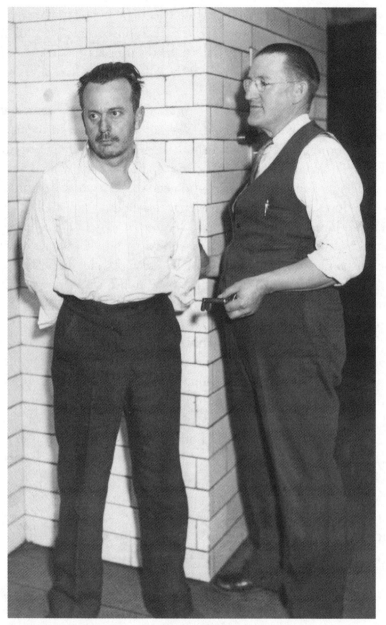

Arthur "Doc" Barker (suspect in Edward Bremer kidnapping) and jailer
William Gates COURTESY OF THE MINNESOTA HISTORICAL SOCIETY

Two short siren blasts issued from the main building of the jail as Ma exited the complex. She glanced back at the other visitors following after her and at the stone walls topped with snaky concertina wire overhead. Once every guest had left the jail, the heavy steel doors were closed behind them.[3]

A Cadillac sedan pulled in front of the detention center and stopped. Ma abandoned the old-lady gait and hurried to the car as though nothing whatsoever was bothering her physically. She pulled off the old coat she was wearing and draped the fur wrap over her shoulders that one of the passengers inside the car handed her through the window. She opened the passenger's side door and slid into the seat. The June 19, 1959, edition of the *Amarillo Globe Times* reported that the Jasper County filing clerk who witnessed Ma Barker leaving the prison saw her removing her hat and straightening her hair as the sedan drove away. "In a few moments she transformed from a somewhat feeble grandmother type to a hearty, rather spirited woman," the clerk described.

Ma Barker wanted the nice things of life: the lovely home, the fine clothing, the money; she was fearless and crafty about gaining them. She learned the intricacies of criminal practice and was smart enough to never get caught. Her boys were not as gifted. By late 1918 they had all gone well beyond playing in Central Park with their crowd. Some were robbing jewelry stores, and others were stealing cars.[4] On July 4, 1918, Arthur stole his first of three Ford roadsters. It was parked in front of a federal building in Muskogee, Oklahoma, and the car belonged to a government employee.[5] A Department of Justice report dated March 4, 1935, noted that Arthur was arrested and charged with larceny of US property. Ma promised to rectify the situation, but before she had a chance, Arthur escaped from jail. He was apprehended and returned to the sheriff of Tulsa County. Ma managed to get the charges against him dropped before his court date. J. Edgar Hoover speculated in a FBI report dated November 19, 1935, that Ma had paid police officers to destroy any proof that Arthur was involved with the theft.[6]

Arthur stole two more Ford roadsters in 1919 and stripped the vehicles of their parts. He was arrested again and placed in the Tulsa County jail where Ma came to see him in early 1920. She had been unsuccessful in persuading the authorities that Arthur was innocent and to release him into her care. She was driven to find another way for her son to be free.[7]

On February 14, 1920, seventeen prisoners, including Arthur, escaped from the jail. A hair saw and sulfuric acid were used to sever the bars on the cell doors. The inmates then made their way through the facility to the roof of the building, where a 130-foot rope was waiting for them. They used the rope to lower themselves down the outside wall and get away. A thorough investigation into the escape was conducted by the warden and his aides. How the inmates acquired the acid and the rope was never discovered. Historians such as Courtney Ryley Cooper and Robert Winer suspect Ma had something to do with it.[8]

Arthur fled to his father's home in Joplin, Missouri. After five days on the run, the authorities tracked down Arthur and arrested him. The moment he was returned to jail in Oklahoma, Ma started working on a way to get him out. Instead of pleading her case to the judge, Ma decided to approach the owner of the vehicle Arthur had taken. Sobbing and wringing her hands, she offered a compelling story about her misunderstood, persecuted son that moved the Ford's owner to withdraw his complaint against Arthur. He was released into the loving arms of his mother in December 1920. Once Arthur was home Ma shifted her focus to her eldest boy.[9]

Herman Barker had been paroled from a Montana prison on April 18, 1920. He made an attempt to go straight. He got a job washing dishes at a café in Casper, Wyoming, but the lifestyle proved too tame for him. By the summer of 1920, he was living in Faribault, Minnesota, fifty miles south of Minneapolis and St. Paul. Shortly after Herman relocated to Minnesota, he fell in with a gang of bootleggers. Prohibition, the restriction of the production, sale, and transportation of alcoholic beverages, had forced underground those who enjoyed a libation or two. Bootleggers smuggled alcohol into the city and sold it to makeshift drugstore owners. Herman had no real interest in bootlegging. He liked the company of those who thwarted the law, but he had a fascination with the fine things, like jewelry, tailored suits, and silk ties.[10]

On September 17, 1920, Herman and a paroled convict named Robert Egan, who had the same preoccupation with jewelry, helped themselves to the diamonds, watches, and gold pocketknives stored inside an unlocked safe at the John H. Ruge Jewelry Company. The pair stole more than $4,000 in merchandise and cash before fleeing the scene. Their plan was to take the midnight train out of Faribault to Davenport, Iowa, but the police intercepted Herman and Robert as they were boarding the passenger car. The two men struggled with the officers. Robert managed to get away, but Herman was apprehended, along with the suitcase containing the stolen property.[11]

Herman was combative with the authorities throughout his arrest and subsequent booking into the Faribault jail. He told police his name was Clarence Sharp and that he was from Minneapolis. He refused to cooperate further. According to deputies at the facility, Herman was intimidating to the other inmates. He always wore a scowl and rarely spoke without cursing. He had multiple tattoos on his arms, chest, and back—some were crude and others obscene. The one Herman seemed to be particularly fond of was the tattoo on his upper chest that read: "A Boy's Best Friend is His Mom." He was placed in a cell alone until Robert Egan was caught and thrown in with him. Robert lied to police about his name just as Herman had. Robert told police his name was Peter O'Brien and that he was from St. Paul.[12]

Shortly after Robert arrived his wife began visiting him on a regular basis. She referred to herself as Katherine O'Brien, and on several occasions she and Robert were seen passing notes to one another. The sheriff suspected the couple were planning something nefarious and stationed additional deputies in the jail to make sure the prisoners didn't do anything foolish. On November 8, 1920, five members of the gang Herman and Robert were a part of attempted to break into the jail to rescue their cohorts in crime. The escape plan failed. Armed with shotguns, the deputies were able to keep the intruders at bay.

Robert was shot and wounded trying to lower himself out a window his friends had burst. Law enforcement was quick to respond to the activity. Herman was never able to leave the cell.[13]

At his trial in December 1920, Herman pled guilty as Clarence Sharp to breaking and entering, larceny, fleeing from police, resisting arrest, and possession of stolen merchandise and money. He was sentenced to ten years at the Minnesota state prison in Stillwater. Herman wasted no time writing his mother to ask her for help in getting him released. Ma decided to approach the parole board about the matter. In a letter dated March 4, 1921, Ma wrote: "Chairman of the Parole Board, I am writing you regarding my son Clarence Sharp. As I understand the parole board meets in July. Mr. Chairman, will you please grant my son parole at this meeting as we need him badly at home as his father is in very bad health. We appreciate anything you do for him. Mrs. Geo. Lavender, 401 N. Cin. St., Tulsa, Oklahoma."[14]

In between writing letters to prison officials and Minnesota state political leaders about how her son Herman had been illegally prosecuted, Ma spent time with several men in the Tulsa area. FBI records note that Ma was "romantically involved" with criminals from the neighborhood who "subscribed to the same loose moral lifestyle she did." She enjoyed frequenting speakeasies and wasn't particular about who accompanied her to the underground saloons as long as they "bought her drinks and treated her like royalty."[15]

On July 15, 1925, Ma welcomed Herman home from the Stillwater prison in Minnesota. He had been given a conditional release and sent on his way. The condition he agreed to was that he would stay out of the state of Minnesota for a two-year period. Ma felt the terms were unfair. The idea that anyone could make such a demand of an innocent person appalled her. She threatened authorities with legal action if Herman was harassed further.[16]

It was difficult at first for Herman to adjust to being at home with his family in Oklahoma after five years of incarceration. Although he and Fred corresponded regularly, Herman felt like a stranger to his brother. Twenty-four-year-old Fred idolized his older brother and tried to be like him in every way. He adopted Herman's fondness for tattoos, nice clothes, and stealing. Ma's boys were close, but Herman felt more at ease with men such as Ray Terrill and Elmer Inman. Both Ray and Elmer were convicted felons with ties to the Barkers that extended back to 1915, when the Barkers first moved to Oklahoma. Since Herman had been in jail, the two men had put together their own gang. They specialized in nighttime burglaries of banks and stores with a unique method of raiding their targets. Using stolen trucks, they extracted safes from the businesses they robbed and transported them to the Radium Springs Health Resort in Salina, Oklahoma. Once the safes were secured at the private resort, a safecracker would open the box and the contents were emptied. The safe would then be hauled to the Grand River Bridge and thrown over the side into the water.[17]

In Herman's absence his brothers had helped keep Ma supplied with comforts their father was never able to give her. She relished the efforts her boys extended to make her life better. In addition to the items her sons gave her, she received expensive gifts from various paramours and managed to buy jewelry for herself with funds she earned providing outlaws with alibis and a place to hide.[18]

In between jobs, Herman drifted in and out of his mother's home. He was restless and wanted to shower Ma with more than she could imagine. He decided to join forces with his little brother to rob a bank in Washington, Arkansas.[19]

On December 16, 1925, Herman, Fred, and two other thieves blasted open the bank safe and helped themselves to $7,000. The police met the bandits as they were racing out of the building. Gunfire was exchanged, and one of the criminals was injured. Three out of the four bank robbers managed to escape. The wounded gangster was taken into custody and questioned. He refused to divulge his partners' names.[20]

Three days later, after what appeared to be a successful bank robbery, Fred Barker, using the name J. Darrow, walked into the Central National Bank of Okmulgee, Oklahoma, carrying several roles of silver dollars, half-dollars, and twenty-five-cent coins. He wanted to exchange the coins for paper money. A teller became suspicious and

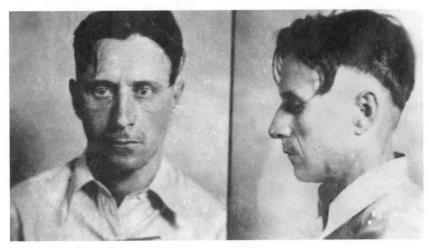

Fred Barker COURTESY OF THE MINNESOTA HISTORICAL SOCIETY

contacted the authorities. When the police arrived and asked Fred about the money, he told them he had won the funds in a poker game in Tulsa the night before. The police searched Fred to find out if he had any more money on him or any evidence of his involvement in the Arkansas bank robbery. They found a receipt for money he had wired Ma as well as a key to a car parked in front of a local hotel. The authorities decided to check out the hotel and learned that the room where Fred was staying was registered to J. Darrow and H. Barker. Inside the room they found new suitcases, new suits of clothing, razors, fountain pens, and a letter to Mrs. G. E. Barker written by Fred, expressing his undying love.[21]

According to the December 21, 1925, edition of the *Ada Evening News*, Fred was arrested on two different charges. "The dapper young man arrested Saturday by police as a suspect in connection with the robbery of a Washington, Arkansas, bank has been identified as a Fred Barker of Tulsa," the article read. "He was wanted by federal authorities on a charge of forging a money order."

While the police worked to find evidence linking him to the bank robbery, Fred insisted that he was indeed J. Darrow. Herman could not be found to corroborate the information Fred offered the police. None of the money from the bank could be found either. With the exception of the rolled coins, which were in unmarked wrappers, there was no physical proof that Fred had anything to do with robbing the bank in Arkansas. The authorities were forced to release Fred.[22]

Herman fled to Salina, Oklahoma, and the Radium Springs Health Resort. It was there he met a Creek Indian woman who managed the business. Carol Hamilton and Herman took an instant liking to one another. Their relationship progressed quickly, and in a short time the two were married. Ma Barker was less than pleased by the news. She didn't trust most women and was particularly leery of those who had spent a considerable amount of time with fugitives. Not that Ma had a problem with fugitives—she just didn't like the idea that Carol knew so much about the crimes Herman and his associates committed. "They'll turn on you," Ma warned her sons about the opposite sex. "There's only one woman you can count on to look out for you and that's me."[23]

Herman disregarded Ma's admonitions and embraced his life with Carol. Herman was so taken by her that he changed his name to Hamilton. The newlyweds operated the resort under the alias Mr. and Mrs. J. H. Hamilton. The popular safe house was heavily armed and equipped with special lighting that could be used to alert any wrong-doers seeking refuge at the resort that the police were on their way.[24]

Marital bliss did not interfere with Herman's criminal career. Between February and May 1926, Herman, Fred, and three members of their gang robbed eight jewelry stores in Tulsa, McAlester, and Muskogee, Oklahoma. The Barker boys and their cohorts stole more than $30,000 in merchandise and cash from the various businesses. They gained entry into the stores via a crawl space or by cutting a hole in the roof and dropping down through the ceiling. Police were at a loss as to who was responsible for the robberies and had no clues to go on until they came across a man's hat at the G. H. Newton Jewelry Store in McAlester. Herman had accidentally left the hat at the scene of the crime. Authorities investigating the burglary at the store traced the hat to a clothing store in Tulsa. The clothing company records noted that Herman had purchased the item.[25]

The authorities began an exhaustive search for Herman. They finally got word he was in Muskogee. Police there recognized him from a description provided by the McAlester investigators. By the time the investigators reached Muskogee, the unsuspecting Barker and his wife had left for Tennessee. The couple was arrested in late May 1926.[26]

At first Herman refused to give the authorities his real name. He insisted that he was J. H. Hamilton and that he was a film distributor. After several hours of interrogation, Herman admitted to serving time in Montana and Minnesota, but he would not confess to being Herman Barker. A search of his personal belongings turned up only a pistol, no jewels or money. There were warrants out for Herman's arrest for burglary in both Tennessee and Oklahoma. On the advice of corrupt former judge Q. P. McGhee, Herman refused to go back to Tennessee. McGhee managed to convince authorities there to drop the charges against his client. Historians speculate McGhee paid the authorities to get them to let Herman go. Police escorted Herman to Miami, Oklahoma. McGhee was able to free him after only five days in jail. No charges were brought against Carol.[27]

On June 7, 1926, Herman and fellow criminal Elmer Inman stole a car from a dealership in Fairfax, Oklahoma, and led police on a high-speed chase from Oklahoma to Kansas. The pair abandoned the vehicle in a field near Fulton, Kansas. Inman was apprehended at once, but Herman got away. Authorities caught Herman purchasing a hat at a store in Fulton. He was turned over to law enforcement agents in Oklahoma and later met with his attorney. McGhee paid Herman's fine, and he was set free.[28]

Back home in Tulsa with Ma, Herman wasted no time planning his next big job. He set his sights higher than a jewelry store this time. He was going to concentrate on banks. On December 23, 1926, Carol rendezvoused with her husband in Claremore, Oklahoma. She brought his burglary tools with her, as he was preparing to rob the state bank in Buffalo. Prior to reuniting with his wife in northeast Oklahoma, Herman had been involved in a pair of major heists: one at the Durnell Dry Goods Store in Muskogee and the other at the Antonovitch Jewelry Store in Bristow, Oklahoma. He stole several fur coats, silverware, jewels, and more than $6,000 in cash. Herman escaped from both crime scenes and left Carol behind to take care of his tools until they saw each other again. He gave the majority of the cash and merchandise to Ma for safekeeping.[29]

On Christmas Eve 1926 Herman and his partners in crime broke into the Oklahoma State Bank and took the safe. The safe contained cash, bonds, money orders, and certificates. On New Year's Eve Herman and his gang broke into the bank at West Fork, Arkansas, and hijacked the safe there as well. The strongbox reportedly contained more than $2,500 in cash and bonds. Both of the safes were finally located on the bank of the Verdigris River near Claremore, Oklahoma. They had been blown open and looted. In both cases Herman had been spotted at the banks several hours before the robberies occurred. Authorities strongly suspected he was the culprit.[30]

Herman didn't let the fact that he was wanted for questioning for two bank robberies interfere with his plans to steal from a third. On January 17, 1927, Herman and fellow gang member Ray Terrill, along with a handful of recruits, broke into the First National Bank of Jasper, Missouri. After forcing open the vault, the gangsters absconded with the contents. The early-morning heist drew the attention of an employee at a business down the street from the bank. The authorities were called, and the thieves scattered when they heard the sirens on the police cars fast approaching. A chase ensued, with police following after the bandits as they tried to get away in two different automobiles. The authorities cornered Herman and Ray in the town of Carterville near Joplin. The police and the gangsters exchanged gunfire for more than thirty minutes. The pair surrendered after Herman was shot.[31]

The January 18, 1927, edition of the *Joplin Globe* reported that Herman was taken by ambulance to St. John's Hospital in Joplin. Ray was escorted to the city jail. The car carrying the other burglars was still at large. The *Joplin Globe* article noted:

While neither of the prisoners would talk about the case, a high-powered sedan their partners were driving was identified by Jasper citizens as one of the two which was used in the attempted robbery. The gun battle was staged when police and other officers surrounded a house at 603 East Main Street, twenty miles from the crime scene.

Barker and Terrill drove up to the house about six o'clock, an hour after they had been routed by posses during an attempt to haul away a bank safe. Officers rushed the house, and Barker ran out the back door. A detective shot him with a sawed off shotgun when he failed to comply with a command to halt and throw up his hands. The officer fired at once and five buck shot took effect, twice in the upper part of one leg, once in the other leg, once in the back, and the other in the pelvis.

A complete outfit of safe cracking tools was found in the car, and the house yielded three revolvers, a shotgun, and a quantity of ammunition. Ashes of what is believed were government bonds, presumably burned when the battle began, were found.

Barker, according to the police records, was arrested here for highway robbery in 1915 and a year later was sentenced at Springfield to two years in the state penitentiary for burglary and larceny. Barker admitted the following aliases: J. H. Hamilton, L. C. Whittier, D. W. Bowers, Bert Lavender, Clarence Sharp, Al Ayers, and R. L. Douglas. He gave the name Douglas when he was captured yesterday.

Both Herman and Ray requested to see their lawyers immediately. For a reward of $500, Herman was released from the Jasper city jail and was to be sent to Fayetteville, Arkansas, to face charges of bank robbery at West Fork. Ray Terrill was to be sent back to Oklahoma. He escaped custody while being transported by authorities in McAlester to serve out his sentence on an old bank robbery conviction. Two weeks after Herman was delivered into the hands of the Fayetteville authorities, he broke out of jail by climbing through a skylight in the roof.[32]

Rumors abounded that Ma Barker, with the help of attorney Q. P. McGhee, was behind the ease in which both Herman and Ray were able to escape. According to the January 19, 1927, edition of the *Joplin Globe*, the Kimes-Terrill-Barker Gang was run by "someone whose capital makes possible the maintenance of an intricate system whereby the maneuvers of each member of the gang are known at all times." The article continued:

Examples of careful schemes used to either liberate or lessen the burden of some members of the gang when he is arrested were cited to police by informers. People are paid to protect the hirelings or look the other way as they get away and sometimes those people are members of law enforcement.

Police went further to say that a resort in Oklahoma, ostensibly a pleasure resort, is one of the rendezvous points of the bandit gang. The other is a modest home in the heart of Tulsa. It is at these locations that the crimes are hatched and carried out. The suave manager of the resort is known to society as an honest, industrious worker, but to his pals he is a clever bandit. Likewise is the so-called old woman who runs the home in Tulsa. Neighbors and some policemen report that the family matriarch is neither old nor possesses gray hair. Both the resort manager and home owner lead a Jekyll and Hyde existence.

Lieutenants of the "brains" whose purpose is to keep in touch with members of the gang go from place to place, aiding the members when they are captured and jailed.

As one instance, police cited a case in which it was the duty of the lieutenant to recover by a clever ruse the property of a prisoner and return it to the gang.

Still another use to which the lieutenant is put, for which a concrete example was cited as a method of getting the bandit out of jail, consisted of authorities pretending to return the prisoners elsewhere for prosecution and the offering of a reward which was supposed to be due the captor of the prisoner for their work.

After Herman escaped from the Fayetteville jail, he and his wife headed west. He still had several buckshot pellets in his legs from the gun battle with police in Carterville, Missouri. Once Herman and Carol reached the West Coast, the Hamiltons, also known as the Barkers, sought medical attention for the injury. Unfortunately, one of the pellets was lodged behind Herman's left kneecap and could not be removed. Subsequently, he was in a great deal of pain and walked with a limp.[33]

On July 31, 1927, the Barkers arrived in Cheyenne, Wyoming. Low on funds, Herman suggested he cash in some stolen traveler's checks he had acquired. Carol was against the idea because Cheyenne was considered to be tough on criminals, and she was afraid of what might happen to Herman if they got caught. Herman didn't believe there was any danger and proceeded to the American National Bank in Cheyenne. Herman told the teller his name was R. D. Snodgrass and requested that the checks he presented be cashed. The teller complied, and Herman left the building. After a quick check the teller discovered the traveler's checks were part of the items stolen from the bank in Buffalo, Kansas. He hurried out of the bank to catch Herman and reached him just as he was getting into his vehicle. Herman was apologetic about the "misunderstanding" as he called it and agreed to return to the bank to correct the situation. The teller turned to head back to work, and Herman sped off in the opposite direction.[34]

Deputy Arthur Osborne of Pine Bluff, Wyoming, received the call about the theft and began looking for the vehicle Herman was driving, which was reported to be heading his way. Deputy Osborne spotted the automobile and began pursuing it. Herman was reluctant to stop but did so at Carol's insistence. Deputy Osborne approached the vehicle calmly and with a smile. "I think you folks are the people I want," Carol later told police the deputy had said.

"I'm sure you're mistaken. You can't want us. We haven't done anything," Herman replied. The deputy disagreed and reached for the door handle. Herman leveled a .32 caliber automatic at him and fired twice. The deputy fell backward onto the ground.[35]

Carol went into hysterics when she heard the gunshots and tried to jump out of the car. Herman stopped her, and the two scuffled a bit before driving away from the scene toward the Wyoming-Nebraska border. The August 4, 1927, edition of the *Helena Daily Independent* reported that a woman matching Carol's description was believed to be the one who shot and killed Deputy Osborne. "This was the theory advanced today by the Denver police after talking with a Denver attorney who came up in an automobile on the highway immediately after the shooting," the article noted. "Hellerstein [the attorney] told the authorities the woman shoved Osborne's body off the highway after he had been shot. The lawyer said she seemed to be leading in the argument, and the man, believed to be R. Snodgrass, was taking orders from her."

The August 10, 1927, edition of the *Anaconda* (Montana) *Standard* reported that there was a reward offered for the person who shot and killed Deputy Osborne. The reward offered for the arrest of the person or persons who killed the deputy by shooting him twice in the back was one hundred dollars.

Law enforcement agents in Colorado, Montana, and Wyoming combined their efforts to find Herman and Carol wherever they might be hiding in the mountainous region. By August 5, 1927, the husband and wife team had taken refuge in a small, out-of-the-way hotel in Tulsa, Oklahoma. They had registered under the name of Mr. and Mrs. Smallwick and were driving a different automobile than the one they had in Wyoming. Less than a week after arriving back in Oklahoma, the pair moved onto a farm in Batesville, Arkansas. The plan was to lay low until the fury of what had happened to Deputy Osborne had subsided. Herman, however, became anxious waiting and was despondent over the fact that they had no money. He left his wife at the farm and set out to fix the problem of their lack of funds.[36]

Herman traveled to Miami, Oklahoma, where he contacted a couple of outlaw friends, Charlie Stalcup and Porter Meeks. He knew they would be open to committing a robbery. The men decided to burglarize the Crystal Ice Plant in Newton, Kansas. Charlie had served time in the Kansas state prison in 1921 and had heard from inmates there that the vaults at the ice plant were easy to bust open and always contained a good sum of money.[37]

On August 29, 1927, the trio of bandits overtook a night watchman guarding the ice plant and broke into the business. The thieves took $200 from the safe and fled from the crime scene in a gray Chevrolet sedan. The battered and beaten watchman managed to contact the police, and officers responded quickly. Motorcycle Officer J. E. Marshall and his partner Frank Bush spotted the gangsters' car speeding through town at 2:00 in the morning. After a short pursuit the getaway vehicle stopped, and Officer Marshall approached the car to confront the offenders. Herman was driving; when the policeman got close enough to look inside the vehicle, he grabbed the officer around the neck, leveled a gun against his face, and fired two shots. Officer Marshall died instantly. Charlie and Porter fired their weapons out of the back window at Officer Bush. Porter jumped out of the car and ran off, still firing his weapon. Officer Bush returned fire, hitting two of the three bandits in the process. Herman put his foot down hard on the accelerator and sped off.[38]

Herman began driving erratically. One of the shots from Officer Bush's gun had hit its mark. Herman had a bullet wound in his upper body, and Charlie had been hit in both of his thighs, his right arm, and his right hand. A witness at an all-night hamburger stand watched the sedan weaving around and jumping over curbs. "God, I'm going blind," Charlie later recalled Herman saying to him. "I'm going blind!" he announced as he crashed into a tree.[39]

"Both of the bandits leapt out of the car and hurried off in opposite directions," the August 29, 1927, edition of the *Emporia* (Kansas) *Gazette* reported. "One of the occupants that left the vehicle drew his pistol and shot himself through the head," the article added, "and the other was found later in a clump of trees."[40]

The police identified the man who had committed suicide as Herman Barker. The August 30, 1927, edition of the *Joplin Globe* reported that the "thirty-three-year-old man was driven to shoot himself in the head because of the pain he was experiencing due to the gunshot wound he had sustained."

In mid-September 1927 authorities tracked down and arrested Carol Barker at a house near the New Salem Church in Neosho, Missouri. "She surrendered without protest," the September 27, 1927, article in the *Joplin Globe* read. Carol admitted that she was trying to make her way back to the health resort in Oklahoma when she learned of Herman's demise.[41]

Herman's body lay in wait at the morgue in Wichita while Ma made arrangements to have him returned to Oklahoma. She was brokenhearted over the loss and pleaded and begged Kansas authorities to turn her son's body over to her. The Kansas coroner's office wouldn't transfer the body until they had a place for Herman to be buried. Given the Barkers' reputation, no city official in Oklahoma was willing to allow the outlaw to be laid to rest in its cemeteries.[42]

Q. P. McGhee used his influence to purchase a plot in the Williams Timber Hill Cemetery near Welch, Oklahoma. Herman Barker's graveside service was held on August 31, 1927. Carol attended the burial in secret. Not only was she wanted by the authorities, but Ma had threatened her with bodily harm if she saw her again. Ma believed Carol had shot and killed Officer Osborne in Wyoming and then blamed Herman for the murder.

When Carol was apprehended on September 19, 1927, she did tell the authorities that Herman was the gunman. She was charged with being an accessory to the killing of the officer and was returned to Cheyenne, Wyoming, to stand trial. "All I want is for the state of Wyoming to end me, and I don't mean life imprisonment," Carol told newspaper and radio reporters. Carol's plea for Wyoming's supreme penalty could not be granted because of the little part she played in the actual killing. She was sentenced to two to four years in the Colorado State Penitentiary.[43]

Ma made it clear to Q. P. McGhee that she was disappointed with the outcome of Carol's trial. She felt that her daughter-in-law had done nothing to protect Herman from harm and that Carol's inability to save him from trouble contributed greatly to his downfall. For that, Ma thought she should be locked away for a lifetime.[44]

CHAPTER FOUR

Losing Lloyd

THE MONUMENT PLACED ON HERMAN BARKER'S GRAVE WAS A MASsive granite stone that stood more than four feet high. The deceased's name was carved into the marble along with his date of birth and the date he died. In the beginning Ma regularly visited the site near Welch, Oklahoma, bringing flowers and some of Herman's belongings from when he was a boy. She laid his things neatly on the mound of dirt that covered his remains. Detective Harrison Moreland, a writer for the *Master Detective* magazine, reported that Ma "turned her back entirely on morality once Herman was gone." There had been a time when she might have lied to George about their sons' criminal activities or tried to dispel the rumors she was spending time with other men, but that all stopped when she saw Herman's bullet-ridden body lying on a slab at the morgue.[1]

George Barker had taken time away from his job at the filling station in Webb City, Missouri, to attend Herman's funeral. Ma paid little attention to her estranged husband. Any comfort she needed during her time of grief was handled by the man who accompanied her to the cemetery, Arthur W. Dunlop, also known as George Anderson. Ma had met Arthur at a club in Tulsa. He had been a carpenter and painter for Sommers Sign System. Ma never let Arthur stray too far from her side; even when George approached her for what he hoped would be a private conversation about where the money for Herman's headstone came from, Arthur was milling around close behind the pair.[2]

Ma dismissed George's question about the headstone but informed the timid, grieving man that Herman and their other boys regularly sent money home for her support. She gushed over how considerate the Barker boys were and cursed those who argued that her sons were anything less. "If the good people of this town don't like my boys," Ma was often heard saying, "then the good people know what to do." George returned to Missouri with the full knowledge that he and his wife would never reconcile and that his sons could never be respectable citizens.[3]

Ma and Arthur planned to return to Tulsa, but before they could go home, Ma wanted to visit Lloyd at the penitentiary in Leavenworth, Kansas, where he had been incarcerated for seven years. According to the May 1935 edition of the *Master Detective* magazine, Herman and Lloyd used to pretend to be outlaws when they were young boys. "The two used to play Jesse and Frank James by riding pinto ponies into Webb City saloons," the article noted. "The Ozark village nurtured legends of old-time bandits, and Herman had heard that one of the James boys' favorite stunts was to ride their horses into a saloon, shooting their guns as they rode." Jesse and Frank James had at one time ridden through Webb City. They had also ridden through Carthage, Missouri, when Ma Barker was ten years old, and she never forgot the sight. She was infatuated with the dashing criminals and later with their mother. Ma admired the way Zerelda James defended her sons and encouraged them to fight against the law when the law wouldn't stop persecuting them.[4]

The Barker boys were reckless, always into trouble, and constantly under the scrutiny of the police because of their illegal activities. Lloyd William Barker was no exception. Born on March 16, 1896, he was Ma's second son. Nicknamed Red because of the red tint in his hair, Lloyd was more of a follower and less an instigator of the various crimes he committed. Records at the Bureau of Prisons note that he did enlist in the army in August 1918. He served as a cook with the 162nd Depot Brigade until mustered out in February 1919. At twenty-one Lloyd was like his brothers, all of whom didn't seem to have any viable means of support, and wandered the streets and alleyways of Tulsa with members of the Central Park Gang.[5]

On June 17, 1921, Lloyd, along with four other hoodlums, robbed a motorized mail wagon in Baxter Springs, Kansas—a town in the southeastern portion of the state. The July 7, 1921, edition of the Joplin Globe reported on the theft of five bags of mail containing more than $3,000 in Liberty Bonds. The bandits fled to Miami, Oklahoma, with the bonds and were attempting to steal an automobile and flee to Arkansas when the authorities caught them and attempted to make an arrest.

"William Green, 21, was wounded in a gun battle between police and four other suspects who robbed mail sacks in Baxter Springs," the *Joplin Globe* article read. "Green was transported to the Miami Baptist hospital where he was formally charged. Lloyd Barker, Gregory O'Connell, Jess Brown, and Fred O'Connell are being held in jail for the federal crime."[6]

A preliminary hearing in the case of Lloyd Barker, also known as Lloyd Anderson, was held on June 18, 1921, in the office of the US commissioner, C. N. Price, in the federal building located in Fort Scott, Kansas. According to the July 16, 1921, edition of the *Fort Scott Daily Tribune* and *Fort Scott Daily Monitor*, "Al F. Williams, U.S. District Attorney of Kansas City, conducted the hearing." The only witness examined was the mail wagon driver, Guy H. Shields. "Shields positively identified Lloyd Barker as the one who held him up and took the five pouches of mail in the process," the *Daily Tribune* and *Daily Monitor* reported. At the close of the hearing, Lloyd was placed under a $10,000 bond. Being unable to give bond, they were committed back to jail.

Ma was frantic when news of what happened to Lloyd reached her. She quickly traveled to Kansas to see her son and to find out if anything could be done to save him from prosecution. Ma's usual approach with the authorities was to cry and plead for her boy's release, but this time she chose another tactic. She was stern and abrasive with the jailers and federal investigators. She demanded nothing but loudly announced to Lloyd her intention to help him get out and come home.[7]

The officers at the Bourbon County jail became worried that Ma would make good on her promise and decided to move Lloyd to another facility. The July 22, 1921, edition of the *Fort Scott Daily Tribune* and the *Fort Scott Daily Monitor* reported that Lloyd Barker was moved to the Wyandotte County jail because the authorities believed efforts might be made to free him from jail. Lloyd was under tight security until his trial began on November 12, 1921. A jury in federal court found him guilty of attempting to rob the mail. Lloyd and two other suspects, Gregory O'Connell and William Green, were sentenced to twenty-five years each for their crime. Their time would be served at the federal penitentiary in Leavenworth, Kansas.[8]

Lloyd's life at Leavenworth was relatively uneventful. Prison records indicate that he was a model inmate. He was employed at the facility shoe factory and also served as an orderly and cook in the tubercular ward of the prison hospital. The May 1935 edition of the *Master Detective* magazine noted that Lloyd and Ma exchanged numerous letters during the time he was incarcerated. He wrote his mother to tell her he hadn't meant to steal the mail bags, and she responded with the wholehearted belief that he was telling the truth.[9]

Lloyd, like his brothers, adored Ma. Harrison Moreland, investigator for *Master Detective* magazine, noted in his article about the notorious gang leader that the Barker boys were devoted to her in a strange, submissive way. "Their letters which I have seen showed it," Harrison recalled in 1935. "They wrote to her almost as if she were a sweetheart."[10] There were several suggestive remarks in the correspondence to and from Ma that would lead one to believe she shared an inappropriate sexual relationship with both Lloyd and Fred. She often boasted to friends and family that those two boys were her favorites.

Lloyd was eligible for parole in 1932, but government officials denied his petition for release. According to the Bureau of Prisons archivists, Lloyd believed his family's criminal activities at the time interfered with parole being granted. He was finally freed on October 29, 1938.[11]

During World War II, Lloyd Barker served as a cook at a prisoner of war camp at Fort Custer, Michigan. He was honorably discharged from the army with a good conduct ribbon.[12]

In 1944 Lloyd headed west and settled in Denver, Colorado, where he became the assistant manager of a restaurant called the Denargo Grill. In February 1949 he married his common-law wife, Jean Wynne, in Brighton, Colorado, and settled in the Westminster area. Jean had two children from a previous marriage, and she and Lloyd had two children together. Less than a month after they wed, Jean murdered Lloyd as he was unlocking the door to their home after a long day at work. It wasn't until Jean's attorney contacted the FBI about the killing that the state police knew Lloyd was Ma Barker's son.[13]

The headline of the March 22, 1949, edition of the *Joplin Globe* announced that "Lloyd Barker Died with His Boots On." According to the article that followed, "Lloyd (Red) Barker, 51, was slain by a blast from a twenty gauge shotgun on Friday, March 18. Barker's wife, Jean, 37, was arraigned in district court on charges she fired the blast. She pled innocent by reason of insanity."

Charles Klein, owner of the restaurant where Lloyd worked, told police that he was surprised to learn of Barker's identity. "He never mentioned it to me," Charles said. "He was even tempered and a good worker."[14]

On April 15, 1949, J. Edgar Hoover issued a memo from his office requesting that his agents in Denver conduct "appropriate inquiries to determine the outcome of charges against Mrs. Lloyd Barker." The directive also instructed that "facts concerning Lloyd's life in Denver subsequent to his release from prison" needed to be documented. Hoover's memo added that the information should be furnished to the bureau in a letter marked "research." "Any inquiries should be made in such a manner as not to elicit press inquiries," Hoover ordered, "and should be casually secured through local authorities."[15]

Sheriff James W. Lail and Deputy District Attorney George Fischer, both from Brighton, Colorado, prepared the response to Hoover dated May 12, 1949. "Jennie Barker shot and killed her husband Lloyd 'Red'

Barker at their home, 3426 W. 73rd Avenue, Westminster, Colorado, on March 18, 1949. She was arrested the same date and placed in the Adams County Jail at Brighton, Colorado, where she readily confessed to the shooting, claiming she was afraid of him, he having threatened her life on numerous occasions. On March 21, 1949, she was tried by jury in the district court in Brighton and entered a plea of not guilty by reason of insanity at the time and since." Upon the testimony of two competent doctors, she was sentenced to life in the Colorado State Insane Asylum at Pueblo, Colorado, where she was confined on April 9, 1949.[16]

Lail and Fischer's response concluded:

> *The only background information concerning Barker as known to James Lail and George Fischer is that he has been employed for several years at the Denargo Grill at the Denargo Market in Denver, and was, at the time of his death the assistant manager of the Grill. He has reportedly been living with Jennie as a common-law wife for approximately seven or eight years, having two children by her. He was legally married to her at Brighton, Colorado, in February 1949. Jennie had two children by a previous marriage.*
>
> *Jennie is described as born February 20, 1912 at New York City, U.S., 5 feet 2 inches, 92 pounds, blue eyes, brown hair, and fair complexion. No further inquiries have been made in this matter in view of the Bureau instructions that the inquiries should be made through local authorities and in such a manner as not to elicit press inquiries. If the Bureau should desire that additional information regarding Barker's life be obtained this information could probably be secured through local newspaper contacts.[17]*

In addition to the research agents supplied Hoover, they also sent along graphic photos of the scene of the crime, showing Lloyd lying on the sidewalk in front of his house in a pool of blood.[18]

The March 23, 1949, edition of the *Sedalia Democrat* featured a picture of Jean Barker flanked on either side by her two oldest children. Virginia Wynne, age eleven, and Ronald Wynne, age fourteen, were photographed comforting their mother before psychiatrists at her court hearing ruled that she was schizophrenic and suffering from dementia praecox.

Lloyd Barker was buried in an unmarked grave at Elmwood Cemetery in Brighton, Colorado. Charlie Klein, the owner of the restaurant where Lloyd worked, closed the eatery that day so that he and his employees could attend the funeral.[19]

Jean Barker died in August 1986 at the Colorado State Insane Asylum. The whereabouts of her children are unknown.[20]

CHAPTER FIVE

Public Enemy

A COLD BREEZE PUSHED PAST THE DILAPIDATED FRAME AROUND THE only window in the dank, stark room where Edward Bremer was being held hostage in the winter of 1934. Blindfolded and bruised, Edward attempted to turn the chair he was tied to away from the frigid air. In a gruff tone Arthur Barker warned him to keep still as he pulled the collar of his coat closely around his neck. The winter in Bensenville, Illinois, was particularly cold that year. Temperatures dipped well below zero. The Barker boys and their associates made little effort to keep their kidnapped victim comfortable. With the exception of the time when Edward was forced to sign his own ransom notes, the ties around his hands were seldom removed.[1]

On January 22, 1934, Edward was instructed to sign a second note to the Bremer family physician with instructions regarding the ransom money demanded. The first note was not taken seriously. In spite of the Barkers' warning not to involve law enforcement, the police came in full force to search for Edward. Note number two was much more forceful and ominous:[2]

If Bremer don't get back to his family, [he] has you to thank. First of all, all coppers must be pulled off. Second, the dough must be ready. Third, we must have a new signal. When you are ready to meet our terms, place a N.R.A. sticker in the center of each of your office windows. We'll know if the coppers are pulled or not. Remain at your office daily from now until 8 p.m. Have the dough ready and where you can get it within thirty minutes. You will be instructed how to deliver it. The money must not be hot as it will be examined before Bremer is released.

We'll try to be ready for any trickery if attempted. This is positively our LAST attempt. DON'T duck it.[3]

Edward remembered hearing a woman's voice from down the hall of the warehouse building where he was held captive. "It was a strong, authoritative voice," he informed federal agents once the incident was over. "In spite of the rough treatment and the frantic move to replace the blindfold and retie my hands, I heard some of what she said." In addition to encouraging the outlaws on the job they were doing, she told them they were "too good for small time," Edward told authorities. "This is where the big dough is made and you don't have to stick your neck out every day."[4]

An Associated Press article written by reporter John Lear in July 1939 noted that Ma Barker engineered crimes that required careful thought and were "low risk but high return." Wherever Ma lived, her home was a community center for convicts and hustlers. Unsuspecting neighbors knew nothing of the regular company she kept. As the illegal exploits of the family became more sophisticated under her direction, Ma was forced to constantly relocate. Posing as an unassuming elderly lady whose sole interest was baking and playing the fiddle, she infiltrated peaceful communities that had no idea her home was under constant suspicion by the police.[5]

The years Ma spent living in Tulsa were consumed with complaints from neighbors about her troubled sons, and there was seldom a time residents weren't peering out the windows or from behind half-closed doors to steal a glance at the questionable activity at the Barker home.[6]

Ma's third son, Arthur "Doc" Barker, was the subject of a great deal of the attention the family received. Among those people coming and going from the Barkers' were Harry Campbell, Ray Terrill, and Roland "Shorty" Williams. All three were ambitious thieves, and Arthur was open to any crime they thought to commit. On the evening of January

9, 1920, the four men attempted to break into the Coweta bank in
Coweta, Oklahoma. Armed with nitroglycerin, picks, and shovels they
had stolen from a hardware store, the outlaws began digging a tunnel
under the bank from the alleyway behind the building. Two men dug
while two men stood watch.[7]

Coweta police officers were making their rounds when they happened upon the four thieves dressed in business suits and carrying
large automatic pistols. They told the authorities their car had broken
down a few blocks away and they were en route to a service station
to get help. The police did not believe their story and escorted the
men to jail until the matter was investigated. The officers found the
vehicle parked in front of a boardinghouse. Inside the vehicle they discovered several rifles and rounds of ammunition. The police extended
their search into the boardinghouse and uncovered three additional
accomplices, including the getaway driver, and eight ounces of nitroglycerin. Arthur and the other four of the robbery detail were arrested
and charged with attempted burglary.[8]

In addition to pressing charges associated with the attempted
bank robbery in Coweta, authorities eventually charged the men with
the robbery of businesses in Tryon and Ripley, Oklahoma, as well. Six
months after the attempted break-in at the Coweta Bank, the daring
quartet were questioned by authorities from Texas and Payne County,
Oklahoma, on suspicion of robbing a bank, a post office, and a general store. According to the January 20, 1921, edition of the *Muskogee
Times–Democrat*:

> *Harry Campbell, Arthur Barker, Shorty Williams, and Ray Terrill
> (also known as G. R. Patton) are at the center of interest to peace
> officers of more places than one.*
>
> *Sheriff Brown of Tyron (Texas County) after seeing the men in
> Coweta, felt strongly of the opinion that they are the young men who
> robbed a bank and a hardware store in town some weeks ago. Busi-
> ness owners from the same county visited Coweta and inspected the
> thieves' arsenals and their accoutrements and positively identified*

a Winchester rifle as one used in robbing the Tyron bank. The picks, shovels, and nitroglycerin collected from the criminals were identified as the items taken from a hardware store in town.

Possession of the burglary tools would constitute a charge sufficient to bind them to the county court.[9]

On June 12, 1921, police sent the four bank robbers by train to the state prison at McAlester, Oklahoma, to be arraigned and to await their trial. The trip was not without incident. Harry Campbell and Shorty Williams jumped from a train window and escaped. Both were eventually recaptured and delivered to the facility.[10]

The four criminals were scheduled to be tried in Wagoner County on July 21, 1921. Ray Terrill pled guilty at his hearing. Harry and Shorty made another daring escape before their case was heard in court but were once again tracked down by the authorities and brought back to the prison. They were found guilty on all charges. Arthur was found not guilty, acquitted, and released. Ma was relieved that her son was free and would return home to her in Tulsa.[11]

Arthur's escape from a long prison sentence did not deter him from continuing with his criminal activities. The close call emboldened him. He believed there was no punishment a judge or jury could hand down from which his mother couldn't save him. Ma had promised her boys she would use every means possible to keep them from ever having to serve a long period of time in prison. However she worked it out, she had proven to be as good as her word, and Arthur was fearless now.[12]

Less than a month after his hearing, Arthur made plans with seven accomplished thieves, some of whom were members of the Central Park Gang, to burglarize the homes of wealthy Tulsa residents. Volney Davis was one of Arthur's closest friends and one of the criminals who participated in a string of robberies in the summer of 1921.[13]

The police paid numerous visits to the Barker home to question the arrogant group of outlaws about their possible involvement. Ma interceded with the usual diatribe about how her innocent boys were being persecuted. To all she gave invitations to search her place for evidence, but first she gave the boys instructions to leave no incriminating evidence in the house. Despite their suspicions, the authorities found nothing to link Arthur, Volney, and the others to the rash of thefts.[14]

On August 26, 1921, the robbers made a fatal mistake that eventually led police back to the Barker house in search of a murderer. Arthur and his cohorts deviated from home invasions to rob a safe at the Fuller Construction Company. Volney had been employed by the business for a short time, and the foreman he worked for always took his wages out of the safe in the work shed at the end of his shift. Volney remembered where the safe was located and approximately how much money was inside but had forgotten there was a night watchman on duty. Armed with .45 caliber revolvers, Arthur and one of the other burglars were the first to enter the construction company office. They came face-to-face with the unsuspecting sixty-eight-year-old watchman, Thomas J. Sherill. Arthur fired a shot into the watchman's head, and the other thief shot the man in the chest.[15]

The Tulsa police were mystified over the murder. The August 26, 1921, edition of the *Ada Evening News* reported that the community was horrified that the guard was gunned down at his post and there was no suspect:

The murder of T. J. Sherill occurred between midnight and five o'clock the morning of August 26, 1921. The aged watchman was found by a gardener living in the vicinity. The body was lying on a platform in front of a little building. A bullet had entered the left cheek and raged upward, coming out at the top of the head. Another had penetrated the body between the stomach and the heart.

Sherill's midnight luncheon had been eaten. This would seem to indicate that he met death after the midnight hour. His rounds were registered in the clock in the hospital and as soon as this clock is opened the time of his death will be approximately arrived at.

Police found the watchman's revolver in his pocket with no cartridges exploded. They believe this clears every doubt as to suicide and they are holding to the theory that an unknown enemy shot the watchman as he stood on the porch in the moonlight.

Thomas Sherill, a work man, declared this morning that he had talked with his father yesterday. The son said his father had been in the best of spirits and gave no hint of trouble or danger. The family knows of no enemy who could have wished his death. He leaves a wife and nine children, all residing in Tulsa.

Thomas Sherill's murder went unsolved for two months. A pair of determined private detectives named F. J. Hays and Walter Duckett worked diligently on solving the crime. Using a marking on the bullet, they managed to match the ammunition to the gun's registered owner in Fort Smith, Arkansas. The detectives questioned the gun owner, and he admitted that he'd loaned his weapon to a man whose sister and friend were living with Volney Davis and Arthur Barker.[16]

In late November 1921 Tulsa police arrested Arthur Barker and Howard Carpenter for the shooting death of Thomas J. Sherill and also took into custody Sylvester Gillard for supplying the guns used to kill the watchman.

The December 6, 1921, edition of the *Morning Tulsa Daily World* carried the news of Arthur's preliminary trial. The paper named him as the leader of the gang that murdered the aged watchman. The article reported:

After a several hour hearing the state rested shortly after 4 o'clock on the 6th and counsel for Barker immediately submitted a demurrer [an objection that an opponent's point is irrelevant or invalid] stating that a short continuance was desired in which to present authority. The hearing will be concluded this afternoon. If the demurrer is overruled, the arguments will be heard immediately because Barker's counsel said the defense would submit no testimony.

Chief witnesses in the hearing were Lee Huntsman, a gardener who lives near the location of the construction company where Sherill was found, William Moore, employee of the Mitchell-Fleming

Undertaking Company which handled the night watchman's body, and gang member Sylvester "Big" Gillard.

Huntsman testified that he found the old man's body and admitted having heard shots and voices during the night but said he thought nothing of it.

With the exception of Volney Davis, who had fled the area before any arrests were made, all the men Arthur had worked with up to and including the burglary of the Fuller Construction Company safe testified against him. Arthur and Volney's girlfriends swore in court that the two men had been with them at their apartment when the crime was committed. The jury did not believe the women.[17]

Ma Barker and her estranged husband, George, attended Arthur's hearing and were there the day the women took the stand on their son's behalf. Ma had expressed her objection to the women coming forward to Arthur and his lawyer. She believed that whatever the pair had to say would only make matters worse for her boy. She was right. Because the women were viewed by the judge and jury to be unreliable witnesses, the court felt all of the witnesses testifying for Arthur were liars and disregarded their testimony.[18]

Ten days after the trial had begun, the case came to a close. Arthur was found guilty of murder. Ma was inconsolable. She rushed to her son and threw her arms around him, sobbing uncontrollably. Once the judge regained order in the courtroom, he announced that Arthur was "nothing but a cold-blooded killer without conscience or remorse." He was sentenced to life in prison at the Oklahoma state prison in McAlester. As he was being led out of the courtroom by officials, he proclaimed his innocence and shouted that he had not received a fair trial. Ma boldly echoed his sentiments and rushed to hold her son again. Both George and Ma were allowed a quick moment with their boy. Ma hugged Arthur's neck and assured him that she would see him soon on the outside.[19]

Prior to Herman's death, a death Ma insisted came at the hands of "blood-thirsty cops," there was no evidence that Ma did more than direct and counsel her boys. From Herman's death forward she grew more and more active and more and more vicious. After Arthur was sentenced Ma became obsessed with getting him out of jail and expanding the membership of the Central Park Gang.[20]

By the early 1930s a number of people had entered the gangster trade. John Dillinger, Al Capone, Bonnie and Clyde, Pretty Boy Floyd, and the Underhill Gang were just a few of the "mighty forces to be reckoned with." The country was in the throes of an economic depression, and men and women were competing for the limited work available. There was a glut of individuals competing in the field of crime. Ma recognized the need to recruit outlaws who would band together to go after specific jobs and decrease the number of culprits who might have plans to attempt the same crimes. She was confident the boys in the gang would do anything she asked of them. Fred, Ma's youngest son, was loyal but impetuous. He was his mother's favorite child and desired nothing more than to follow in his brothers' footsteps.[21]

Born in 1901, Fred had a close relationship with Ma. She doted on him and confided in him. Historians note she had a similar relationship with Arthur when he was in his teens. Both men were involved with a variety of women and were accused of being abusive to their paramours.[22]

Fred was twenty when he committed one of his first violent crimes that culminated in a shoot-out with police. On August 6, 1922, Fred and sixteen-year-old Willie Roberts stole a car from a couple in Tulsa, Oklahoma. Armed with a revolver, the pair of thieves then drove the vehicle to Kansas City, Missouri. The trip was a deviation from their original plan. They initially spoke about robbing a bank in Picher, Oklahoma, but according to the police "the pair got cold feet."[23]

Fred and Willie were speeding when authorities attempted to pull them over. Fred, who was driving, refused to comply, and a chase ensued. He eventually stopped, and both men jumped out of the car and started running. Fred was shot in the leg. The two criminals were arrested and held in a Kansas City jail while awaiting Oklahoma authorities to retrieve the carjackers and transport them back to a facility in Tulsa.[24]

Less than a month after being released on car-theft charges, Fred committed his first federal offense. In early September 1922 he and six other individuals, two women and four men, robbed a US mail truck near Miami, Oklahoma. The seven were detained in the Ottawa County jail while their crime was thoroughly investigated. The September 7, 1922, edition of the *Morning Tulsa Daily World* recounted that all of those arrested claimed Tulsa as their home. The article also noted:

> *The seven were taken into custody Monday while driving through Miami toward home from a camping trip in the extreme eastern edge of the county. They had bathing suits and other camping paraphernalia and explained they'd been on an outing trip.*
>
> *Charles A. Carter, driver of the mail truck, who was robbed, took a good look at the men, but could not identify any of them as the three who stuck him up and took the registered pouch containing $14,200 from him. Carter said that two of the men resembled the robbers, but he was not sure.*
>
> *The men admitted having shady reputations, but they deny all knowledge of the robbery. The detained parties give the name of Fred Barker, W. C. Crabb, Glen Lamberson, Edward Minson, Wayne Evans, Mrs. May Deshane, and Mrs. Elizabeth Lowery.*
>
> *Barker limps a little and is said to admit that he is the man whom the Kansas City police shot at recently while he was in possession of a stolen Cadillac car.*[25]

Neither Fred's close encounter with the law or witnessing his brothers' hardships because of their own criminal activity deterred him from continuing his illegal ventures. Using more than ten aliases, Fred's crime spree expanded beyond Oklahoma. He was wanted for questioning in a string of auto thefts and the robberies of three service stations in Kansas.[26]

On January 6, 1923, Fred and another bandit armed with revolvers forced their way into an auto repair shop in Tulsa, Oklahoma, and robbed a group of men playing poker. They escaped with $600 of the card players' money. Police were called to the scene, and the owner of the shop, who had recognized Fred, told the authorities Fred was the culprit. The police tracked Fred to the home of one of his friends and found him hiding under the house. He was ordered to come out with his hands up. Fred did as he was told; as he was surrendering an over-anxious police officer shot him in the hand.[27]

Although he maintained he was innocent, Fred was tried for the robbery of the card game and sentenced to five years in a reformatory. Before he turned himself in to the officials at the reformatory, he was ordered to court in Huntsville, Texas, to stand trial for car theft. In October 1923 he walked out of the state prison in Huntsville, Texas, where he had served time for stealing cars, and was rearrested in Tulsa on a charge of mailing morphine to inmates at the McAlester penitentiary in Oklahoma.[28]

Fred's parents were present when the authorities escorted him to the reformatory in Granite, Oklahoma. Ma wept bitterly at the sight and pleaded with the judge to reconsider and release her son into her custody. The judge refused her request. She left the courtroom vowing to get even with the law for robbing her of her sons. By late October 1923 three of her boys were incarcerated.[29]

Fred was released from the reformatory on November 4, 1925, and by Christmas he had run afoul of the law again. He was suspected in connection with the robbery of a bank in Washington, Arkansas, and wanted by federal authorities on a charge of forging a money order stolen from a post office in Jenks, Oklahoma. He was arrested again in late December 1925, but after a full investigation, federal agents said they could find no hard evidence to link the youngest Barker to the Arkansas bank robbery or the theft of money orders; they were forced to let him go.[30]

Fred met his brother Herman soon after Herman was released from jail in Okmulgee, Oklahoma. The headquarters for the gang the Barkers ran with was located in Miami, Oklahoma. Herman took Fred under his wing, and along with six other outlaws, they set about robbing jewelry and clothing stores in Vinita, Tulsa, Muskogee, and McAlester, Oklahoma. Together they stole more than $100,000 in cash, jewels, and other merchandise. The group separated in early spring 1926 to keep from being captured by the law, which was in hot pursuit. Herman believed they stood less of a chance getting caught if they went their separate ways.[31]

The authorities found Fred Barker at the Hotel Marion in Little Rock, Arkansas, where he was registered under the name F. R. Lang. The police were confident that when they raided the crook's room they would find the lion's share of the money and items Fred, Herman, and the other bandits had stolen. Unfortunately, all that was found in Fred's possession were two diamonds. He was arrested and placed in jail at Fort Smith, Arkansas, where he was held over for trial.[32]

The Barkers' family attorney, Q. P. McGhee, along with a crooked Miami County, Oklahoma, deputy named Frank M. Warner, offered the judge set to hear the case against Fred an unspecified sum of money to rule that there was insufficient evidence in the case and to allow the accused to go free.[33]

In November 1926 Fred reteamed up with his older brother and idol Herman to burglarize stores in Winfield, Kansas. It was late when a Cowley County, Kansas, deputy stopped a man who appeared to be breaking into the Tharp Grocery Store. The suspect ran away before the law enforcement officer could question him. The deputy chased the culprit down the street and lost him in the shadows. That's when the officer spotted a young man sitting on the hood of a car and ordered the man to drive in the direction of the thief he was running after. The man, later identified as Fred Barker, was reluctant to do as he was asked and used the excuse that he couldn't leave because he was waiting for his mother. The officer suspected he was lying and demanded that Fred drive him to the police station. Fred grudgingly did so.[34]

At the station the police grilled the outlaw further. They wanted to know the real reason he was out so late. Fred insisted he was waiting for his mother to return from the drugstore; even when he was informed that the drugstore had been closed for hours, he didn't deviate from the story. Fred told the officers his name was Ted Murphy and that he was from Miami, Oklahoma. The police searched him for identification and found a large roll of cash in his suit pocket. Fred refused to say another word to the officers about anything else.[35]

A thorough search of Fred's car was made, and police found a .32 Colt automatic pistol and burglar tools, including a large hammer and bolt cutters. There were also items that looked suspiciously like stolen goods.[36]

It was soon discovered that the money Fred had in his possession was the exact amount that had been taken from the safes at a furniture store and a butcher's shop. The thieves were well on their way to stealing funds from another business when their crime was thwarted by a quick-thinking deputy making rounds.[37]

Fred was taken into custody and charged with burglary. His bail was set at $14,000. Try as she might, there was nothing Ma could do to help. Fred was a repeat offender; at his trial he was found guilty of the offenses and sentenced five to ten years in the Kansas State Penitentiary in Lansing, Kansas. He was moved from the Cowley County jail to the state prison on March 12, 1927.[38]

Fred Barker's prison intake information noted he was an American from Missouri with a sixth-grade education. His occupation was listed as laundryman, and it was noted he had no religion. The intake form also read that he had been married to Billie Orr, had no children from the union, and that his parents were living at 401 Cincinnati Avenue in Tulsa, Oklahoma.[39]

In times of crisis, when Ma's boys alone could not turn a disastrous situation around, she depended on the other members of the Central Park Gang, Q. P. McGhee, and McGhee's associates for help. McGhee employed a variety of tactics to obtain the Barker boys' freedom when they, or their cohorts, were in an Oklahoma jail. If the outlaws pled guilty, he would arrange for them to be immediately paroled. McGhee would work out deals with the corrupt district attorney's office by either paying them a fee or promising them a particular service in exchange for allowing the Barker boys and their gang members to go free. He would also offer substantial cash rewards if the arresting officer turned the accused over to Deputy Sheriff F. Warner in Tulsa County. Such was the case when Fred was taken into custody in Winfield, Kansas. McGhee and Deputy Sheriff Warner arrived at the jail with a card offering a reward of $25 for the return of the car Fred was driving at the time he was arrested as well as a $300 reward for the accused.[40]

The January 27, 1927, edition of the *Miami Daily News-Record* conveyed that the Winfield police "refused to give up Barker, who was being held to face a charge of burglary."

On those rare occasions authorities would not cooperate with McGhee, he would carry on and try to find another way to free his client. That was not to be the case in Kansas. McGhee and lawman Warner were held by Winfield police, and the men were later charged jointly with harboring, aiding, and assisting a person guilty of a felony. Unbeknownst to McGhee, an investigation had been initiated by Houston B. Teehee, Oklahoma assistant attorney general, into the questionable procedures used to secure the Barkers' releases from state prisons and county jails. The investigation had reportedly extended into other states besides Oklahoma, and Assistant Attorney General Teehee hoped to persuade the FBI to look into the matter as well.[41]

McGhee was released on bail and continued conducting business as he usually did. Although he suspected his every move was being monitored by the government, he managed to provide Ma with legal assistance. On October 24, 1927, McGhee was "found guilty of aiding criminals to escape arrest and prosecution." The jury left the decision of the degree of punishment with the court. McGhee appealed the decision and was allowed to go free on an appeal bond. His association with known criminals was not interrupted during this time.[42]

The comings and goings of the Barkers and associates like McGhee did not escape the attention of FBI director J. Edgar Hoover. He was anxious to wage war against crime gangs. Those that concentrated in the panhandle, like the Barkers, and major organizations in the Midwest, like Al Capone and his boys, were averaging a yearly income of $108 million.[43]

Since robbers and corrupt lawyers operated across state lines, Hoover pressed to have their crimes recognized as federal offenses so that he and his men would have the authority to pursue them. He wanted them to be known as public enemies. Hoover believed the term public enemy (which didn't become popular until 1930) best described individuals whose activities were seen as criminal and extremely damaging to society.[44]

In December 1927 Hoover presented a report of the work his bureau had completed that year and argued that the police section of the department was the natural choice to track and apprehend repeat offenders like the Barkers. According to the December 8, 1927, edition of the *Index-Journal*, in a year's time Hoover's men had procured "ten life sentences, other sentences aggregating 7,090 years, fines totaling $149,045,000, and recovered property valued at $6,014,483." The article concluded by noting that "Hoover's bureau operated on an expense of $2,012,860, the smallest since 1923."

Hoover was an ambitious man who set his sights on apprehending not only the Barkers and their associates but the person he held responsible for all their misdeeds, Ma Barker. "Ma learned the intricacies of criminal practice and schooled her boys well," Hoover is quoted as saying in the May 1935 edition of the *Master Detective* magazine. "She cast her lot with their criminal activities—in as much as she was more intelligent than any of her sons," he wrote about her in a FBI report. "She controlled them and found this expression of dominance easily exerted because of the submission of her sons Fred and Arthur."[45]

Ma worked with furious determination to get her boys out of the various state prisons in which they found themselves in 1927. The extent to which she would go and the men she partnered with to see the jobs done earned her a top spot on Hoover's public-enemy list.[46]

CHAPTER SIX

Murder in Wisconsin

A DILAPIDATED FORD MODEL T PICKUP SLOWED TO A STOP IN FRONT of the Barker home in Tulsa, Oklahoma, in mid-May 1931, and Alvin Karpis climbed out of the bed of the vehicle. Alvin was a tall, self-confident man, well dressed but not flashy. He carried a small duffle-style suitcase containing all the belongings he had in the world. He studied the weathered house in front of him, taking notice of its state of disrepair. The homes on either side were not in perfect condition; it was a low-income neighborhood, and everyone seemed to be strug-gling, but the Barkers' house was in a sorry state in comparison.[1]

A man and woman inside the Barker home were arguing. The exact nature of the disagreement was not clear, but the sound of doors slamming and glass breaking made it apparent that the fight had esca-lated into a war.[2]

Alvin removed a cigarette from his suit jacket pocket and lit it while contemplating what to do next. Ma Barker exited the front door carrying a hammer and nails. She didn't pay much attention to Alvin. Her lower lip was bleeding, but she didn't pay much attention to that either. She was focused on fixing a portion of the screen that had been torn from the corner of the door.[3]

"Are you Mrs. Barker?" Alvin asked, walking toward Ma and tak-ing a drag off his cigarette.

"I am," Ma said turning around to face Alvin.

"I want to get ahold of Freddie," he told her.

Ma looked Alvin over suspiciously. "Who are you?"

"I'm the guy who called with Freddie in Lansing," Alvin told her.

"Oh, yes, he told me about you," Ma replied. "He told me you'd be getting out soon. He came to visit me when he got out. He's a good boy."

Ma let her guard down, and Alvin stepped onto the porch. He told her he was a thief and that he'd been sent to the Kansas State Penitentiary in Lansing for attempting to rob a pool hall. It was just one of many crimes Alvin told Ma that he'd committed.[4]

Alvin was born in Montreal, Quebec, on August 10, 1907. When he was ten years old, his parents moved to Topeka, Kansas. His father ran a farm and also worked for the Santa Fe railroad as a design painter. Alvin's mother took care of the home and the four children. Alvin was the Karpises' only son. He was not a fan of hard work and frequently found a way out of doing chores around the homestead. In 1917 Alvin met an eighteen-year-old lawbreaker who had spent much of his youth in and out of reform schools. The two boys struck up a friendship and became partners in crime. They broke into grocery and hardware stores, taking money and merchandise. Before the law could catch up with the juvenile delinquents, Alvin's father moved the family to Chicago.[5]

For more than two years, Alvin abandoned his criminal activities and took a job with a drug company as a shipping clerk and errand boy. The lifestyle proved to be too mundane for Alvin, and at eighteen he returned to Chicago and crime. He went into business with a friend and opened a hamburger stand that doubled as a base for selling alcohol. Alvin and his partner broke into warehouses and storage facilities, stealing everything from pocketknives to tires. He snuck onboard trains, which deposited him in towns in Iowa, Missouri, Oklahoma, Arkansas, Ohio, Michigan, and Wisconsin. During his travels he familiarized himself with the merchants who brought in the most money.[6]

Alvin was finally caught riding the rails for free by an ambitious railroad guard. Authorities sentenced him to serve thirty days with a group of prisoners. The prisoners were chained together and performed both menial and challenging work. Shortly after Alvin completed his punishment, he was arrested for robbing a warehouse in a small Kansas town. The judge who heard Alvin's case was furious with his behavior and sentenced the repeat offender to a five- to ten-year sentence in a reformatory in Hutchinson, Kansas.[7]

The Hutchinson Correctional Facility housed a number of violent young men who were more than willing to share their criminal experience with Alvin. Lawrence Devol was one of those who relished talking about his illegal ventures. He was raised in Tulsa and had become a member of the Central Park Gang by the age of twelve. At thirteen he was arrested for larceny. On August 19, 1927, he participated in his first bank robbery in Vinton, Iowa. Devol and three other thieves stole more than $70,000. The following February Devol and his group broke into a bank in Ohio and stole a quarter of a million dollars.[8]

Alvin idolized Devol. He was a daring and accomplished thief; not only did he know a great deal about breaking into banks, but also he could handle nitroglycerine—a dangerous but most effective tool.[9]

In 1929 Alvin, Devol, and two other inmates escaped from the reformatory and embarked on a crime spree that included heists in Oklahoma, Nebraska, and Missouri. They stole money, clothing, shoes, guns, and cars. When authorities apprehended the pair in Kansas City, Missouri, on Sunday, March 23, 1930, the outlaws admitted to a total of forty robberies. Using the aliases Leonard Carson and Raymond Hadley, the twenty-four-year-old and eighteen-year-old men had been on the run for several months before authorities managed to get a lead on their whereabouts.[10]

The March 24, 1930, edition of the *Miami Daily News-Record* reported that the fugitives were taken into custody after they had aroused the suspicions of two policemen who watched them drive by a certain downtown street corner several times in a motorcar with an Oklahoma license plate. "The youths," police said, "admitted the car had been stolen in Tulsa two weeks prior." A suitcase containing what police said were burglary tools was found in the car. Police also told reporters:

The youths confessed to taking $5,000 in loot from filling stations and small stores. They only had $500 in their possession when they were arrested. The remainder of the $5,000 had been lost in gambling.

Among the towns in Oklahoma in which Carson and Hadley admitted their participation were Quapaw, Henryetta, Chandler, Sapulpa, and Tulsa.

Oklahoma authorities were notified of the youths' capture, and they are being held pending action by officials of that state. They told police they came to Kansas City planning to engage in robberies here and that they were to meet a man whose name they gave as Harry Borders. They were seeking him when they were arrested.[11]

Both Alvin and Devol were eventually tried for their crimes and sent to the Kansas State Penitentiary in Lansing, Kansas, on May 19, 1930.[12]

At some point the conversation Ma and Alvin began on the front steps of the porch moved inside the Barker home. Alvin wasn't too impressed with the interior of the house. According to his autobiography it was "little more than a shack accentuated with handbags, fine clothes, new dishes, furs, trinkets, and jewelry scattered about." All were mementoes from crimes in which the Barker boys had participated.[13]

Alvin continued to be forthcoming with Ma about his past. While he and Fred were in jail, Fred had explained to him that there was nothing he could tell Ma that would make her shudder. Alvin told her that he'd managed to walk out of the state penitentiary a free man on May 2, 1931. He had taken a job working with a detail in the coal mines near the facility. Prisoners who worked in the mines could either earn time toward an early release or they could earn funds to use in the commissary. Inmates serving exceptionally long sentences only cared about accumulating money. Alvin convinced the long-timers to donate their time to him in exchange for his pay. In two months, he earned 108 days.[14]

Alvin shared with Ma what his life had been like in the penitentiary

$1,200.00 REWARD $1,200.00

Twelve Hundred Dollars.

WANTED

For the Murder of C. R. Kelly, Sheriff of Howell County, Missouri, on December 19, 1931

Gangsters of
Kimes-Inman
Gang of
Oklahoma
Missouri
Kansas and
Texas

ALVIN KARPIS   **FRED BARKER**

DESCRIPTION: ALVIN KARPIS, alias George Dunn, alias R. E. Hamilton, alias Ray Karpis, alias Raymond Hadley, alias George Haller; Age 22; Height 5-9¾; Weight 130 lbs.; Hair-brown; Eyes-blue; Scars-cut SC base L. hand; Occupation, Worked in bakery.   FPC   1-R-II-5

1-U-UU-8

Karpis is ex-convict having served State Reformatory Hutchinson, Kansas, 1926, No. 7071   Also State Penitentiary Lansing, Kansas, May, 1930, Crime Burglary.

DESCRIPTION: FRED BARKER, alias F. G. Ward, alias Ted Murphy, alias J. Darrows; Age 28; Weight 120 lbs.; Height 5-4; Build-slim; Complexion-fair; Hair-sandy; Eyes-blue; Teeth-lower front gold, two upper front gold. Sentenced State Reformatory, Granite, Oklahoma.   Robbery 1923.   Sentenced State Penitentiary Lansing, Kan., March, 1927.

FPC   29-I-20

20-O-22

These men acting together murdered Sheriff C. R. Kelly, West Plains, Missouri in cold blood when he attempted to question them.

The Chief of Police and Sheriff at West Plains, Missouri, will pay a reward of $300.00 each for the arrest and surrender of either of these men to Howell County, Missouri officers. $200.00 additional will be paid on conviction.   We will come after them any place.

An additional Reward of $100.00 each will be paid for the arrest and surrender to Howell County officers of A. W. Dunlop and Old Lady Arrie Barker, Mother of Fred Barker. Dunlop is about 65 years of age; slender, white hair, full blood Irishman. Mrs. Barker is about 60 years of age. All may be found together on farm. We hold Felony Warrants for each of these parties.

Police and other authorities: Keep this Poster before you at all times as we want these Fugitives.   If further information is desired Wire Collect Chief of Police or Sheriff at West Plains, Missouri.

James A. Bridges   Mrs. C. R. Kelly
Chief of Police   Sheriff

West Plains, Missouri

JOURNAL PRINT, West Plains, Mo.

Reward poster for Alvin Karpis and Fred Barker

and described his first meeting with Fred. Fred and Alvin took an instant liking to one another and spoke often of working together once they were released. Fred was released from the Kansas State Penitentiary on March 29, 1931. He stopped by Ma's house in Tulsa and had planned to stay with her, but Arthur Dunlop proved to be a problem. Dunlop was Ma's live-in boyfriend. He drank too much, and the drinking led to arguing with whomever was around. Fred had decided to move to Joplin to live with his father for a while. Before traveling to Missouri, he paid a visit to his brother Herman's widow. Ma did not like Fred seeing Carol. She never liked her and referred to her as a "hussy." Ma believed that Carol aided the authorities in tracking down Herman, and nobody could convince her otherwise. She feared Fred's life would be cut short too if he spent any time with Carol.[15]

Shortly after Alvin confessed all to Ma, she changed her clothes and set off for the Western Union office to send a message to Fred. He got word back to Ma the following morning with instructions for Alvin to take the train to Joplin. Fred met Alvin at the station.[16]

Fred was happy to see Alvin and excited to have him meet his friend, twenty-six-year-old W. H. Geers, also known as James Edward Creighton. Creighton was a bank robber who three months prior to meeting Alvin had robbed the National Bank of Hastings in Nebraska. He had escaped from police investigating the crime and was hiding out in Joplin. The three men decided to room together at a boardinghouse and there began talks to form a gang. Creighton had a wife and a child and preferred not to have his name attached to a known group of criminals. He wanted to disappear in the background after a job. Fred was audacious and had more experience with breaking the law than Alvin, so it was decided the group would be known as the Barker-Karpis Gang.[17]

The first job Fred proposed the three take on together was robbing a bank in Mountain View, Missouri. Fred recruited two additional ex-offenders to help with the daytime heist. They were William Weaver and Jimmie Wilson. On October 7, 1931, Alvin and Weaver broke into the small-town bank at 3:00 in the morning. Wearing handkerchiefs over

Ma Barker with her paramour Arthur Dunlop

their faces and carrying guns, the two men laid in wait for employees to open for business. A pair of employees arrived on the scene before 9:00 a.m. and were made to open the safe. The thieves removed the money and deposited the two bank employees inside the vault.[18]

Fred was waiting outside the building in the getaway car. As soon as Alvin, Weaver, and Wilson, their lookout, ran out of the bank, Fred was revving the engine of the vehicle. While speeding away from the crime scene, Wilson scattered two-inch roofing tacks on the road in their wake to slow up any police that gave chase. When the Barker-Karpis Gang was far out of town, they stopped to count the money. They had successfully made off with $7,000.

A month prior to the Mountain View robbery, Fred used money he stole from jewelry stores in Oklahoma and Kansas to move Ma out of Oklahoma to a farm in Thayer, Missouri. Ma was tired of the police watching her every move and questioning her about crimes the authorities couldn't solve. She had experienced police harassment for a number of years and feared they would do whatever they could to connect Fred to robberies in the area. Ma knew that nothing short of leaving the state would keep the police at bay.[19]

Ma made the trip to Missouri in an expensive sedan. Much to Fred's displeasure Dunlop accompanied her. Dressed in the new hat and suit Ma purchased for him and sporting a fresh haircut and shave, he rode alongside her, sipping alcohol from a silver flask.[20]

Thayer was a small railroad town near the Arkansas state line. Ma's home was a wood-framed structure sitting on ten acres of land. It sat back from the road and had a view in every direction. She had Fred and his cohorts put a barbed wire fence around the property. A long cable affixed to the front gate at the end of a gravel road and attached to a bell inside the front door would ring whenever someone came onto the property. In the evening, two cars were always stationed behind the house, one parked facing one direction and the second facing the opposite direction. Ma would leave nothing to chance in Thayer.[21]

When Ma wasn't preoccupied with Dunlop and his drinking, she was in the kitchen cooking meals for Fred and his associates. Alvin shared some of the kitchen duties with Ma. He had served as a baker in prison, and one of his only legitimate jobs had been as a pastry maker. "In time I became one of Ma's boys," Alvin boasted in his autobiography. "She and I grew very close. Right from the start Ma and I had a feeling for one another." According to Alvin, Ma was a "good sport and never put up a fuss when it was time to go to work."[22]

In the early hours of December 18, 1931, Alvin and Fred robbed a clothing store in West Plains, Missouri. After selecting $2,000 worth of the most expensive garments in the shop, the pair sped away in a 1931 DeSoto sedan. The next day while members of the local West Plains police force were investigating the clothing-store theft, Alvin, Fred, and William Weaver were waiting at a garage in town for two flat tires to be fixed. One of the mechanics replacing the tires noticed that the suits the outlaws were wearing looked a lot like those reported as stolen. The mechanic phoned the owner of the clothing store and asked him to come to the garage to see if the items were from his shop. The mechanic also informed Sheriff Roy Kelly about the incident. The sheriff was coming out of the post office when the mechanic raced over to him to tell him what was happening.[23]

Before deciding to question the suspects, Sheriff Kelly retrieved his gun from the backseat of his car. Fred saw the sheriff approach the car and motioned to Alvin. Shots rang out just as the sheriff opened the car door. Alvin jumped out of the vehicle, reloading his weapons as he fled, and made his escape. Fred drove the car out of the garage as fast as he could. The car hit a curb and bounced. In a flash the DeSoto had disappeared. Sheriff Kelly lay on the ground in a heap. He had been shot twice in the chest and twice in the left arm. He was dead before the ambulance arrived.[24]

The December 21, 1931, edition of the *Marysville Daily Forum* reported that Sheriff Kelly "was slain by the fire of two men" and that "bullets of different calibers were found in an examination of the garage where the shooting occurred."

Raymond H. Tiner, an employee in the garage, identified Fred Barker from a photograph as one of the men who shot the sheriff. The December 22, 1931, edition of the *Joplin Globe* reported that authorities were searching for an old man and an old woman in connection with the case. Some newspaper accounts speculated that the old man and woman were Ma Barker and Arthur Dunlop.[25]

The police located the Barker hangout two miles from Thayer, Missouri, but no one was at the farmhouse when they arrived to question the tenants. Officers did find numerous articles of clothing identified as having been taken from the West Plains store. Authorities also found a drawing of the First National Bank of West Plains among the items strewn about a table in the front room of the house. Some of the other items found were letters addressed to members of the gang and newspaper clippings telling of the sentencing of several men believed to have been known by the gang members.[26]

Ma, Arthur, Fred, and Alvin took refuge at a farm that belonged to one of the Barkers' old friends in Joplin, Herbert Farmer. Farmer was happy to see Ma and her brood, but given the trouble that was sure to follow them, he suggested they hurry along to St. Paul, Minnesota, where they would be safer.[27]

In the 1930s virtually every major gangster, kidnapper, or bank robber in America took refuge in St. Paul. The city was one of three locations in the country that were safe havens for criminals. The other two were Hot Springs, Arkansas, and Cicero, Illinois. St. Paul was the most popular destination. It was well situated for making bootleg liquor and breaking the Prohibition law. Water was needed to make liquor, and the Mississippi River was a rich source. The city had the added advantage of being close to the Canadian border. Liquor could be imported and exported over the Canadian border with relative ease. By 1931 the city had become the epicenter for bootlegging and bootleggers. Public officials and police who were taking bribes to allow the liquor to flow freely encouraged major criminals to come to St. Paul.[28]

Desperados who provided generous compensation to law enforcement agents and to city and state politicians were allowed to live in St. Paul without fear of reprisal. As long as they promised not to kill or rob anyone within the city limits, the outlaws were left alone.[29]

Herbert Farmer, who possessed an extensive criminal record, knew of St. Paul's reputation. That's why he instructed Ma and the boys to go there.[30]

J. Edgar Hoover was aware of the city's reputation as well. He referred to St. Paul as "the poison spot of America." His goal as director of the FBI was to apprehend the corrupt individuals who created the sanctuary. Hoover wasn't able to realize his goal until Congress passed the Federal Kidnapping Act in 1932, more popularly known as the Lindbergh Act, which was intended to let federal authorities step in and pursue kidnappers and later bank robbers once they had crossed state lines.[31]

Ma was as underwhelmed by St. Paul as she was Hoover, at least in the beginning. Although Ma didn't complain, Alvin recognized that she was unhappy. He noted in his autobiography how much she had loved living on the farm. Once the gang had settled in Minnesota, Alvin took Ma out on the town to show her some of his favorite nightspots. He took her to dinner often at the Green Lantern Bar and Supper Club. "It was a perpetual party," Alvin wrote of the famous hangout frequented by high-profile gangsters. "There was probably never before as complete a gathering of criminals in one room. . . . There were escapees from every major US penitentiary. I was dazzled."[32]

Ma was overawed as well. When she and Alvin were out together, they laughed and talked, danced and drank. The only time their evenings were spoiled was when Arthur Dunlop insisted on tagging along. "She let him sponge off of her," Alvin remembered years later. "He looked presentable enough. He was a slim, gray-haired guy, about a head taller than Ma, who kept himself reasonably neat and tidy. But he was a pain in the ass. When I took Ma out to the movies, I'd have to take Dunlop along, too. When we were buying food and clothes, we always had to remember to pick up a share for him. And Dunlop did nothing in return—didn't work, didn't go on scores, didn't help out around the house. He didn't even do a good job of keeping Ma happy."[33]

From the time Sheriff Roy Kelly was discovered gunned down in West Plains, Missouri, in late December 1931, a posse of fifty officers and citizens had been searching for the men who shot him. Members of the posse followed every lead and questioned numerous suspects. On January 13, 1932, the authorities tracked two men who had been bragging about the murder to a house in Mansfield, Missouri. After blasting the home with tear gas, Reuben Hensel, twenty-eight, from Hallowell, Kansas, and Al Bissel, forty-five, from Reeds Springs, Missouri, exited the premises with their hands up. Officers realized shortly thereafter that the pair did not match the descriptions of the murderers they were hunting. The police made similar mistakes in Chicago and Oklahoma.[34]

In May 1932 officials received reliable information that the Barker-Karpis Gang was in Minnesota. A body floating facedown in a lake just over the state line from Illinois prompted the authorities to travel to the northeast to investigate.[35]

The Van Buren, Missouri, newspaper the *Current Local* reported on May 5, 1932, in detail the slaying of Arthur W. Dunlop in Webster, Wisconsin. "Fred Barker and Alvin Karpis were present at the killing but escaped," the article announced. "It was fully determined that these were the men implicated in killing Sheriff Roy Kelly when he attempted to arrest Barker and Karpis in West Plains last December."[36]

According to Alvin's auto-biography Arthur Dunlop's demise was necessary. His drinking and consistent complaining about having to relocate to avoid the police wore on Fred and Alvin's nerves. Arthur was combative with members of the Barker-Karpis Gang, particularly Fred. He resented taking orders from "young punks." Fred disliked Dunlop intensely, and he wasn't shy about how he felt. He never spoke directly to his mother's lover or called him by name. He referred to him only as "the old bastard."[37]

Dunlop was belligerent and abusive when he was drunk and blamed Ma for all the ills in his life. Ma tolerated his insulting remarks and backhands across her mouth, but Alvin made a habit of stepping in between them and warned Dunlop to

George Anderson (aka Arthur Dunlop), Ma's paramour, was killed for talking too much about the family business.
COURTESY OF THE MINNESOTA HISTORICAL SOCIETY

leave her alone. Dunlop resented Alvin's interference and made veiled remarks that Alvin and Ma were more than friends.[38]

One evening in late April 1932, Dunlop was acting particularly aggressive and hurling insults at both Ma and Alvin. As Dunlop was preparing to leave the house, Alvin spotted a revolver in his back pocket. Alvin stopped him as he was headed out the door and lured him back into the kitchen with the promise of another drink.[39]

"When we were out of Ma's hearing, I told him to let me have the thirty-eight [Dunlop's gun]," Alvin recounted in his autobiography.

"He told me to go to hell, and I pulled out my own .45. 'Don't raise your voice and don't make a wrong move. Try either one and you're a dead son-of-a-bitch. Just hand over the gun and shut up.' Dunlop did as he was told but left the house in a fury."[40]

When Dunlop wasn't making himself comfortable at the Barkers' residence, he was frequenting some of St. Paul's finest speakeasies and talking too much to anyone who would listen. Fred and Alvin were told by the new criminal connections they'd made in the area that Dunlop's public behavior was worrisome. Fred and Alvin agreed. Dunlop knew enough about the gang's activities to cause sufficient trouble. Something had to be done.[41]

Before the gangsters could confront Dunlop, they received word from a police informant inside headquarters that the authorities had been tipped off about where to find Fred and Alvin. An unconfirmed snitch had delivered a copy of *True Detective* magazine to police headquarters in St. Paul that featured photographs of Fred and Alvin. The snitch told authorities where the Barker-Karpis Gang was hiding out. Dunlop had shared details of the gang's whereabouts with a source Alvin believed was their landlord's son. The gang's contact inside headquarters was stalling a raid on the home until Fred and Alvin were tipped off.

When Alvin was made aware of what was happening, he hurried to relocate Ma and Dunlop to another hiding spot. Alvin confronted Dunlop, and he admitted what he'd done. He blamed his behavior on being drunk and pleaded with Ma and Alvin to forgive him. Alvin was disinclined to grant his request. He drove him to a hotel and checked him in using a different name.[42]

Ma was extremely distressed with what Dunlop had done. She and Alvin drove around for hours talking about what had to be done next. "I told Ma she'd be better off without him," Alvin later recalled telling her. "She agreed. Out of loyalty, she didn't want to criticize Dunlop, but I gathered she'd had her fill."[43]

Alvin explained that he and Fred would take Dunlop to Kansas City, Missouri, until the excitement in St. Paul subsided. The plan was then to send Dunlop on to Chicago. Ma was convinced it was the best scenario. She cried, and Alvin wiped away her tears before taking her to a friend's house to stay until the business with Dunlop was settled.[44]

Dunlop didn't make it to Chicago. On April 26, 1932, the seventy-year-old man was shot in the back of the head and the right side of his body. His remains were found on the shores of Lake Fremstad, five miles outside the town of Webster, Wisconsin.[45]

The coroner's report revealed that Dunlop had been stripped of his clothes and his mustache had been partially severed and left hanging. When questioned by the authorities, gas station attendants near the spot where Dunlop was killed identified Fred Barker and Alvin Karpis as the two men who purchased gas shortly after the time of death. The pair was driving a car with four new tires, presumably the ones purchased in West Plains in December 1931.[46]

Alvin insisted in his autobiography that neither he nor Fred killed Dunlop. He pointed the finger at Jack Peifer, owner of the Hollyhocks Casino in St. Paul and friend of Fred and Alvin. Peifer had hired the gangsters to do several distasteful jobs while they were in Minnesota, and Alvin later wrote that Peifer "wanted to return the favor."[47]

Ma frequently confessed to Alvin that she didn't miss Dunlop. His drinking and brutish behavior was distracting. She now lavished her affections on Fred, Alvin, and the other hoodlums who associated with the pair and redirected her focus back on the family business. Ma and her boys left Minnesota and sought refuge in Kansas City, Missouri. Fred and Alvin posed as insurance salesmen, and Ma claimed that both men were her sons. By the end of early June 1932, the three had recruited four new gang members—all of whom were convicted bank robbers.[48]

CHAPTER SEVEN

Careless Crimes

ALVIN KARPIS, HARVEY BAILEY, AND BERNARD "BIG PHIL" COURT-
ney walked quickly out of the Citizens National Bank in Wahpeton,
North Dakota, on September 30, 1932. Each was wearing a long
overcoat, and if not for the Thompson machine guns or .45 caliber
revolvers they carried in their hands, they could have passed as bank
examiners to the casual observer. An alarm screamed behind them,
and Fred Barker and Lawrence Devol charged out the double doors of
the bank, each having a female hostage in front of him. Fred pulled a
tommy gun from under his coat and opened fire on law enforcement
agents collecting on the sidewalk across the street from the bank. The
police didn't dare exchange bullets with the bank robbers for fear of
hitting one of the captives.[1]

The bandits kept careful eyes on the reinforcement of officers that
quickly arrived. Alvin shot at the incoming officers, forcing them to
take cover behind parked cars and streetlights. The hostages screamed
and tried unsuccessfully to break free. Thomas Holden, driver for the
Barker-Karpis Gang, revved the engine on the 1932 Hudson passenger sedan and drove it evenly and quickly out of the nearby alley.[2]

The gangsters loaded into the vehicle as it paused momentarily.
They shot more rounds at the officers to keep them pinned to the
ground. The police cowered under the gang's gunfire. Both Fred and
Lawrence pulled the hostages onto the running boards of the car. The
women were panicked but complied. The vehicle roared away from the
bank as the women cried out for help.[3]

In a few short moments, law enforcement was chasing after the gangsters in their police vehicles. The police were careful when they returned fire because the women were still being used as human shields. The pursuit was slowed when one of the bank robbers broke open the rear window and threw two five-gallon milk jars full of roofing nails onto the road. The police swerved their vehicles to miss the objects. Some didn't make it. They hit the nails and their tires blew. A flurry of fast gunfire from the fugitives dissuaded the officials from traveling too close to the getaway car.[4]

The September 30, 1932, edition of the *Bismarck Tribune* noted that the Barker-Karpis Gang entered the Citizens National Bank at 10:05 in the morning and, using profane language, ordered the dozen patrons and employees to the floor. "One man was armed with a submachine gun, three with revolvers, and one with an iron bar," the *Bismarck Tribune* article read, continuing:

> *One of the men approached the cashier of the bank and informed them that a holdup was in progress. "This is a holdup and no fooling either. We mean business." That was the order of the bandit leader. As soon as the victims raised their hands they were ordered to drop to the floor. While one of the gunmen stood guard, the others proceeded to rifle through the drawers in the cashier's cage and loot the vault.*
>
> *Then as the raiders were looting the bank, the burglar alarm sounded. The alarm was touched off by the cashier. The bandit standing guard slugged the cashier on the head and knocked him senseless.*
>
> *Hurriedly gathering up all the available cash while the alarm sounded, the bandits ran through a rear door. They made no attempt to lock the victims in the vault.*
>
> *The robbers escaped with $7,000 and two hostages. They were dumped off the bandit's car at a deserted farm house twenty miles southeast of Wahpeton on the Minnesota side of the river in the course of a desperate flight from a sheriff's posse, which at 1 p.m. was still on the trail.*

The hostages were severely wounded by the time Harvey Bailey drove the car across the river and down a dirt road concealed by trees. The bandits had outdistanced the police by five miles and were comfortable no one could catch them. The women continued screaming and crying as Harvey maneuvered his way over rocks and pastures toward an old abandoned schoolhouse. Alvin and the other gangsters jumped out of the vehicle as soon as it came to a stop to check on the victims. Both had been hit by bullets, and one of the women had a broken leg. The robbers laid the injured hostages on the ground, and Alvin retrieved a medicine bag from the car. His cohorts in crime held the women down as he shoved syringes filled with morphine into their arms.[5]

The gang's car had not survived the getaway intact. A couple of the tires had been shot, and the gas tank was leaking. Leaving the wounded hostages behind, the gangsters limped along in the vehicle for another mile before it gave out altogether. Fred and the others walked to a dilapidated farmhouse and inspected an old Essex car sitting in the yard. The man who owned the home, his wife, and children hurried out of the ramshackle home to greet the curious strangers.[6]

"Does it run?" Alvin asked the farmer in an even tone.

"Yeah, it runs," the man replied. "It doesn't have hardly any brakes and there's kind of a short in the wiring, but it'll run. What's this here all about?" he inquired, eyeing the gun in Fred's hand.

"We just robbed the Wahpeton bank," Alvin said matter-of-factly, "and we need a car to get out of here fast. We're taking yours and leaving ours and we'll give you some money to square it."

Lawrence Devol handed the farmer a wad of cash as the gangsters eyed the man, impatiently waiting for him to answer.

"You robbed the bank, did you?" he said. "Well, I don't care. All the banks ever do is foreclose on us farmers."

Not another word was said as the gang quickly loaded into the car and sped away.[7]

The Barker-Karpis Gang fled to St. Paul, Minnesota, where they would lay low for a while, set their sights on future heists, and reflect on the robberies in which they participated. The year 1932 had been a busy one for Fred Barker and his associates. The Citizens National Bank in Wahpeton, North Dakota, was just one of more than a half dozen robberies the criminals had orchestrated.[8]

The gang had stolen more than $250,000 in cash and merchandise. Ma was proud of her brood. "Ma Barker was a she-wolf," J. Edgar Hoover told reporters in mid-January 1935, "a veritable beast of prey, encouraging her sons to loot and kill. She helped plan the crimes and sat back and waited for the gang to make it happen."[9]

Ma used a portion of her share of the thievery to rent a cottage at White Bear Lake, one of the largest lakes in the Minneapolis–St. Paul metropolitan area. Posing as a widow named Mrs. Hunter, Ma moved herself, Fred, and Alvin into the quaint home. She invited all the members of the gang to come and relax at the lake. She cooked for them, played a few songs on the fiddle for them, and talked business. Ma wanted the next robbery to include her sons Arthur and Lloyd. She strongly suggested the gang wait until she could get her boys out of jail before they went back to work. "Three sons could make more money than one," she reasoned.

Arthur had been released from prison on September 10, 1932. Ma had never abandoned her efforts to secure an early out for him. In the later part of June 1932, she'd hired a private investigator from Leavenworth, Kansas, named Jack Glynn, to assist her. Jack was a well-liked former police chief who acted as a go-between for convicts and corrupt political figures. He let the duplicitous officers know the amount of money Ma was willing to offer for her son's freedom and oversaw the transaction.[10] Arthur's release from the Oklahoma State Penitentiary came with the condition that he was never to return to Oklahoma again. The same amount of funds was offered for the release of Lloyd, but the powers-that-be at Leavenworth could not be bought.[11]

Any member of the Barker-Karpis Gang who was apprehended as a result of a crime orchestrated by the family could always expect Ma to do whatever was necessary to get them out of jail. Those she hired who failed to do their best were disciplined by her boys. Criminal lawyer J. Earl Smith was retained to defend Harvey Bailey after he was caught

Mugshots of Kate "Ma" Barker (right) and Fred Barker (left) COURTESY OF THE LIBRARY OF CONGRESS, LC-USZ62-125405

by the authorities with a Liberty Bond from a bank robbery the gang pulled in June 1932. Smith was unable to convince a jury of Bailey's innocence. On Ma's orders Fred lured the attorney to a meeting, and his bullet-ridden body was found on a golf course the following day.[12]

When Arthur left the penitentiary, he boarded a train for Neosho, Missouri, and set off on his way to visit his father. After a three-month stay, he traveled to St. Paul, where he was reunited with his mother, his brother, and the old friends he knew from the Central Park days in Oklahoma, including Volney Davis, who had been released from prison in November 1932. After Fred introduced his brother to the newest members of the Barker-Karpis Gang, they sat down and began making arrangements for the next bank robbery.[13]

As soon as the details of the burglary were addressed and the routes for the getaway established, Ma left for Chicago, where she was to stay until the heist was completed. Before she left her boys, she praised them for their loyalty to her and challenged them to set their sights on "bigger prizes."[14]

In addition to helping orchestrate the "jobs" for the gang, Ma secured "safe havens" for some of the gang to run to after holdups. Chicago was one of her favorite cities to hide. She enjoyed the night-life, the stores, and getting lost in a sea of like-minded criminals.[15]

The effects of the Great Depression were evident across the Mid-west; hundreds of thousands of people struggled to find food and work. The land throughout the prairie states resembled the lunar sur-face—want and need were omnipresent. After dark in Chicago the lights from the dance halls and juke joints blinded the underworld from seeing anything but prosperity. Ma liked the escape from truth.[16]

On December 14, 1932, Ma made an urgent call to her boys in Saint Paul. She told them she was having heart palpitations. Ma had "hit the panic button," Alvin noted in his autobiography. "One of us had to go to her—and in a hurry. I was the only one who knew my way around Chicago, so I was elected."[17]

The time Alvin spent with Ma relieved her anxieties and stabi-lized her heart rate. What services he provided the Barker matriarch is unknown. Alvin was romantically involved with Herman's widow, Carol Hamilton, at the time. Ma was jealous of Carol and wasn't shy about telling Alvin what she thought of her. Alvin returned to St. Paul the evening of December 15, 1932, but before he left he promised to escort Ma around Reno, Nevada, in the near future. She was not opposed to employing whatever means necessary to keep her boys away from their women. More often than not Ma's boys put her first above all other females.[18]

Arthur Barker led the charge into the Third Northwestern Bank of Minneapolis on December 16, 1932. Fred was fast on his heels, followed by William Weaver and Verne Miller. All were armed with revolvers and Thompson submachine guns fitted with extralarge clips. It was 3:00 in the afternoon, and the sun shone brightly through the large glass windows of the triangular-shaped building. Ordinar-ily, accomplished thieves like the Barker-Karpis Gang avoided banks with an abundance of windows near major intersections. The Third Northwestern National was not only exposed on three sides, but two of the city's busy thoroughfares ran in front of the building. "It was like working in a greenhouse," Alvin wrote in his autobiography, "but sometimes we did things like that deliberately, maybe to interject some extra excitement into our work."[19]

Arthur leveled his tommy guns at the heads of the stunned bank tellers holding their hands in the air. Alvin and Verne Miller forced the bank customers to the floor, facedown. The one or two who argued against the instruction were slapped or knocked in the head with the butt of a pistol. While Fred, Arthur, and William were ushering one of the bank tellers to the vault and demanding that he open it, the traffic outside, including the streetcar, had slowed to a crawl. Curious bystanders were watching the action inside the bank. Lawrence Devol stood guard at the bank's entrance. Customers were screaming and pleading for help. Fred and Arthur emptied the vault, and the other gang members inside the building scooped all the cash in sight into large canvas bags.[20]

Suddenly, the bank alarm began howling; one of the tellers had managed to set it off. The gang didn't panic but continued collecting the money from the drawers and vault. While planning for the robbery, they learned the best time to strike was when the police officers on the day shift were going off duty and the evening shift was coming on. Fred, Arthur, and the others did not anticipate a quick response from law enforcement. Two officers running behind schedule a short mile from the bank heard the bank alarm sound and decided to proceed to the location.[21]

Hearing the siren on the fast-approaching police car, Lawrence snapped a drum onto his machine gun and stepped into the street just as the squad car arrived on the scene. Before the policemen exited the vehicle, Alvin and Arthur riddled the windows of the bank from inside with a hail of gunfire. All the gangsters rushed out of the building.[22]

Jess Doyle drove the getaway car to the front of the bank, opened the driver's side door, and sprayed the police vehicle with bullets. Lawrence followed suit. As he was hurrying to jump into the getaway car, he slipped and fell. His fingers were still on the trigger of the gun. He was firing like crazy into the sky. A stray bullet blasted through one of the tires, and Jess noticed it as he got to his feet and all the members of the gang hopped inside the vehicle.[23]

Verne Miller took over as driver and, according to Alvin, did an amazing job hauling the gang out of the area before the full force of the Minneapolis Police Department was on them. The rubber on the flat tire eventually broke free from the wheel well and all that was left was the rim. Having thought out the crime well, the robbers had another vehicle, a green sedan, parked and ready for them when they reached the St. Paul city limits. To further thwart the pursuit of the police, a third vehicle, a Chevy, was used to take the gang to their meeting place in Como Park in St. Paul.[24]

During the stop to change vehicles, gang members worked quickly to exchange the license plates from the hot car to the safe car. The job was almost done when two men in an old jalopy drove over to the hurried criminals to ask if they needed help. Fred waved the pair off and told them to "get going." The driver leaned out the window to get a better look at the action. Fred pulled his gun and shot the man in the head. Covered in blood, the passenger quickly moved his friend's lifeless body from behind the wheel of their car, took over the driving, and sped off. The Barker-Karpis Gang finished changing the plates, loaded into the vehicle, and headed to Fred's apartment.[25]

Reports of the outlaws' heinous actions of that day were printed in newspapers across the country. The December 17, 1932, *Salt Lake Tribune* announced:

A policeman was killed and two other persons critically wounded today by bandits who held up the Third Northwestern National Bank and escaped with approximately $20,000 in cash and $10,000 in securities. Six patrons and ten employees were in the bank, located in a small neighborhood community two miles from St. Paul. An employee pressed a burglar alarm button and Patrolmen Ira L. Evans and L. R. Gorski arrived just as the bandits rushed out.

A fourth bandit, armed with a machine gun, followed and opened fire as the police car drove up. Evans felt more than twenty wounds. Gorski, who received at least five wounds, had only a slight chance to recovery. The bandits then drove to Como Park, St. Paul, shooting Oscar Erickson, peddling Christmas wreaths nearby. He was not expected to live.

Police of both Minneapolis and St. Paul surrounded the park soon after but the bandits escaped.

Oscar Erickson, twenty-nine, died from the gunshot wounds he sustained, as did Officer Gorski. Alvin lamented in his autobiography that the money they stole was a "paltry sum in view of the shooting and lives lost, not to mention the loss of the vehicles."[26]

After splitting the stolen funds, the Barker-Karpis Gang decided to go separate ways for a time and meet in Reno once things had settled down. Alvin traveled to Chicago to spend a few days with friends. Verne Miller planned to head in that direction too and find a place to get rid of the Chevy the gang used as one of the getaway cars. Fred, Arthur, Jess, and William were going to drive to Nevada. Lawrence planned to go to Oklahoma.[27]

Police officials in Minnesota had cast a wide net over the state and were feverishly looking for the gang. They had no real leads until December 18, 1932, when Lawrence was arrested for drunk and disorderly conduct while at a party in his apartment complex in St. Paul. When the authorities searched his apartment, they found money from the Third Northwestern Bank robbery. A notebook containing the addresses of those believed to have aided Lawrence in various robberies was also found. Police were immediately dispatched to those locations.[28]

On December 19, 1932, the front page of the *Appleton Post-Crescent* featured an article that reported several arrests had been made in connection with the Third Northwestern Bank holdup:

St. Paul Police Chief T. E. Dahill announced that one of four men seized yesterday had admitted participation in a bank robbery that resulted in three deaths.

At the same time Minneapolis police, watching an apartment where two men were arrested in that city, took a fifth into custody.

Chief Dahill said Lawrence Barker alias De Volt [sic] confessed verbally to complicity in the Third Northwestern National Bank raid Friday, but refused to name his companions. He also refused to sign a written confession.

Minneapolis police said the man arrested had a green automobile similar to that which the robbers changed in a St. Paul park after leaving the bank.

Officers asserted he carried $750 in travelers' checks issued by the Midwest National Bank in Lincoln, Nebraska and that the checks were not completely filled out. The man refused to give a statement and the police refused to give his name.

The men held gave their names, police said, as James Colton alias Clarence De Volt, Owen Lewis, and Robert Newburn.

Lawrence Devol (newspaper accounts often misspelled his name) was positively identified by witnesses who had been at the Third Northwestern Bank the day he helped rob it. It was later determined that the three men arrested with Devol had no connection with the Minneapolis bank robbery, but they were initially bound over for trial in the matter. Robert Newburn and Clarence De Volt were acquitted of the charges and released. Owen Lewis, also known as Leonard Hankins, denied any involvement in the bank robbery and confessed to the police. He was found guilty of the offense. Witnesses accused him of being one of the shooters who killed the two police officers at the scene. On January 10, 1933, Lawrence Devol pled guilty to a charge of second-degree murder and was sentenced to life in prison in the Minnesota state penitentiary at Stillwater, Minnesota.[29]

The Barker-Karpis Gang and some of their paramours reunited in Reno, Nevada, at a club called the Rex. Although they considered what happened to Lawrence unfortunate, the outlaws were amused that authorities had arrested and prosecuted someone else for their crime. To celebrate their good fortune, Ma hosted a party on Christmas Day at a furnished home she rented with Fred and Alvin. A number of people in the same line of work as the Barker-Karpis Gang, including Lester Gillis (Baby Face Nelson), attended the holiday festivities.[30]

When Alvin wasn't preoccupied with prostitutes whom he visited on a regular basis, he and Ma spent a considerable amount of time together at the popular clubs around town. They liked to play keno and attend the shows at the various casinos. "In Reno," Alvin recalled years later, "we felt a million miles away from Minneapolis and all its problems."[31]

Alvin and Ma enjoyed keeping company with Lester and his wife and children. They all became great friends, and when Lester had throat surgery in Vallejo, California, in January 1933, Ma and Alvin accompanied him to the hospital and stayed by his side until he was in recovery. Hospital director Thomas Williams was smitten with Ma, and the two had a brief affair. Thomas's facility catered to the gangsters who needed care but couldn't go to any other hospital for fear of being arrested for their crimes. A generous donation to the hospital and to Thomas ensured secrecy.[32]

When Alvin and Ma left Lester, they traveled to San Francisco to see the sights. Before returning to Reno, they drove around Lake Tahoe and spent a few days in the town of Truckee.[33]

More than a month had passed since the Barker-Karpis Gang robbed the Third Northwestern Bank in Minneapolis. Tension had mounted between the hoodlums. They'd been in Reno too long, and they were restless and anxious to get back to work. By early February 1933 the lawbreakers had relocated to the Chicago area and were residing in apartments in a neighborhood called Oak Park. Between dinner at Ma's place and drinking and dancing at the O. P. Inn (a popular hangout for mobsters in Maysville, Illinois), the gang planned a robbery that proved to be the most dangerous of its career.[34]

The citizens of Fairbury, Nebraska, were beginning their Tuesday workday when machine-gun fire at the First National Bank interrupted their regular routines. At 9:00 in the morning on April 4, 1933, members of the Barker-Karpis Gang, armed with tommy guns, burst through the front door of the bank, demanding that all the money from the vault be turned over to them.[35]

Fred and Arthur Barker and Alvin Karpis were the lead gunmen, followed by veteran bank robber Frank "Jelly" Nash. Volney Davis and Earl Christman stood guard outside the entrance of the building. Eddie Green waited at the back door ready to shoot any police officers who dared enter. Jess Doyle waited across the street in a black Buick to drive the bandits away from the scene.[36]

Sixteen employees and an unknown number of patrons were in the First National Bank when the robbers entered. All were ordered to get on the floor and keep their faces "buried in the pavement." Fred put a pistol in cashier R. S. Wilfley's face and demanded to see the bank president. Petrified and shaking, the cashier managed to tell the gun-wielding thief that the president hadn't arrived for work yet. Fred wasn't deterred by the news. He pushed the cashier toward the vault and instructed him to open it.[37]

Cashier Frank Nelson was made to follow his coworker to the vault to give him a hand. A gun was shoved into his ribs, and Nelson slowly and nervously began turning the dial. "I guess we will have to kill someone around here if there isn't more speed," Nelson heard one of the robbers announce. He tried to hurry and turned the combination more quickly. As soon as the vault door was opened, the cashier was pushed out of the way, and Arthur and Frank stepped inside and began relieving the space of all the money. Fred and Alvin kept their guns trained on the customers and the bank employees lying on the floor. Passersby glancing inside the bank noticed the action taking place and called out "Robbers!" Earl Christman fired his gun at the curious onlookers, and people screamed as they scattered.[38]

Deputy Sheriff W. S. Davidson and a gun salesman named Glen Johnson, who supplied the sheriff's department with weapons, rushed toward the bank. They had received a call about the robbery in progress from the owner of a nearby business.[39]

Both Volney Davis and Earl Christman were shooting at Fairbury residents who dared try any heroic moves. When Deputy Sheriff Davidson arrived at the scene of the crime, he aimed his gun at one of the two gang members standing outside the bank and began firing. Several shots were returned by the bandits from inside the bank, and glass flew outward onto the sidewalk. Deputy Sheriff Davidson and Glen Johnson took cover behind the cars lining the street.[40]

As Glen Johnson and Sheriff Davidson carefully peered over the vehicles protecting them, they spotted the robbers start to emerge from the bank with a pair of hostages. Captives Keith Sexton and Olive Halleck did not struggle. Earl Christman loaded a fifty-bullet drum onto his machine gun and opened fire on law enforcement officials approaching the building. A bank security guard jumped up from the floor and shot at Earl. Earl quickly returned fire and hit him. The police shot back, hitting Earl in the stomach. Volney bombarded the officials with a hail of bullets.[41]

Fred and Alvin recognized the gang would not be able to exit the front door unscathed and decided to shoot the glass in the windows alongside the entranceway. As the robbers stepped over the window frame, the police fired on them. Keith Sexton was shot five times in the abdomen, and Olive Halleck was struck in the side.[42]

Hearing the gunshots, Eddie Green ran from the back of the business to the front, arriving just in time to see a fray of ammunition strike the walls of the building. He quickly dropped to the ground and escaped being struck. The fleeing bandits tossed their injured hostages aside and grabbed two women exiting a nearby medical clinic. More gunfire was exchanged between police and the robbers. Fairbury citizens screamed and shouted warnings to one another to "stay put." Earl Christman was hit several more times by flying bullets. Jess Doyle sped the Buick toward the front of the bank and stopped long enough to let his fellow gangsters pile inside the vehicle. The women were placed on the running boards on both sides of the car. Fred and Alvin continued shooting at the police. Jess slammed his foot down on the accelerator, and the car zoomed down the street. The two women cried out for help as the vehicle disappeared around a corner. The gangsters opened the back windows of the car and tossed boxes of roofing nails onto the road to slow down or stop anyone in pursuit.

Jess brought the getaway car to a stop fifteen miles outside Fairbury. No one had followed them. After depositing the frightened and panicked hostages on the side of the road, the vehicle sped away. As soon as the Buick was out of sight of the women, Jess stopped the car again, this time to check on Earl. He was bleeding badly and in a considerable amount of pain. Alvin poured whiskey over the wounds and packed them with towels and gave the suffering bandit a shot of morphine.[43]

The extent of the damage left behind by the Barker-Karpis Gang in Fairbury and what was stolen from the First National Bank were covered in various newspapers the following day. "Eight people were seriously injured. Three men were wounded by machine gun fire in a gun battle with six robbers. . . . The men escaped with $27,643.00," the *Belleville Telescope* reported. The article continued:

> *Deputy Sheriff W. S. Davidson was in his office in the courthouse across the street when the robbers came out with their hostages. With him was Peter Glynn [sic] Johnson. With drawn guns, the sheriff and Johnson ran into the street and opened fire on the robbers. Davidson was wounded in the leg and Johnson in the shoulder. Keith Sexton, bank employee forced into the street by the robbers as a shield, was wounded five times when he came into the line of fire of the submachine gun, with which the robbers used to return the officer's fire. His condition is critical.*
>
> *In their haste, the bandits left a briefcase in the bank lobby. In the bag was a set of Kansas automobile license plates and an automatic pistol. Officers said the car in which the men fled carried Iowa license plates.*[44]

The gang of outlaws made it out of Nebraska and into Kansas. They drove to the home of Verne Miller in Kansas City. According to Alvin, Verne's house was at the location where most gangsters went when they needed medical treatment. He knew doctors who would tend to injured criminals on the run for a fee.[45]

Shortly after the robbers arrived at Verne's home, Fred, Alvin, and Eddie decided to travel on to St. Paul with the stolen money. Arthur, Volney, and Jess opted to stay behind with Earl. Once his condition stabilized they would join the others. Earl died in the early hours of April 5, 1933. The three gang members who were with him until the end buried Earl in a secret location outside of town.[46]

Before all the gangsters converged at the designated location in St. Paul, Arthur and Alvin were persuaded by Ma's friend George Ziegler to hijack a Federal Reserve Bank handcart. The cart was regularly transferred from the bank in downtown Chicago to the main post office a few blocks away. George believed the cart contained money. Alvin summoned Fred to the setting, and he agreed that the gang should overtake the cart en route to the post office. The details of the crime were planned almost entirely by Alvin. He arranged for a place to hide out, acquired a car for the heist, and selected the gang members who would take part in the robbery.[47]

Stealing the money from the cart proved to be the easiest part of the job. With treasures in hand the five gangsters, including William Weaver and Harry Campbell, loaded into the getaway vehicle and raced out of the city. While traveling to the safe house, another vehicle collided with the bandits' car.[48]

Several on-duty police officers patrolling the streets quickly arrived at the crash site. Outraged at the situation, Arthur shoved his automatic weapon out the car window and fired. The officers dove behind whatever barriers were available to keep from being hit by bullets. As Arthur continued to shoot at the police, his partners in crime hopped out of the getaway car and ran toward a vehicle they hoped would run. Monty Bolton, a newcomer with the gang, shot his machine gun in the direction of the police. Eager to escape the barrage of retaliating fire, he took his eyes off the direction he was shooting but kept his finger on the trigger. Arthur's left hand got in the way of the flying bullets, and he yelled out in pain.[49]

The back end of the four-door sedan the hoodlums used to take them away from the action was riddled with bullets. No one but Arthur had been hit. The mailbags stolen from the handcart were secured inside the misappropriated car. When the gang finally reached a safe spot to search inside the mailbags, it was revealed they'd only swiped checks.[50]

Arthur was returned to Ma at the hideout in Elmhurst. He was bleeding and angry. Alvin noted in his autobiography that Arthur was not as upset about the wound as he was about the fact that the bullet had blown a diamond out of his favorite ring.[51]

Ma was fiercely unhappy that the boys had added a job to their schedule in which the reward was not assured. George Ziegler tried to explain why he believed the mailbags contained cash, but Ma wasn't interested. "All those mistakes," Alvin recalled later in his life, "All that carelessness. It was enough to make a guy shudder."[52]

The risks involved with robbing banks had increased in the seven years the Barkers had been in that line of offense. Ma felt it was time her family expanded into an area where the reward was greater than the danger.

CHAPTER EIGHT

Pleasing Ma

Fred Barker sat in a dark corner at Tallman's Grill in Kansas City, Missouri, enjoying the music of a jazz troupe. He was situated behind a lavishly decorated table loaded with steaks, oysters, and frogs' legs. He was waiting for his date, Paula Harmon, also known as Polly Walker. She attracted more than casual attention when she finally arrived. The amply built, full-fleshed woman with reddish-blond hair wore a stylish gown suited for an evening out. A silver fox-fur cape was draped over her shoulders, and on her left hand was a ring studded with eight diamonds. She was twenty-nine years old and had a reputation for treating men with flirtatious condescension, as if they were children.[1]

In spite of objections from friends and family, Fred enjoyed Paula's company. She possessed an average face, hazel eyes, and a scarred nose, which gave the impression that she had been struck by a heavy instrument. She greeted Fred with a kiss, and he helped her into her chair. The two always had a great deal to talk about; they had a lot in common. Fred liked to shower her with gifts as well, and Paula liked to accept them.[2]

"Girls liked Freddie and he didn't mind spending money on them," Alvin Karpis wrote in his memoirs. "But he wasn't always lucky in the type of broad who hooked him. Paula Harmon turned out to be a rotten choice, though you couldn't tell that to Freddie when he got stuck on her. Paula was a drunk too."[3]

Fred wasn't the first gangster to overlook Paula's drinking. She was the widow of bank robber Charles Harmon. Charles died from a gunshot wound in the neck he received fleeing the scene of a bank robbery in Menomonie, Wisconsin. Paula, a native of Georgia, earned her living operating a house of ill repute in Chicago. Patrons referred to her as "Fat Witted" because she had a sharp tongue when provoked.[4]

Paula and Fred met at Herbert Farmer's homestead near Joplin, Missouri, shortly after her husband died. The Farmers were good friends who helped her through the loss and protected her from questions the police might have wanted to ask her. Fred thought Paula was charming, and she liked the attention he gave her.[5]

After helping rob the bank in Fairbury, Nebraska, Fred made it clear to his associates that he wanted to spend time with a woman, away from the business. Verne Miller's paramour suggested he reacquaint himself with Paula. Fred and Paula met again in mid-April 1933 in St. Paul and then traveled to Kansas City for a brief vacation. The pair used the alias of Mr. and Mrs. J. Stanley Smith. Mrs. Smith was a housewife, and Mr. Smith posed as a salesman for the Federated Metal Company of St. Louis.[6]

While Fred was busy with Paula, Alvin was keeping time with a seventeen-year-old girl named Dolores Delaney. Her two older sisters were involved with outlaws, and the rebellious teenager was fascinated with Alvin because of his background as a lawbreaker. Dolores was spontaneous and playful and, not unlike Alvin's wife Dorothy Slayman, wanted to be with him all the time. Dorothy was working at a massage parlor when she met Alvin in mid-1931. They married in the fall that same year and set up house in Chicago. That's where he abandoned her two months after they wed.[7]

Alvin's relationship with Dorothy was so short-lived he never had an occasion to introduce her to Ma. That wasn't the case with Dolores; the two women took an instant disliking to one another. Dolores resented any time Alvin spent with Ma; Ma thought Dolores was too young and inexperienced to keep Alvin happy for a long period of time. She believed Dolores would eventually turn on him and the gang. She felt the same about Fred's girlfriend Paula.[8]

Anytime Ma overheard the women say anything disparaging about her boys, she would report that information back to them. She didn't see it as undermining their relationships but protecting them from harm.[9]

Arthur wasn't as desirous for full-time female companionship. According to many of the wives and lovers of the Barker-Karpis Gang members, Arthur had spent so many years in prison he had learned to live without a regular partner.[10]

Members of the Barker-Karpis Gang who were close to Ma generally kept the women they were seriously involved with away from her. "It was a crazy system," Alvin admitted years later, "and often created friction with our women who couldn't understand why we were so careful with her feelings." The boys preferred to avoid Ma's jealous anger. They were devoted to her and considered her contribution to their organization invaluable and something they would not jeopardize. Not only did she recruit and school the hoodlums who joined the group, but she was always a foolproof cover for the gang. Ma could project an innocence and wholesomeness to rival Whistler's mother, but she could be fiery and obstinate.[11]

Alvin went out of his way to express his admiration for Ma. The pair attended the World's Fair in Chicago together in early June 1933. The focus of the fair that year was on the science and technology of the future. Although there was no exhibit that included advancements in unlawful acts, Ma predicted her boys would be involved in crimes that would break new ground. "Bank robbery is beneath our dignity," the FBI files quoted Ma as saying. "Bigger game is in our future."[12]

One year after President Herbert Hoover signed into law the Lindbergh Act that made interstate kidnapping a crime punishable by the national government, millionaire William Hamm Jr. was kidnapped while walking home from his office in St. Paul. The Barker-Karpis Gang, which was behind the abduction, demanded $100,000 for his return. Failure to meet the demand would result in the man's death. This was the "bigger game" Ma had in mind for her boys.[13]

The idea to kidnap William Hamm was presented to Fred and Alvin by Jack Peifer, owner of the Hollyhocks Casino in St. Paul. Jack wanted 10 percent of the ransom for bringing the opportunity to Ma's group.

Once they all came to an agreement regarding the terms, select members of the Barker-Karpis Gang met at a rented cottage at Bald Eagle Lake in Ramsey County, Minnesota, to begin planning the abduction.[14]

Thirty-nine-year-old William Hamm Jr. was a descendant of one of the richest families in the state. He was president of Theodore Hamm's Brewery and worth an estimated $4.5 million. He was targeted because he was rich.[15]

On June 15, 1933, Fred and Alvin grabbed Hamm off the street outside his office at 12:45 p.m. and forced him inside the backseat of a black coupe. His face was shoved into the floor, and a hood was slipped over his head as the car sped away.[16]

The gangsters transported Hamm to the home of a postmaster in Bensenville, Illinois. "Once the car stopped I was gently pulled out of the vehicle by the icy cold, small hand of what I think was a woman," Hamm reported to police once he had been released. Historians speculate the hand was that of Ma Barker.[17] FBI director J. Edgar Hoover reported that Ma was diabolically clever at conceiving "getaway charts." Before a kidnapping Ma would drive through every inch of an escape route, coding every twist, turn, and bump in the road, recording speeds on curves and through congested areas in both wet and dry weather. She left nothing to chance.

Prior to Alvin phoning Hamm's business manager on June 16 to let him know his boss had been kidnapped, William was forced to sign four different ransom notes. The notes explained that the ransom was to be paid in twenty-, ten-, and five-dollar bills.[18]

Despite the gang's insistence that the police not become involved, Hamm's mother was adamant they help her find her son. Unbeknownst to the Hamm family, the Barker-Karpis Gang had a man working for them on the inside, St. Paul police chief Tom Brown. For a share of the ransom, Tom's job was to keep the outlaws updated on law enforcement's activities and misdirect them when possible.[19]

News of the kidnapping made the headlines of papers throughout the state. The June 17, 1933, *Oshkosh Daily Northwestern* informed readers that authorities suspected Hamm was being held by a gambler and liquor runner named Verne Sankey. "Sankey is accused of collecting a total of $72,000 in ransom from relatives of Charles Boetzcher II, Denver, and Haskell Bohn, St. Paul, in abductions during 1932," the article read. The report continued:

> *Grave concern for Hamm's safety was expressed early today after kidnappers failed to keep a contact they arranged for 5 o'clock last night. News of the kidnapping was not made public until late last night after William Dunn, business manager of the brewing company, and police received a communication from the kidnappers and a note from Hamm himself saying, "Do as they tell you."*
>
> *Police suspected Verne Sankey was the plotter of the kidnapping. Orders to shoot Sankey on sight were issued from the St. Paul police chief. At 5:15 p.m. on Friday, William Dunn received a telephone call saying, "Billy Hamm has been killed. We want $100,000."*

Shortly afterward, Dunn received another telephone call. This time the voice said: "We know this is a shock to you but we are in dead earnest. Have $100,000 by Friday. The money must be delivered in a Hamm brewery truck. Have the sides removed so we can see that no policemen are concealed in it."[20]

Less than five hours before the ransom was to be delivered, Jack Peifer contacted Fred and told him that the St. Paul police force had set a trap for the members of the gang assigned to retrieve the money. Tom Brown, the police chief informant, had warned Jack that a machine gunner would be hiding on the floor of the truck ready to shoot the kidnappers once the doors of the vehicle were opened. The first attempt to deliver the money was called off by the gang.[21]

Negotiations for a new drop were made, and this time the police did exactly as told, with no surprises planned. While watching for the kidnappers to release her son, Hamm's mother, Marie Scheffer Hamm, collapsed from worry and exhaustion. A physician and nurse were called to the Hamm home. Marie died of heart failure before she knew what became of her son.[22]

After four days the ransom was paid; Hamm was returned unharmed. The June 30, 1933, *Decatur Herald* announced to readers in the Midwest that Hamm was released and that he had every intention of cooperating with authorities to bring the kidnappers to justice. "Although it was a trying experience I was treated with utmost respect and courtesy," Hamm told the *Herald* reporters. "But like the old adage, home sweet home is the best place of all."

Hamm's attorney, M. F. Kinkead, assured the press that "every law enforcement body, including the Ramsey County police department and my office, will go the limit to clear up this outrage."[23]

"Hampered by the lack of adequate clues and the fact Hamm was forced to avert his face from the kidnappers when he was not wearing goggles lined with cotton and a white hood, authorities pressed their investigation with the utmost speed," the *Decatur Herald* noted. The article continued:

> *Hamm only saw his captors but dimly. . . . The windows of the house in which he was placed in a second floor room were boarded up. "I never saw the men because when I didn't have on my goggles they made me turn my face toward the wall when they came into the room. They were very nice to me. I asked for anything I wanted and ordered anything I wanted. The meals were good and simple, nothing elaborate but whoever did the cooking knew their way around the kitchen."[24]*

Federal government and state law enforcement officials worked together investigating the kidnapping. They determined that the crime was perpetrated by Roger Touhy and his band of criminals. Touhy was an Irish American mob boss and bootlegger with ties to Al Capone. He and three others were indicted in August 1933 for Hamm's abduction.

Immediately after William Hamm was released, the Barker-Karpis Gang fled to Chicago. Fred, Arthur, and Alvin stayed at Ma's home in Oak Park. The other members of the gang found their own apartments nearby. When they all came together to discuss the division of the $100,000 ransom, Alvin declared the criminals' latest job "another successful Barker-Karpis production."[25]

Alvin and his cohorts believed they had once again gotten away with a crime and that the authorities had no evidence linking them to the kidnapping. Unbeknownst to Ma's boys the FBI had been developing a program called latent fingerprint identification. In July 1933 the identification unit of the FBI's division of investigation established a fingerprint file.[26]

The file contained a collection of fingerprints of known gangsters, kidnappers, and extortionists. Each fingerprint was classified separately and filed in a designated sequence so that latent fingerprint impressions found at the scenes of crimes could be checked against them to establish the identity of suspects. According to the September 11, 1933, edition of the *Salt Lake Tribune*, "Latent fingerprints are fingerprint impressions left upon some object at the scene of a crime, which impression, while not obvious at first, may be brought out by application of chemical powders."

In August 1933 Hoover reported that forty latent fingerprints were examined and identifications established in six instances. During the same period the main fingerprint collection, which contained the prints of 3,870,910 individuals, was instrumental in the arrest of 340 fugitives from justice.[27]

On September 6, 1933, the latent fingerprint identification system was used on the four ransom notes prepared by members of the Barker-Karpis Gang in the Hamm kidnapping. Alvin Karpis's and Arthur Barker's fingerprints were found on the notes.[28]

"The Freddy Barker gang of Missouri and Oklahoma has become the focus of investigators in the search for the kidnappers who held William Hamm," the June 27, 1933, edition of the *Moorhead Daily News* reported. "Search for the Barker gang was started after police located the hideout where the wealthy brewer was held captive after the seizure. Police refuse to make known the location but indicated the photographs of Barker had been identified as those of a man seen in the hideout's vicinity while Hamm was held."

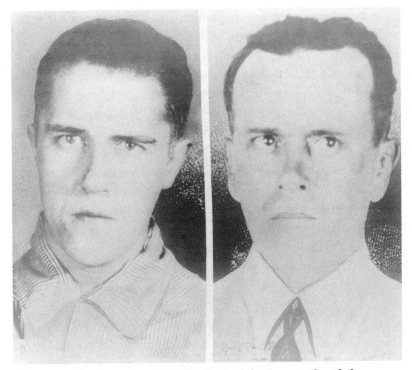

Alvin Karpis (left) and Arthur "Doc" Barker (right), who were identified as members of the gang that kidnapped Edward G. Bremer in St. Paul, Minnesota
COURTESY OF THE LIBRARY OF CONGRESS, LC-USZ62-134472

Although authorities strongly suspected the Barker-Karpis Gang as the culprits behind the kidnapping, they continued to hold Touhy and his men and started building a circumstantial case against him. Al Capone thought Touhy was encroaching on his business territory and wanted him out of the way. Capone enlisted the help of St. Paul police chief Tom Brown to keep Touhy locked behind bars.[29]

While the police were busy trying to connect Touhy to a series of serious crimes, Ma Barker and Alvin were meeting with Capone about work they had done in the Chicago area. The pudgy, brutally violent gangster warned the pair that if they ever decided to hide any kidnapped victims in his city, they would be charged rent. Ma and Alvin reluctantly agreed.[30]

Alvin noted in his autobiography that law enforcement tried to beat Touhy and his men into confessing to the Hamm kidnapping. Touhy refused to admit to the abduction. In August 1933 a special grand jury was convened in St. Paul to hear fifteen witnesses testify that Touhy and his group were responsible for taking Hamm. The Touhy Gang was bound over for trial and in November 1933 was acquitted of the kidnapping. However, Touhy and his men had been found guilty of abducting John Factor, a wealthy market speculator who paid a $70,000 ransom in July 1932. Touhy hanged himself in jail with his own necktie before a sentencing hearing could take place.[31]

Ma and her boys concluded that Capone was behind Touhy's suicide. The Barker-Karpis Gang resented the stranglehold Capone had on the Windy City but were not motivated to challenge him. The public in Chicago and surrounding midwestern states resented the stranglehold gangsters had as a whole. On more than a dozen fronts, the agencies of the US government were fighting crime.[32]

On July 26, 1933, President Franklin D. Roosevelt let it be plainly known to his constituents that he was fully behind the establishment of a super-relief force of federal investigators to step in to check the growth of organized crime, especially kidnapping. Hoover was pleased by the news and the additional authority he was given to track down notorious outlaw gangs terrorizing law-abiding citizens.[33]

Ma and the boys were not as intimidated by Hoover as they were by Capone. Ma yearned for a bold and profitable caper that would raise their reputations in the underworld. While plans were being made for such a scam, Fred and the group decided to hold up two Railway Express company employees at the door of their office in St. Paul.[34]

Wearing masks over their faces, eight members of the Barker-Karpis Gang burst into the office, brandishing weapons. They escaped with two large cash boxes, which police said contained $60,000 to $100,000.[35]

"Cashboxes were on a hand truck outside the door of the express company office, near the Union Station, ready to be taken to Minneapolis," the September 11, 1933, *Monroe News Star* reported, also stating:

The police said the eight men backed a big sedan under the depot concourse not far from the express office.

As T. J. Mangan, a guard, and S. Moles, messenger, opened the door of the office to wheel out the truck carrying the cash container, five robbers surrounded them.

The leader, armed with a sawed-off shotgun, commanded the company employees, "Stick 'em up and face the wall."

Two men guarded the victims while the others loaded the cash boxes into the automobiles. After disarming Mangan and Moles, the robbers sped away in their car. They fired two shots in the air as they went.

Two days after the railway station heist, the Barker-Karpis Gang robbed the Union State Bank in Amery, Wisconsin. According to the September 13, 1933, *Ironwood Daily Globe*, four members of the gang broke into the bank the evening before the holdup and hid inside the building. The men overpowered two employees when they reported to work in the morning. The *Globe* also reported:

More than $43,000 in cash and securities were stolen. The loot included between $11,000 and $12,000 in cash and approximately $35,000 in securities, most of them negotiable.

The gunmen used the same kind of automobile that was used in the raid on the St. Paul Railway Express Agency on Monday, September 11, 1933. This and other angles have led authorities to believe the same gang was responsible for both crimes.

The four, armed with a rifle, a shotgun, and two pistols, threatened to kill O. M. Olson, the assistant cashier, if he made "any false moves" and kicked him several times while he was opening the safe which was under time lock set for 8 a.m. They met him as he entered the bank shortly before that time.

Olson was forced to lie on the floor in a back room as three raiders waited for the return of the fourth that had left to get their automobile, parked some distance away. Vice President B. H.

Christenson then entered and was forced to lie on the floor along-side Olson.

Before hurrying away the gunmen emptied two loaded shotguns and two rifles owned by Olson and Christenson and kept in the bank. They also took the keys to Olson's car to avoid pursuit.

Police indicate that the descriptions of the four matched with those of them who robbed the Union Depot in St. Paul.

Arthur rested his bloody hand on Ma's kitchen table in Chicago. He was in shock and shaking. Ma gently lifted his arm and hand and placed a sheet under it. Within a few moments the sheet was soaked through. A sweat broke out on Arthur's forehead as she saturated the wounded appendage with an antiseptic called tincture of iodine. A bullet had struck the tissue between his thumb and index finger on his left hand and exited through the flesh on the other side. The necessary pressure Ma used to wrap the gunshot with cotton bandages made Arthur cry out in pain. Ma demanded an explanation about what happened from the frazzled gangsters around her watching the action.[36]

The boys had been involved in a shoot-out with Cook County law enforcement officers on September 22, 1933. Against Ma's better judgment that they stay away from bank jobs, Fred and Alvin had urged the gang to participate in the robbery of a pair of bank messengers. The messengers were traveling from the bank to the post office when they were robbed shortly after midnight. An article in the September 22, 1933, edition of the *Logansport Pharos-Tribune* reported that "estimates of what was stolen ranged as high as $500 thousand in the total amount of checks, securities, coupons, and cash obtained in the murderous mail holdup."

Timing the robbery to a split second, the gang descended on the bank car in which two messengers and two guards were riding just as it pulled up to the Federal Reserve door in the heart of Chicago's financial district. The *Logansport Pharos-Tribune* noted that the criminals operated with ruthless rapidity, shooting down Officer Miles A. Cunningham in the process. Officer Cunningham was killed by machine-gun fire from the gang when their flight away from the crime was temporarily halted by a collision.[37]

A total of six members of the Barker-Karpis Gang, including George "Machine Gun" Kelly, participated in the robbery, using two cars equipped with a smoke-throwing apparatus, police sirens, and red and green lights like those used on squad cars.[38]

A number of patrolmen responded to the activity and took cover behind signboards and mailboxes when the bullets began flying. Law enforcement agents shot at the bandits but failed to stop the men from getting away. During the escape from the police, the driver of the gangsters' vehicle crashed into a car on the street. The outlaws leaped out of the damaged getaway car and loaded into the second vehicle. Clues found in the abandoned car and the daring nature of the crime led authorities to suspect that George Kelly and Verne Miller were part of the band of miscreants.[39]

Police captain R. Patrick told reporters that "officers suspected Kelly and Miller because of the special machine gun equipment." Among the items found in the car the gang left behind were five automatic revolver clips, one machine-gun drum, and three automatic rifle clips.[40]

During the exchange of gunfire with law enforcement, Arthur was hit in the hand. Ma considered the gang to have been lucky to have gotten out of the foolhardy experience with their lives. By the time she had finished dressing Arthur's bullet wounds, the group agreed to focus on the next kidnapping.[41]

On the morning of January 17, 1934, Edward G. Bremer, St. Paul banker, stepped from the white front door of his brick mansion on fashionable East River Boulevard, leading his nine-year-old daughter by the hand. It was 8:15 a.m. and bitterly cold. Deep snow lay in the streets; an icy wind was sweeping down from Minnesota's white-blanketed prairies. Edward and his little girl climbed into a big, blue Lincoln sedan.[42]

Their route took them along Goodrich Avenue to Summit School, which the Bremer girl attended. Each morning her father dropped her at school then drove downtown to his office in the Commercial State Bank of St. Paul.[43]

As soon as the car stopped, Edward's daughter climbed out, ran to the front door, and then turned to wave good-bye to her father. He waved back and drove away from the building into the snow. Straight ahead was Lexington Avenue, an arterial highway. As Bremer slowed down in preparation to stop at a stop sign in the near distance, another sedan came slowly along Lexington Avenue on his left. Both cars stopped simultaneously. Then suddenly the left door of his sedan was thrown open. A gun was thrust toward Bremer's head and a gruff voice exclaimed, "Move over, or I'll kill you."[44]

Edward Bremer was the second millionaire the Barker-Karpis Gang had kidnapped. Once the reward of $200,000 was paid, the banker was released after being held for more than twenty days. Just after midnight on February 7, 1934, servants at the home of Adolph Bremer answered the frantic ringing of the doorbell. Adolph followed closely behind the servants as they swung open the door. Edward Bremer was on the other side, and he collapsed into his father's arms. He was sobbing; his thin, unshaved face was cut and bruised. His wife, Emily, met him in the hallway; her arms went around him and she wept tears of joy. Federal agents and St. Paul police authorities hurried to the house. They waited for the moment when Edward Bremer could talk to them.[45]

An hour later, Special Agent Harold Nathan, Chief of Police Thomas E. Dahill, and Inspector Charles Tierney entered the bedroom where the kidnapped victim sat in bed, propped up with pillows. He recounted his observations during his time as a hostage:

> It was morning when we left the house where I'd been held. My eyes were bandaged, and I was placed in the bottom of a car surrounded by gasoline cans. They drove for hours; they made frequent stops. It was after dark when one of my guards said that others had left to find out if the money was marked. After another hour, the missing guard returned and said the money was alright.

We were nearing Rochester and they said, "We'll put you off on a dark street. You get out of the car, count up to fifteen very slowly before removing the bandages from your eyes. Then turn about and go to the Rochester bus depot. Catch the bus for St. Paul. Don't take a taxi, don't telephone your family, don't notify anyone. We'll be watching you."[46]

So the kidnap car was stopped; Edward Bremer was helped from the floor of the backseat and put out of the vehicle. As he counted to fifteen, he heard the car drive away. He pulled the bandages from his eyes and threw them into a snowdrift, but days and nights of living behind bandages had spoiled his sense of equilibrium; he staggered and forced himself to walk in circles until his feeling of balance returned. Moving with painful slowness he finally reached the bus station.[47]

The pursuit of the Barker-Karpis Gang soon became an epic in persistence with flaming highlights. In the month that followed, Hoover's federal agents never relaxed. They raided a farmhouse in Oklahoma, capturing several criminals, but missed Fred, Arthur, and Alvin by less than an hour.[48]

On March 23, 1934, the Department of Justice issued a report to the public positively identifying Arthur and Alvin as two gang members who took part in the kidnapping of Edward Bremer. The official report also noted that Arthur and Alvin were wanted for two murders. The men were being sought for the killing of Sheriff C. Kelly of West St. Paul. Photos of the three gangsters were circulated across the nation's midsection.[49]

Ma and her boys were keeping low profiles in various apartments throughout the Chicago area. The money had been divided among them, and the gang members were informed not to spend large quantities of cash. They suspected the money was marked, and if circulated in big amounts, it could lead the authorities to the places where they were hiding. Alvin turned more than $10,000 over to a man named Boss McLaughlin. For a fee Boss would peddle the money through legitimate businesses to make it appear that it came from lawful sources. If

Boss was successful the gang would hire him to launder more of the ransom. He was not successful. A few days after Arthur turned the $10,000 over to him, Boss was arrested by the FBI on suspicion of dealing in unlawful currency.[50]

In early April 1934 federal authorities learned that John Dillinger was passing some of the "hot money." On April 22 federal agents raided the Little Bohemia resort near Mercer, Wisconsin, where the gangster was hiding. Alvin was also there at the time, and he, Dillinger, and his men responded to the raid with mass machine-gun fire and shot their way out of the place. Alvin's fingerprints were found on a deck of playing cards at the resort, and more money from the Bremer ransom was discovered at the scene as well.[51]

Informants in the underworld sent word to Hoover in Washington that the Barker-Karpis Gang had dissolved. He was told that Ma Barker's nerves in particular had become frazzled under the constant strain of his agency's pursuit. Director Hoover believed at long last he had a "clear mental picture of the iron-willed woman his men were trailing," even though her whereabouts remained a mystery.[52]

CHAPTER NINE

Dangerous Criminals

COLD WIND AND SPITTING RAIN ASSAULTED PATRONS OUTSIDE THE Rialto Theatre in downtown Chicago in late April 1934. Inside, smartly uniformed ushers escorted excited moviegoers to their seats. They hurried along the plush, carpeted aisles, chattering about the film they were about to see and the violent weather that had threatened to keep them away. The ticket holders paid little attention to anyone outside the friends or family with them. Ma, Fred, and Alvin were pleased by the moviegoers' preoccupation. Although the three weren't trying to hide their identities, they did not want people to take undue notice of them. They sat quietly in their seats, waiting for the movie to begin. A hush fell over the audience when the lights were dimmed and the projector came on. Fred sunk down in his seat, and Alvin draped his arm affectionately around Ma's shoulders.[1]

A Universal International Newsreel flashed on the giant screen in front of the group. The footage included a press conference of German foreign minister Konstantin von Neurath denouncing France for "destroying at a single blow the result of lengthy negotiations for disarmament," a report about the death of American sportswriter and editor Joe Vila, and an announcement about the American government's war against dangerous and criminally prolific gangsters.[2]

A shot of a federal agent reviewing a stack of files appeared on the screen. The names on the tops of the file folders read Charles A. Floyd alias "Pretty Boy," Homer Van Meter, Vernon C. Miller, and John Hamilton. The agent reached inside a couple of the folders and

John Dillinger, one of the many gangsters on the FBI's Public Enemies List, which included Ma Barker COURTESY OF THE LIBRARY OF CONGRESS, LC-USZ62-112142

removed photographs of some of the men. A clip of heavily armed federal investigators racing to their vehicles to chase after thugs followed the criminals' pictures. "G-Men fight to protect citizens from dangerous lawbreakers," a banner across the bottom of the screen read. "These men are public enemies," the next banner announced. More pictures were shown—John Dillinger, Baby Face Nelson, Fred Barker, and Alvin Karpis. "Remember, one of these men may be sitting beside you."[3]

According to Alvin Karpis's autobiography: "The lights went on in the theatre, and everyone looked to their left and right to see if a face matched the pictures. People were giggling. They didn't believe that any public enemy could ever be sitting beside them." Ma smiled at Fred and Alvin, and the three chuckled along with the audience. "She [Ma] had just got [sic] the first real confirmation that her boys were more than ordinary crooks," Alvin continued.[4]

Dozens of agents in dozens of cities were on the lookout for the Barker-Karpis Gang. With the exception of Arthur, the outlaws decided to leave Illinois and relocate to various spots in Ohio. Some of the boys and their girlfriends moved to Lake Erie, Grand Forest Beach, and Toledo. Ma and Fred rented an apartment in Cleveland. In June 1934 the gang members reunited at the Harvard Club in Newburgh Heights, Ohio. The Harvard Club was one of the largest gambling operations between New York and Chicago. Several of the criminals wanted their share of the ransom received for Edward Bremer, and they met at the location to discuss the matter. The majority of the cash had yet to be laundered, so the participants in the kidnapping agreed to only take $18,000 each until the remaining balance was safe to put into circulation.[5]

Reports in newspapers such as the *Moorhead Daily News* conveyed that federal authorities had alerted banks across the Midwest to check the serial numbers on all the cash coming and going out of their facility against the list the government provided. The June 1, 1934, edition of the *Moorhead Daily News* noted that law enforcement agents were at a loss as to where the bulk of the ransom money and the Barker-Karpis Gang had disappeared. Federal bureau agents cited the raid on Dillinger's hideout at Little Bohemia in Wisconsin as the reason for the gang's silence. Investigators speculated that the criminals were fearful of getting caught and had been broken into two groups to keep from being apprehended. John L. McLaughlin, one-time political leader of Chicago's West Side and latterly reputed overlord of city gambling concessions, told police that he had handled $53,000 of the ransom paid for Bremer's release.[6]

The *Moorhead Daily News* explained:

McLaughlin's son, John Jr., was arraigned in May before a United States commissioner and held under $50,000 bond when agents testified he had $35 of the ransom money. Arraigned with him was Phillip Delaney, 34, a bartender. Melvin Purvis, chief Department of Justice agent, revealed that Delaney was arrested at the same time the senior McLaughlin was held. He was said to have passed $24,000 of Bremer's money. A third man being held was arrested with $2,665 of the Bremer money in his possession.

United States Attorney Davis H. Green announced that the Department of Justice agents would continue to question the four while arrangements were made for their indictment in St. Paul.

Federal men searched the entire Southwest for two notorious gangsters, Arthur (Doc) Barker and Alvin Karpis. Several weeks ago Attorney General Homer S. Cummings announced that Barker and Karpis had been identified as the men who actually kidnapped Bremer from an exclusive St. Paul residential district. The four men held here are accused only of aiding in disposing of the ransom money.[7]

With the exception of Arthur, the Barker-Karpis Gang members were satisfied to stay in the shadows for a while. A woman by the name of Mildred Kuhlman drew Arthur out of hiding. He met her through an Ohio gangster by the name of Ted Angus. Twenty-year-old Mildred was an attractive woman with dark eyes and dark hair. She and Arthur had spent a few evenings together drinking and gambling at the Casino Club in Toledo. Their relationship was platonic until Arthur witnessed one of Mildred's former lovers choking her. Arthur dropped by to visit Mildred at her apartment when he saw the abusive man grab her neck and backhand her. Arthur intervened and nearly beat the man to death for his behavior. Mildred stopped Arthur from killing the man.[8]

Indebted to Arthur for saving her life, Mildred agreed to travel to Chicago, where Arthur promised to shower her with gifts and good times. He provided her with funds to rent an apartment and an expensive room at the Morrison Hotel for their romantic rendezvous. Ma told Arthur that his actions were putting himself and the other members of the gang in jeopardy. He dismissed her warning, telling her not to worry or let "a case of jitters rule their lives."[9]

The girlfriends of the outlaws, Paula Harmon and two other women, Wynona Burdette and Gladys Sawyer, were taking chances with the health and well-being of the gang. They frequently socialized together at various clubs in the Cleveland neighborhood where they lived. One particular evening the women had too much to drink and were causing such a disruption at a local tavern the police were called in to control the situation.[10]

Paula resented the way the authorities were treating her and let them know she had friends that would make them regret their actions. The three were arrested and taken to the police department. Still under the influence, Paula let a few names of the gang slip and threatened the lives of the officers if she wasn't immediately released. As soon as Paula was sober, the authorities questioned her extensively about what she knew of the Bremer kidnapping and the Barker-Karpis Gang. Eventually, she made long, detailed statements about the inner workings of the gang. It was all as Ma had once predicted: The lives of the boys were in question because of the women with whom they had become involved.[11]

When Fred received word that Paula was being held by authorities, he and Alvin decided to leave town. They met with Arthur in Chicago to discuss the recent events. Alvin announced that he was going to take his pregnant girlfriend, Dolores, to Havana. Fred's plan was to run with Ma to Florida. Arthur refused to leave Mildred and Illinois. He returned to Mildred's apartment on Pine Grove Avenue, a high-class residential district on the north side of the city.[12]

Unbeknownst to Arthur, the Chicago office of the Burns Detective Agency had received a tip that a gangster had been spotted coming in and out of the apartment. Federal agents arrived at the location hoping to find Russell Gibson, one of the Barker-Karpis Gang members they believed had assisted in the kidnapping of Bremer. Federal investigator Harold Nathan began watching the Pine Grove Avenue apartment night and day. Nathan was anxious. He realized the developing situation could prove to be the key to putting an end to the Barker-Karpis Gang. His men learned that the tall, thin criminal Gibson, his wife, two other men, and a woman were constantly in and out of a certain second-floor apartment.[13]

These men were killers; a raid was dangerous, but it had to be staged. Late in the evening of January 8, 1935, Agent Nathan and sixteen of his men surrounded the apartment house. Some agents entered by the front and some by the rear doors; others were planted beneath the windows of the marked apartment. The windows were all alight; shadowed figures passed back and forth behind the shades.

As Nathan and his men went up the front and back stairs, they unlimbered submachine guns, drew automatic pistols, and removed tear-gas bombs from their overcoat pockets. Then the men on the front stairs stopped. From above they heard light, carefree footsteps; a pretty, fifteen-year-old girl appeared, staring at their grim faces and guns. She was Geneva Fisher, a schoolgirl who had been visiting friends in an apartment above.[14]

"Go back!" whispered Nathan, and the girl's frightened face disappeared as she ran up toward the third floor.[15]

The agents stopped before the door of Mildred's apartment. They knew their associates had reached the back door by this time. They listened, then pounded on the door. There was no answer. With terrific force one husky agent drove his boot against the door just below the knob. There was a crash of splintering wood; the lock broke. An agent pushed the door open and threw a tear-gas bomb into an empty hallway. The other agents with machine guns leaped forward, shoulder to shoulder, shouting, "Stick 'em up!"[16]

No one was in sight. Russell Gibson's tall figure had run toward the back door. Two other men and two women were waiting in a room for the invaders. Russell wore a bulletproof vest and carried a high-powered machine-gun pistol as he threw open the back door.[17]

He came through the door into the back hall, his head down, his gun before him flashing fire and spraying shots fan-wise. As Russell gained the back hall, his pistol jammed. He was surrounded by federal men with machine guns. Their guns answered his with a deafening roar, and the tall bandit plunged forward upon his face, his mouth spurting blood.[18]

Meanwhile, Nathan and the other agents had charged into the front hallway. They turned to the left, toward the room where the two men and two women waited. The tear-gas bombs had done their work; these four people were choking and sputtering from the fumes. Neither of the men had a gun out, and all four individuals were taken prisoner.[19]

In Russell Gibson's pocket $5,000 in cash was found, some of it Bremer money. The tall bandit refused to talk, dying within an hour at the American Hospital. Agent Nathan simply announced afterward that Russell's wife, another woman, and two unknown men had been taken into custody.[20]

However, the two men were not unknown. One of them was a most important capture. A letter was found in the pocket of this prisoner that made Agent Nathan's eyes gleam with excitement. It caused the machinery of the division of investigation to move in an entirely different direction, in pursuit of Ma Barker. "This is a helluva time to be caught without a gun," Arthur Barker remarked to Agent Nathan, who was beaming with pride because he'd apprehended a key member of the Barker-Karpis Gang.[21]

Russell Gibson, member of the Barker-Karpis Gang COURTESY OF THE MINNESOTA HISTORICAL SOCIETY

Reports of Arthur's arrest didn't make the news until ten days after it occurred. The January 18, 1935, edition of the *Sedalia Democrat* noted that the gangster was transported to St. Paul to stand trial for the $200,000 kidnapping of banker Edward G. Bremer. The article also noted:

> *Barker's arrival was a day and a year after Bremer was kidnapped from his automobile. Handcuffed and heavily manacled with leg chains, Arthur (Doc) Barker arrived under a heavy guard of deputy United States marshals and agents of the department of justice.*
>
> *George F. Sullivan, United States district attorney, announced that Barker would be tried at the April term of court. Also scheduled for trial at the time are John J. McLaughlin, William Vidler, and Phillip Delaney, all of Chicago, arrested in the city charged with having handled Bremer ransom money.*

A small arsenal was recovered from the apartment where Arthur was arrested. FBI files revealed that special agents seized one .32 Colt automatic pistol, one .38 Colt Police Positive revolver, two Browning 30.06 automatic rifles, one Auto and Burglar 20-gauge Ithaca Gun Company shotgun, one .351 rifle fitted with front-machine-gun grip and Cutts compensator, and large quantities of ammunition for each weapon.[22]

In addition to the guns and ammunition, several letters and cards were recovered with aliases of who sent the items and to whom they were written. The postmarks on all the correspondence were from Florida. A map that was also found at the scene had a pencil circle around the town of Ocala, Florida.[23]

A memorandum prepared by the FBI team under Special Agent in Charge E. J. Connelley for Director Hoover explained what transpired once Arthur Barker was placed in custody. "Monty Carter [an informant who had worked with the Barker-Karpis Gang] assisted agents in tracking Arthur and now that Arthur was arrested felt free to offer the details. He gave the FBI a 'line-up' on the kidnapping as to whom kidnapped Bremer, who held him, and who negotiated for the ransom money."[24]

Alvin Karpis and his wife returned from Cuba, completely unaware that federal authorities had tracked Arthur and two other members of the gang to Mildred's apartment in Chicago. Alvin came back to the United States when he learned that the man the boys had hired to launder a sizeable amount of the Bremer ransom had taken the money to Havana to exchange it for unmarked cash. The character the Barker-Karpis Gang paid to take care of the funds was supposed to route the money through Caracas and Mexico City.[25]

With the help of a friend named Joe Adams, Alvin managed to rent a house for himself and Dolores in Miami. He also purchased a 1935 Buick Special to drive. The first road trip Alvin took in his new car was to Lake Weir, four hours north of Miami, to visit Ma and Fred. Using the name Blackburn, the pair had rented a house fifty yards from the water. One of the gang members, Harry Campbell, and his girlfriend Wynona arrived on the scene at the same time, and the group enjoyed time together fishing, boating, and picnicking. "A stone fence about waist high surrounded the property," Alvin recalled in his autobiography, "and the grounds were crowded with grapefruit, orange, and lemon trees. It was a small paradise, and Ma had the luxury of a maid and a gardener."[26]

Alvin and Ma sat for hours on the bank of the lake, talking and discussing future jobs. They planned to go back to work in the winter. Ma believed that if the gang continued to focus on sophisticated crimes, her boys would be unstoppable. From the start of the FBI investigation of the Barker-Karpis Gang, Hoover believed it was "Ma's agile and mature mind that was behind the violent punks she reared and mentored."[27]

The group that had assembled at Lake Weir for several days seldom left one another's company. Ma cooked every meal for her guests, and in the evenings they listened to the phonograph and danced to the music. All was going well for them until Harry was involved in a car accident. He was driving drunk and slammed into a vehicle that had run through a stop sign. Harry was bruised and rattled from the crash. The driver of the other car and his wife were killed. The infant son the couple had with them survived. The police arrived to investigate the crash, and for a brief moment it seemed to Fred, Ma, and Alvin, who heard the accident take place and raced to the scene, that the wanted criminals' locations might be uncovered. "If the sheriff took Harry's fingerprints and sent them to Washington," Alvin cringed at the memory in his autobiography, "the FBI would descend on him and the rest of us."[28]

Harry talked his way out of having prints made with inquiries about where he could purchase a new vehicle. The sheriff at the accident mentioned that his best friend was the Ford dealer there and that Harry could buy a vehicle from him. The officer escorted him to his friend's dealership, and Harry bought a car from the salesman. Before leaving the business Harry donated $250 to the care of the baby who lived through the collision. The authorities thanked Harry for his generosity and sent him on his way.[29]

Ma wept when Alvin announced he needed to get back to Dolores in Miami. She asked him to let them know when his baby was born. Alvin promised to do so and to return soon with his wife and child. "I could tell by her expression that the kid would be welcome, but Dolores not so much," Alvin remembered years later. "She hadn't shown Dolores much warmth in the past. When I pulled away from the place by the lake, I was looking forward to seeing Ma, helping out, taking care of Dolores and our kid."[30]

Bonnie and Clyde, outlaws in the 1930s who met with a violent end, just like Ma Barker COURTESY OF THE LIBRARY OF CONGRESS, LC-USZ62-134474

While Alvin was traveling to Miami, planes carrying armed federal agents were making their way southward toward Florida; other agents were traveling to the state by train. It represented a quiet, unobtrusive converging of forces at the town of Ocala in middle Florida. The federal agents stayed at different hotels and didn't seem to know one another. Some of their members drove into the nearby country and seemed to be especially interested in the charming village of Ocklawaha. There were secret conferences; days passed.[31]

FBI director Hoover's drive to rid the country of its enemies had proven successful. In 1934 alone his team of investigators helped bring down Clyde Barrow and Bonnie Parker, Charles Arthur "Pretty Boy" Floyd, and John Dillinger. With those top criminals out of the way, Hoover could focus on capturing Ma Barker and her boys. While waiting for just the right time to overtake the desperate outlaws, federal agents divided their efforts in order to track down all members of the Barker-Karpis Gang.[32] The January 9, 1935, edition of the *Belvidere Daily Republican* reported that law enforcement had located Russell Gibson, ex-convict and suspect in the $200,000 Edward G. Bremer kidnapping at a North Side Chicago apartment. He tried to shoot his way out of the federal men's trap and was killed.[33]

"Tear gas bombs hurled into the apartment by the government raiders forced the surrender of Byron Bolton of St. Louis, Missouri, and two women, one of whom was said to be Russell's wife," the *Belvidere Daily Republican* article noted. Russell died after being struck with multiple bullets. Although hit with four bullets, only one, a steel-jacketed missile fired from a high-powered rifle, penetrated the ex-convict's bulletproof vest. The article continued:

In Gibson's pockets authorities found $5,000 in large bills. The serial numbers were being traced to determine whether the money was part of the Bremer ransom. Government operatives who attempted to question the dying gangster said he stubbornly refused to talk of his recent activities and the whereabouts of Alvin Karpis. . . .

Gibson was shot down as he raced out of the rear door of the Pine Grove Avenue apartment. Five government agents met him and opened fire as his pistol jammed after firing only one shot. Gibson fell with a bullet in his lung.

Sixteen agents had surrounded the apartment building. They were armed with tear gas bombs, machine guns and rifles. Occupants of Gibson's first floor apartment were called upon to surrender, and a few seconds later Gibson emerged from the rear door with gun in hand.

The officers in the front began flooding the flat with tear gas, forcing Bolton to come out on a small balcony with his arms raised in surrender.

US attorney general Homer Cummings was pleased with Hoover's bureau's dedication to bringing to justice the high-profile criminals terrorizing the country. The January 8, 1935, edition of the *Dothan Eagle* carried an article from leaders in Washington congratulating the FBI on the job it had done:

Uncle Sam's efforts against the underworld were recounted in unromantic statistics today by Attorney General Cummings who informed Congress of the FBI's accomplishments and informed elected officials that the government obtained 3,531 convictions in the fiscal year.

Cummings' annual report covered the period when Dillinger, Floyd, and Nelson were wiped out. He let Congressmen know that the department was at work building a coordinated, nation-wide crime-fighting machine to press the attack against men of that type.

Justice officials heard with much interest President Roosevelt's pronouncement in his message that he would consult Congress on the strengthening of our facilities for the prevention, detection, and treatment of crime and criminals.

A far-flung arrangement for the cooperation of federal, state, and local authorities was represented as the goal of the adminis-tration. The task is called large. The Justice Department regarded as most reliable. A calculation by those that gather statistics note that in 1934 there were probably a minimum of 1,300,000 serious crimes known to the police of this country.

To accelerate the campaign that started last year when Con-gress widened the powers of the Justice Department, Cummings plans to shortly establish a crime institute—a national center to coordinate activities against evil-doers.

Federal authorities worked closely with Florida state police to pos-itively identify that the inhabitants inside the Lake Weir home near where law enforcement agents had gathered were indeed Ma Barker and her son Fred. Plainclothes officers moved into the area to learn all they could about the pair. Neighbors innocently shared stories about the people they knew only as the Blackburns. Among the accounts was that the Blackburns kept the radio inside their home on twenty-four hours a day. The two automobiles they owned were also equipped with radios, which were blaring whenever mother and son were driving. A few Lake Weir citizens had seen Fred and Alvin pilot a boat in the area, pulling a live pig behind. They were using the animal as bait to lure Old Joe the alligator out in the open so they could shoot him with their machine guns.[34]

Other residents of the small community said that Fred was lav-ish in his use of money in town, paying for small, inexpensive items with bills of large denominations and not waiting for change. The local barber confirmed the fact that Ma's boys were not shy about letting citizens know they had money. He received a fifty-dollar tip for giving haircuts to three members of the gang.[35]

Carson Bradford, the owner of the house Ma and Fred rented, had told the authorities that the woman he spoke to about the property had a "hillbilly twang" and claimed to be from Arkansas. She said her name was T. C. Blackburn and that her son was called Blackie. Ma shared with Bradford that she was a churchgoer who sometimes had members of the congregation visit her on Sunday for dinner. Several months later, Bradford learned the congregation she was referring to were members

Charles "Pretty Boy" Floyd, fellow gangster and friend of the Barker-Karpis Gang COURTESY OF THE LIBRARY OF CONGRESS, LC-USZ62-134475

of the Barker-Karpis Gang. Ma's cohorts knew it was safe for them to visit when they saw that the green light outside the boathouse was on. When the red light appeared, it meant the boys should stay away.[36]

It was almost dawn on January 17, 1935, when more than fifteen figures surrounded the two-story white house where Ma Barker and her son were living on Lake Weir. A moon floated across the silvery treetops. Nothing about the scene suggested violence except that the dark figures carried machine guns.[37]

When dawn came, the figures in plain clothes had mounted machine guns on all sides of the house, but the guns were pretty well out of sight. No sound came from within; apparently, the inhabitants were fast asleep.[38]

According to veteran newspaperman Vernon Lamme, law enforcement agents rerouted traffic around the road leading south into Lake

Weir from Ocala. "It was day break and several men wearing long coats were directing cars away from the vacation town," Lamme later wrote. "Recognizing immediately these men were strangers, I parked and approached them, showed them my press badge and credentials and learned they were FBI agents and that they had the Barker gang holed up in a two-story, frame house. They said that Ma Barker and her son Fred were inside. The FBI wanted them."[39]

Lamme noted in his book *Florida Lore Not Found in History Books* that one of the agents initially sent into the area to investigate the Blackburns was one of the youngest. The man looked like a high schooler and posed as a magazine salesman. He visited stores, pool halls, and several other local spots when he overheard a customer mention the "suspicious" fisherman renting a large house near the lake. The agent walked to the home where the fisherman was to ask them to buy a magazine subscription.[40] The Barker-Karpis Gang suspected nothing, invited the agent inside, and even offered to take him on a fishing expedition.[41]

"The agent had been forewarned that Fred had a tattoo on his arm and that was how he could be identified. He joined the family at the lake the next morning. During the heat of the day Fred pushed up his sleeves, revealing the tattoo, and the agent knew then the man indeed was Fred Barker."[42]

It was just before 5:30 in the morning when the first signs of life were observed by officers watching the home Ma Barker rented. Then one federal agent left his machine gun, moved across the porch, opened the screen door on the front porch, and knocked on the door.[43]

CHAPTER TEN

Gunfight at Lake Weir

FIFTEEN FEDERAL AGENTS STOOD IN RAPT SILENCE OUTSIDE THE home of Mrs. Blackburn and her son in Lake Weir, Florida. Mrs. Blackburn was really Ma Barker. At 5:32 in the morning on January 16, 1935, an investigator had knocked on the front door of the house and shouted: "We are Department of Justice men. Come on out!" He heard naked feet patter along an inside hallway and doors on the second floor of the home opening and closing. The FBI believed Ma and Fred were inside the house but were not certain if anyone else was with them.[1]

The agent who had dared approach the two-story residence walked backward to a spot behind one of the many oak trees on the property. He exchanged a glance with the other agents under cover around him. Their lips were grim, their hands loose upon their machine guns. No one said a word for several long moments. Finally, Ma responded to law enforcement's demand that she and her son Fred come out.[2]

"Who are you?" she asked.

"Federal officers," the lead agent replied.

More time passed; then Ma called out, "All right, go ahead."

The special agents interpreted the remark to mean that Ma and Fred were going to surrender, but they were wrong. Fred suddenly appeared in the front doorway, bareheaded, in a white shirt and gray trousers, and with a spitting machine gun. As Fred's bullets crashed toward the agent, Ma's high, shrill voice came like a cry of doom: "Let 'em have it!" Fred's machine-gun fire was answered by tear-gas bombs, rifle fire, and machine-gun fire from weapons in the hands of the FBI agents.[3]

Across the way from the white house, Mrs. A. F. Westberry was awakened by the roar of gunfire. It seemed to come from all sides of her house; it was close up, and it seemed to shake the building. In abject terror she jerked herself to a sitting position as bullets crashed through her closed bedroom door and buried themselves in the head of her bed.[4] She later told newspaper reporters:

I got out of bed . . . opened the door a crack, and more bullets came through the window and hit the face of the door above my head. I looked out the window and saw the yard was full of men. From Mr. Bradford's house across the road there was a lot of shooting. I could see streaks of fire from the guns. I could see the blazes from the men's guns on the outside. There was a lot of rapid fire like machine guns. My daughter was in bed. I broke open the back window of our room and told her we had to get out. About that time some more bullets came smacking through the dining room window and hit the wall.

My daughter and I climbed through the window and got down on the ground. We were going to run to my neighbor's house, about fifty yards back of our house. The house from which the bullets were coming was only about a hundred feet in front of my house.[5]

As we lay down on the ground for a moment, we heard the firing coming louder. We got up and started to run to Mrs. Rex's house. As we ran, some men yelled at us to stop. We did not stop.

They began shooting at us. I learned later it was the federal men. We kept on running and they kept yelling and shooting. They must have shot at us two dozen times. They didn't know who we were. It was still a little dark. Finally we got to Mrs. Rex's house.

There appeared to be fifteen or twenty federal agents. The shooting kept on all morning. Just before noon it stopped. We saw all of the federal men go into the house. Some of them came out in a few minutes. It was all over.

My daughter and I went back to our house and inspected the damage. There were three holes in my bed just above where my head had been. There were two holes in the door facing. In the window were two holes looking as if ten or twelve bullets had come through at the same time.[6]

Federal agents did not know how many gang members were actually inside the house. Shots came at intervals from all the windows. Authorities weren't sure if the house was manned by a large group of criminals or if Fred and Ma were running from window to window. The persons inside were using machine guns, so the answering fire suggested a dozen defenders in action.[7]

At one point during a lull in the gun battle, investigators moved in on the servants' quarters, several yards from the main house. Willie Woodbury and his wife lived in the small cottage. They were the cook and maid for the property. The couple was sleeping when the gunfire began. The quarters had sustained several shots during the initial exchange, and agents felt the time was right to see if anyone was inside. Officers pounded on the door, demanding that the inhabitants come out with their hands up. A petrified Willie shouted back that if the authorities wanted them, they would have to knock down the door. The agents did as suggested and found Willie and his wife huddled together on the floor, too frightened to move.[8]

Federal agents shouted to Ma Barker to surrender. The answer came in renewed flashes of fire, shooting from first one window, then another. Occasionally law enforcement officials could see Ma's gray head or Fred's dark-red hair as they darted like phantoms across the corner of a window. Hours passed and the fight continued with intermittent bursts of shooting. News of the battle had spread throughout the surrounding country; crowds were arriving, but they kept well back from the line of fire.[9]

It was just before noon when the fusillade died out. Agents carefully inched their way out of their hiding spots and rushed toward the house. They lobbed tear-gas shells into the upstairs windows and waited for it to take effect. Federal authorities sent Willie Woodbury into the house to find out if anyone inside was alive. Agents reasoned

The Lake Weir home in Florida where Ma Barker and her son Fred were shot and killed by J. Edgar Hoover's G-Men

the Barkers wouldn't shoot the loyal servant. Willie entered through the back door, moving slowly and cautiously. A minute later, he stuck his head out the upstairs window, coughing and wiping his eyes. The tear-gas fumes were overwhelming. "They are all dead," he called out to the investigators below. An armed agent hurried into the building to confirm Willie's findings. It was true. The Barkers were dead.[10]

Ma Barker and Fred were found lying side by side. Her arm was around her youngest boy, his blood staining her breast. Eleven machine-gun slugs were taken from Fred's corpse, but one shot in the head had killed Ma. Her pudgy hands clasped an empty machine gun. According to the FBI report, a .45 caliber automatic pistol was found near Fred's body. The report also said:

A search of the house after the battle had disclosed $14,000 in $1,000 bills, and an investigation revealed that these $1,000 bills were a part of those that had been obtained by Cassius McDonald in Havana, Cuba, in exchange for the Bremer ransom money. There was also found other currency of smaller denominations totaling approximately $293.00.

A small arsenal was located in the house which consisted of: two Thompson submachine guns, one Browning .12 gauge automatic shotgun, one Remington .12 gauge pump shotgun, two .45 caliber automatic pistols, one .33 caliber Winchester rifle, and one .380 Colt automatic pistol, together with machine gun drums, automatic pistol clips, and a quantity of ammunition.

There was also found in the house a letter signed by B. L. Barnes which was a letter to Fred Barker from his brother Arthur. The letter read as follows: "Hello ever [sic] one how is that old sunshine down there fine I hope. Boy it is not so hot up here, for we are having some winter. I Bet you and Buff are not catching no fish now for I think I caught them all when I was down there. I took care of that Business for you Boys it was done. Just as good as if you had did it yourself. I am Just like the standard oil always at your service ha ha. Tell, Bo, you know the Boy with the rosey [sic] cheek that Moxey is up here looking for him and if it is alright to send him down. I have not seen c——k yet I have Been Busy on that other he was perrty [sic] hard to locate. But will see him right away, and see if he wants come down there. Tell mother that deer was mighty fine and I said hello and her and the squaw had better not let you Bums Beat them in a catching fish ha ha well I will close for this time as ever you [sic] Big Bud. B. L. Barnes."[11]

The letter Arthur wrote to his family provided officials with information about what became of fellow gangster William J. Harrison. William was the "business" Arthur was referring to. He had been a member of the Barker-Karpis Gang and participated in the kidnapping of Edward Bremer. Authorities found William's charred remains in a barn on January 6, 1935, near Ontarioville in Du Page County, Illinois. It is believed that Arthur lured him to the abandoned spot and shot him. The body and the barn were saturated with paraffin before a match was tossed in. Investigators surmised that Arthur murdered William to keep him from talking to police about the specifics of the kidnapping.[12]

Media outlets from Baltimore to San Francisco carried reports of how the Bremer kidnap suspect and his domineering mother were slain by US agents in a six-hour siege. Pictures of the victims were plastered across magazines and newspapers. Articles containing the specifics of the machine-gun fight varied from city to city, but the main detail was always the same: Ma and Fred had been killed. "Crime never pays," began the notice in the January 16, 1935, edition of the *Denver Post*. It continued:

Fred Barker, long sought for the $200,000 kidnapping of Edward Bremer, wealthy St. Paul banker, and his mother "Ma" Barker were shot to death by the Department of Justice agents.

Just after the furious battle ended, the federal agents said two men and a woman had been killed, but a later look disclosed that only the Barkers were slain. After a blasting encounter with the guns, the agents resorted to teargas. Barker immediately made a break from the barricaded house and was promptly mowed down by the withering fire of the federal men.

The agents suffered no casualties. The beautiful summer home belonging to Carson Bedford, president of the Biscayne Kennel Club at Miami, who had rented two months ago to a man who gave his name as T. C. Blackburn, was shot full of holes.

When Ma Barker fell in the house, federal agents said she was holding a machine gun in her hand and part of the drum of cartridges had been exhausted. The agents said they had fired 1,500 rounds of ammunition into the house.

The bullet-ridden room where Ma and Fred Barker were found dead by J. Edgar Hoover's G-Men

The cache of firearms and ammunition Ma and her boys had with them at the time of their demise

According to the March 29, 1936, edition of the *Kansas City Star*:

The big, white house at Ocklawaha came under surveillance after Arthur Barker was arrested. One morning came a knock at the door. Ma Barker opened the door merely a crack. "Well?" she demanded.

"We're federal agents," the visitor said: "If you'll come out one by one, there'll be no trouble."

The eyes of the old woman gleamed meticulously. "To hell with you—let the Feds have it!" Then the shooting began, fifteen federal agents answering machine gun burst for machine gun burst. Finally, after six hours, those within the house were silenced. And when the officers finally entered they found Fred Barker and his mother there alone, both dead.

FBI director Hoover made a public statement about the end of Ma Barker and her boys. He expressed his personal gratification that Ma and Fred had been "eliminated" and that a number of other members of her group had been apprehended. "We have another member of the mob and several other women who were involved with the gang locked up in Chicago," the January 17, 1935, edition of the *Moberly Monitor-Index* quoted Hoover.

Hoover received constant calls from field operatives about the gun battle in Ocklawaha, Florida. Speaking of Ma Barker, he referred to her as a "jealous old battle axe." "She dictated who her sons' lady friends were to be. We even heard that when they wanted to go out on a party they would go to another town from where she was. She taught her boys never to be taken alive. Ma Barker was the brains of the gang, a domineering woman of about sixty years, so clever that she never had been arrested."[13]

Alvin Karpis and Harry Campbell had just returned from a fishing trip in the Gulf Stream when they found out about Ma and Fred being shot and killed. Alvin's girlfriend Dolores and Harry's paramour Wynona were waiting outside the Karpises' home to let the pair know about the incident at the rented home at Lake Weir. "I felt two emotions when Dolores told me about Freddie and Ma, grief and fear," Alvin recalled years later in his autobiography. "I'd lived through a lot with both of them. But I was scared, too. If the FBI got them, then they might get me. Dolores and Harry and Wynona next. I had to keep cool. Freddie and Ma were gone, but we were still free and loose."[14]

According to the FBI report, it was time for Alvin and Harry to renew their flight. Plans for their departure were made hurriedly, and the gang's new errand boy, an orchestra leader by the name of Henry "Duke" Randall, was dispatched to the El Comodoro Hotel in Miami, where $1,200 was secured for Alvin from Joe Adams, who had been holding the same for the fugitive. The night of January 16, 1935, found Dolores Delaney and Wynona Burdette aboard a train bound for Atlantic City, New Jersey. They carried with them as credentials a note signed by Henry "Duke" Randall addressed to William A. Morley, part owner of the Dunmore Hotel, Atlantic City, New Jersey. The message requested Morley to take care of his friend Mrs. Graham (Dolores, who was in her last month of pregnancy) and to see that she obtained a good doctor and good care.[15] The FBI report noted:

The women arrived at Atlantic City, New Jersey, about 2 o'clock on the afternoon of January 18, 1935, and registered at the Dunmore Hotel as Mrs. A. B. Graham and sister of Macon, Georgia. At about 1 o'clock in the morning the following day Karpis and Campbell appeared at the Dunmore Hotel driving a Buick sedan bearing Florida license D-5-306. Karpis registered at the hotel as R. S. Carson, and Campbell used the name of G. C. Cameron. Special Agents had learned of the license number of the car in the possession of Karpis and a description of the car and the desperate character of its occupants were broadcast.

Early on in the morning of January 20, 1935, police officers located the car in the Coast Garage at Atlantic City, New Jersey, and this officer with two fellow officers, of the Atlantic City Police Department, then proceeded to the Dunmore Hotel to investigate. The officers approached the third floor of the hotel with drawn guns.

In the hallway they found a frightened man dressed only in his underwear and when questioned by the officers he stated that he would be glad to have the man who was in the room in which the officers were interested to come out in the hallway. The ruse worked. Karpis dashed into Campbell's room and they came out together firing a machine gun and after an exchange of shots with the officers, Karpis and Campbell succeeded in perfecting their escape.

Dolores Delaney was wounded in the leg. She and Wynona Burdette succeeded in escaping from the hotel and crouched in the alley, awaiting the arrival of Karpis and Campbell to rescue them. However, during the period of time they were waiting for the fugitives they deliberated upon the safety of their men and it was decided that to continue their flight with Karpis and Campbell at this time, due to the condition of Dolores Delaney, would only hinder their flight. The women remained in the alley until taken into custody by officers.[16]

Dolores's injuries were not serious. She was taken to a local hospital where the wound was dressed, and she remained at the facility in anticipation of childbirth.[17]

The Department of Justice agents continued their aggressive search for the remaining members of the Barker-Karpis Gang. "Shoot first and talk afterward," was the advice from Chicago, where officials thought Alvin might seek a new hideout.[18]

Driving a stolen Pontiac Alvin and Harry tried to find where Dolores and Wynona were being held. The attempt was unsuccessful, and fearing they would be caught, they fled the area. On January 20, 1935, they abandoned the vehicle in Pennsylvania and hijacked a car and driver in Allentown. Doctor Horace Hunsicker was the owner of the vehicle. He had stopped to see his parents while en route to the state hospital. Alvin was prompted to steal the car after he spotted a doctor's emblem on the back of the vehicle. The criminals stuck a machine gun in Doctor Hunsicker's side and forced him to drive them to Guilford Center, Ohio.[19]

Once the gangsters arrived in Ohio, Alvin and Harry pushed the doctor out of the car. They tied his hands and feet and gagged his mouth before abandoning him in an empty town hall. The gangsters proceeded on to Toledo. With the help of contacts the pair had in the city, they ditched the car and took refuge at a house of ill repute owned by a madam named Edith Barry.[20]

Meanwhile, federal agents scoured the country looking for the escaped gang members. According to the February 7, 1935, edition of the *Ironwood Daily Globe*, law enforcement thought Alvin might have fled to Northern California. "Recent findings of a cached machine gun, and identification of a man unduly interested in the movement of gold from mining operations as a member of the Barker-Karpis Gang, led officers to believe Karpis was hiding out below the snowline in the Sierra Nevadas," the article read.

A hotel owner in Yorkville, Illinois, reported that Alvin and Harry had checked into his establishment and were holed up in their rooms with alcohol, machine guns, and prostitutes. Law enforcement responded to the business but found no one there matching the description of the fugitives.[21]

Alvin read the news about the birth of his son in the Ohio newspapers while continuing to hide out at the brothel. Dolores had a son weighing seven pounds and four ounces. Alvin's parents traveled to Philadelphia, where the baby was born, to take custody of the infant. Dolores and Wynona were taken to Florida to face charges of harboring criminals.[22]

Alvin tired of waiting around Edith Barry's brothel for federal agents to become disinterested in him. Harry and Alvin made plans to steal the payroll from the Youngstown Sheet and Tube Plant in Warren, Ohio. Despite the difficulties Alvin and Harry had working with new outlaw recruits, the heist was a success. The total amount stolen was $72,000.[23]

Government officials arrived on the scene of the robbery and quickly linked the job to the last remaining remnants of the Barker-Karpis Gang. The FBI posted photographs of the criminals in newspapers around the country. Well-meaning citizens reported seeing Alvin and Harry in Saratoga Springs, Florida; Des Moines, Iowa; and Hot Springs, Arkansas. The pair was linked to the robbery of the First National Bank and Trust Company in Springfield, Ohio, and a series of drugstore robberies in Waterville, Ohio.[24]

In August 1935 news that Alvin sent threatening letters to FBI director Hoover in Washington surfaced. Details of the letters were lacking, but they were reported to have been about how he was going to kill Hoover for killing Ma. The report of the letter was posted in the July 21, 1935, edition of the *Dayton Daily News*. Officials pronounced it "authentic," indicating that handwriting and fingerprint experts scrutinized it. Years later, Alvin claimed the accusation was "merely a hoax to try and lure me out of hiding."[25]

Alvin Karpis was listed as public enemy number 1 by the FBI for more than a year. He and Harry split up and went their separate ways in hope of further eluding the authorities. Investigators eventually tracked the kidnapper to New Orleans. On May 1, 1936, the number-one bad man of the United States was captured without resistance by officers led by Director Hoover. The May 2, 1936, edition of the *San Bernardino County Sun* reported:

> *A few hours later, the man who succeeded John Dillinger as the most wanted criminal was placed aboard an airplane heavily guarded and manacled and taken from the city with the destination unannounced.*
>
> *Without a shot, Karpis was taken into custody along with Fred Hunter, 37, a suspect in the $34,000 Garretsville, Ohio, post office robbery and a woman known only as "Ruth" as they emerged from an apartment building about half a mile from the center of the business district.*
>
> *Hoover made the announcement of the capture with the simple statement, "We've captured Alvin Karpis, generally known as Public Enemy No. 1—but not to us. They were taken without firing a shot."*

Within the past two weeks, the justice department placed a $5,000 price upon Karpis' head, and added a $2,500 price for information leading to the capture of his pal, Harry Campbell.

Four days ago, the postal inspection service followed the justice department lead and added a $2,000 reward for Karpis bringing his price to $7,000 and $2,000 more for Campbell.

Hoover said the bureau of investigation had known that Karpis had been in and out of New Orleans for the past several months. He, himself, had come here several days ago to direct the man hunt. Hoover, smiling slightly, made his announcement of the capture in the bureau office in the post office building here about an hour after the raid saying, "I've got something interesting to tell you."

Hoover did not say how many men took part in the capture but there were reported to have been between fifteen and twenty. "They were in an apartment on the first floor of the building and were leaving the house to enter an automobile when the agents surrounded them," Hoover said. "The agent called upon them to surrender and they were taken without the firing of a shot. Shackles were placed on the hands and feet of Karpis and the shackles then bound together. He and the others were taken to the post office building."

The plane carrying Director Hoover, various FBI agents, and Alvin Karpis landed in St. Paul, Minnesota, on May 2, 1936. Alvin was taken to the federal building downtown and locked in a cell. Alvin's former partner Arthur Barker was held at the same facility during his trial.[26]

US district attorney George F. Sullivan of St. Paul led the team of prosecutors at Arthur's hearing in April 1935. They began the trial with a look at his criminal history. The government called an agent from the Oklahoma Bureau of Investigation to tell the jury about Arthur's background.[27]

The agent identified Arthur as the man whose picture and fingerprints he had taken in 1922, the date of Arthur's first encounter with the law. It was anticipated the government planned to show that the

Alvin Karpis captured by federal agents and brought to St. Paul in connection with the
Hamm and Bremer kidnappings COURTESY OF THE MINNESOTA HISTORICAL SOCIETY

fingerprints corresponded to those on equipment used in the Edward
Bremer kidnapping and definitely linked Arthur with the abduction.[28]

Four gas cans the government claimed bore Arthur's fingerprints
and a funnel found on a highway near Portage, Wisconsin, were offered
as evidence in the kidnapping trial. The cans were used to refill the car
transporting Bremer from the point where he was taken hostage in St.
Paul to the location where he was held in Illinois.[29]

In addition to the physical evidence against Arthur, several witnesses
took the stand to share what they knew about the criminal's behavior and participation in abducting Edward Bremer. Adolph Bremer,
Edward's father, was one of the individuals to take the witness stand.[30]

According to the April 18, 1935, edition of the *Marshall Evening
Chronicle*, Edward Bremer's elderly, white-haired father broke down as

he related in a voice shaken with sobs the days of anguish the family suffered while his son was in the hands of the kidnapping gang.

"Tears welled into the eyes of the aged man, president of a brewing company and personal friend of President Roosevelt, as he told of the family's suffering while kidnappers held his son for $200,000 ransom," the *Marshall Evening Chronicle* article reported.

Several people accused of conspiracy in the case confessed to their deeds and pled guilty rather than stand trial. Not only did they admit to their wrongdoings, but they implicated Arthur in the process. Chicago bartender Phillip Delaney told authorities how he "peddled" (or laundered) $24,000 of the $200,000 ransom, which he said was given to him by John J. "Boss" McLaughlin, a member of the Barker-Karpis Gang. The money was said to have been given to McLaughlin by Arthur. The bartender's confession was admitted into evidence.[31]

An article in the April 26, 1935, edition of the *Bismarck Tribune* reported that "additional sums of the 'hot' money were disposed of by a man simply known as 'Bill' while McLaughlin and Delaney waited in an automobile and watched."

The activity surrounding the case wasn't limited to the courtroom. Mobsters who feared they might be implicated in the proceedings sent death threats to the prosecuting attorney's office and warned that they would intercept officials transporting Arthur from the jail to the courtroom. According to the January 22, 1936, edition of the *Sandusky Register*, four suspicious characters loitering outside the jail in St. Paul created a panic among the deputies guarding the gangster. "One of them carried a violin case," the article quoted a guard as saying, "a machine gun fits handily into violin cases."

The suspicious-looking men turned out to be clergymen who came to conduct services at the jail. The violin case contained a violin.[32]

Arthur Barker sat through the proceedings in utter silence, glaring as the various witnesses took the stand against him. His sharp, criminal eyes had no effect on the witnesses. Wynona Burdette kept her eyes on the prosecuting attorney when she took the stand. The former radio singer spoke in a low, polite voice of raids by federal men from which leaders of the gang barely escaped and of what she knew about Arthur beating Edward Bremer when he was taken hostage.[33]

The government's most telling blow against Arthur was delivered by Byron Bolton, former machine gunner with the Barker-Karpis Gang. The nervous gang member accused Arthur and Alvin Karpis of the Bremer abduction.[34]

Neither Arthur nor his court-appointed attorney offered a defense to the accusations, and Arthur did not take the stand on his own behalf. The prosecuting attorney concluded his portion of the case by demanding Arthur's conviction on evidence that was neither "rebutted nor undisputed." According to the May 15, 1935, edition of the *Greenfield Daily Reporter*, the prosecuting attorney told the jury that "Arthur Barker has figured in this picture from the beginning and helped stage the crimes of the country."

The jury deliberated for one day before rendering a decision in Arthur's case. He was found guilty. Federal judge M. M. Joyce, who had been overseeing the trial, sentenced the gangster on May 17, 1935. "Arthur Barker, you have no defense in this case," Judge Joyce announced at the sentencing. "No one could doubt your guilt. You have had a fair trial. Kidnapping is one crime that the people of this country will not tolerate."[35]

Arthur was sentenced to life in prison. His face remained stoic during the reading of the sentence. His penalty brought the number of life sentences for kidnapping to eighteen since the passage of the federal Lindbergh Act.[36]

On May 25, 1935, Arthur was handcuffed and shackled and transferred from the jail in St. Paul to the Leavenworth penitentiary. He was hopeful of being allowed to work as a printer. He was a printer during a previous stay at the facility and had told Ma and his brothers that he liked the work.[37]

In a crowded court clerk's office in St. Paul in July 1936, Alvin Karpis was charged with four counts of kidnapping, two relating to the Bremer abduction. Bail was set at $500,000. Worried the habitual criminal would try to escape, a federal agent was ordered by Hoover to be with Alvin at all times. He wasn't allowed to be alone for any reason, not even when he met with his attorney. Against his lawyer's advice, Alvin pled not guilty at his arraignment. He noted in his memoirs that the US district attorney tried desperately to work out a deal with him. "He promised that if I pled guilty on the four counts and tell what I knew about others involved with the crime, he'd get me a prison sentence and not death, and that the sentence would be of such a length that I would eventually get out and not die inside the penitentiary."[38]

Alvin refused to cooperate. His trial was scheduled to begin on July 13, 1936. One hundred witnesses were on call, and numerous newspaper and radio reporters had descended on the federal building to cover the hearing. Alvin looked exhausted and discouraged when the guards escorted him into the courtroom. An article in the July 1936 edition of the *Reading Times* noted that "the gangster who once boasted 'I'll never be taken alive' had laid aside his braggadocio and appeared in a mood to give up the fight and take his medicine."[39]

Alvin had reconsidered his initial plea, and just before court was called into session, he informed his attorney that he wanted to plead guilty. The judge hearing the case ordered Alvin to stand up and say "guilty" after the charges against him were read aloud.[40] An editorial in the July 16, 1936, edition of the *Alton Evening Telegram* read:

> *The name of Alvin Karpis is to be added to the long list of one-time "tough" gangsters who rode high and wide at the expense of others. Karpis was a king of gangland, and with his henchmen conducted a rule of gun and crime. Others more notorious than he had felt the pinch of the law, and it was inevitable that the time would come for Karpis, too.*
>
> *Karpis was captured. More intelligent men than he—and braver men, too—took him into custody. Came the time for his trial, Karpis found that defending his kind had become less popular—that the law was less flexible; and that a case has been made against him. He could not, as his jargon has it, "beat the rap." So he pleaded guilty to kidnapping.*

*The day of the gangster like Ma Barker and her boys are gone
from America. The criminal has found out that the law means
business. And when the law means business, the criminal, however
notorious, whatever his one-time power, cannot go on.*

Twenty-seven-year-old Alvin Karpis showed no emotion when
he was sentenced to life in prison on July 28, 1936. In Washington,
DC, Department of Justice officials said that Alvin would be taken to
the penitentiary at Leavenworth, Kansas, and later to Alcatraz in San
Francisco.[41]

On Thursday, August 6, 1936, an iron-barred railway coach brought
twenty convicts into Oakland, California, after a three-day journey from
Leavenworth. Alvin was one of the prisoners in tow. According to the
armed guards watching over the prisoners, "Alvin acts like he's going
to a picnic." Standing near the grilled windows, he smiled to railroad
employees and answered their questions with handcuffed gestures. A
launch met the guards and convicts in Oakland and transported them
to the grim rock in San Francisco Bay that offered no hope of escape.
Three other members of the Barker-Karpis Gang, including Arthur
Barker, would also serve out their life sentences at Alcatraz.[42]

With Alvin and Arthur behind bars, Ma and Fred dead, and many
of their cohorts arrested and awaiting trial or being pursued by government officials, FBI director Hoover believed the American public
could begin to feel safe again.[43]

An article in the July 11, 1936, edition of the *Evening News* echoed
Hoover's sentiments:

*There is a feeling that though most of us probably failed to notice it,
an era in American history—an ugly, unsavory era withal—has
recently come to a close. This era was that of the gangster. It began
about 1920 and petered out a few weeks ago with the bringing
to justice the specimens as Alvin Karpis, Ma Barker, and "Lucky"
Luciano. And in the study of its rise and fall there is a wealth of
illumination about the ways and customs of the American people.*

The principal bit of illumination is the not entirely surprising fact that we did it all ourselves. We brought on the era of crime and we cut it off.

We had gangsters because we were what we were and we at last taught them who is boss because, by the grace of Providence, we are what we are. The good that is in us and the bad that rides along with it played equal parts in the era of the gangster.

It is easy to say that we wished the gangster on ourselves by passing the prohibition law. Easy-and-exact. For, although prohibition gave the city tough his chance, he didn't come in out of the void. We had set the stage for him, the "eminent respectables" supported him—and in fact had given him a spear to carry long before.

We did that chiefly by forgetting one of the race's oldest axioms—that where there is no vision the people perish. And there was precious little vision during those dark and feverish years: or if there was foresight, it was clouded over so that we seldom saw it.

We tolerated crooked politics, fixers of high and low degree, four-flusher, go-getters: we let the wealth-at-any-price spirit steal over us, decided that the man who had the most money must of necessity be the finest citizen and figured that any city with tall skyscrapers and handsome boulevards must be flourishing. We were, in other words, on the make pretty steady. We sowed in disregard of the spirit, and we reaped—among other things—gangsters. We got just about what we asked for and we had nobody to blame but ourselves.

But there is a brighter side to it. It didn't, after all, last forever. The country did wake up, finally. Once more, as of old, it showed that American wrath can be a terrible and deadly thing when it is roused: and it swept over the underworld in an irresistible tide.

The era is over now, one hopes.

CHAPTER ELEVEN

Waiting for a Grave

THE BODIES OF MA BARKER AND HER SON FRED WERE TAKEN TO the Pyle Mortuary in Ocala, Florida, after they were killed in the shoot-out with federal agents. On January 16, 1935, mother and son were laid on stainless steel slabs, their frames covered with sheets from their necks down. Marion County officials and federal agents posed for photographs with the dead gangsters, and reporters negotiated with morgue employees for a chance to see the well-known criminals lying in state.[1]

The deceased outlaws were the town's top attraction for eight months. Their iced-down bodies, riddled with bullet holes, were still and bloated, waiting for somebody to come bury them. The FBI encouraged the Barkers' extended stay in Florida, hoping that gang members still at large might drop by to make sure the two gangsters were indeed Ma and Fred Barker. No gang members showed, but tourists came from all over the country to view the bodies.[2]

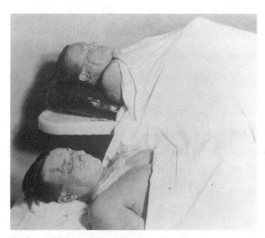

Bodies of Ma and Fred Barker after the shoot-out in Florida in January 1935 COURTESY OF THE FBI

George Barker, Ma's estranged husband, was notified of the death of his wife and son on January 17, 1935. The January 18, 1935, edition of the *Springfield Daily News* noted that George, now sixty-seven, wasn't interested in hearing about the pair. "I don't care when and how Fred and Kate are buried," he told reporters. "I don't care to have them brought back here. I wouldn't care to attend the funeral. I'd like to be left out of all this. They chose their path some years ago and I followed mine. I haven't seen any of them in years."

George was a solitary man who had worked at a gas station and as a caretaker of a campground in Joplin, Missouri, since he and Ma had gone their separate ways in 1928. An article in the October 14, 1935, edition of the *Pulaski Southwest Times* reported that George rarely, if ever, spoke to his estranged wife and children. He was visited often by law enforcement agents who speculated that members of the Barker-Karpis Gang might use his home and business as a place to hide from the law. George's friends and neighbors said he was honest and upright and that his only solace came in knowing that at least one member of the family remained respectable.

"After the Barker boys began to get in 'big time' crime they tried to lure their father away from Joplin," the *Pulaski Southwest Times* article read. "They told him he would not have to worry anymore about money the rest of his life. George, however, chose to remain in Joplin barely earning enough to live on."

The government strongly encouraged George to assume the legal responsibility for taking care of burying his family. It wasn't until George learned that Ma and Fred would be given a pauper's funeral and laid to rest in Florida that he decided he wanted to bring them home. The problem was he didn't have money for his estranged wife and son to be transported to Oklahoma to be buried next to Herman. It would take George several months to gather enough funds to get the job done.[3]

In the meantime George learned that he and another gentleman named Frank Dixon were named coadministrators of Fred's estate. The money discovered at the Florida home where Fred and Ma were killed had been confiscated by the FBI. The serial numbers on the bills did not match those on the ransom money from the Bremer kidnapping, but the bureau had a reasonable expectation that the cash had been acquired from some illegal activity. The government would not release the funds to Fred's estate and refused to give George a receipt for it.

Attorney Claude B. Kenney came forward to represent George in the matter. The January 24, 1935, edition of the *Joplin Globe* included an article about the legal efforts to obtain the $10,000 found in the "death house":

> *Co-administrators George Barker and Frank Dixon gave bond in the sum of $20,000, estimating the estate as consisting of personal property worth $10,000 and no real estate. Information given to Probate Judge Adolph McGee was that the administrators would send their attorney to Ocklahawa, Florida, where Fred Barker and his mother were killed, to seek and obtain from authorities the money reportedly found in the house.*
>
> *It is the contention that the money, unless identified as belonging to other parties, is the property of the Barker estate. Frank Dixon is a proprietor of a tourist camp where George Barker is employed. The $20,000 bond also was signed by A. W. Wolfenbarger and S. L. Wolfenbager, business associates of Mr. Dixon.*
>
> *The application gives the heirs of the deceased Fred Barker as the father, a brother, Arthur Barker of Joplin and a brother, Lloyd Barker, of Leavenworth, Kansas.*

The inventory and appraisement records on file in the Jasper County Records and Research Center revealed that Ma had a number of personal items hidden away in storage units in Illinois and Minnesota. Using the name Mrs. F. E. Gordon, Ma rented a facility in Chicago that contained the following property: one white-gold ring set with diamonds; lady solitaire set with diamond; small, yellow-gold ring; wedding ring; wearing apparel; a living room suite; two bedroom suites; dining room suite; radio; electric sweeper; two floor lamps;

three large rugs; five small rugs; three trunks and contents; three or
four suitcases and contents; and other small articles, including:

1 secretary desk—$12.50
1 3-piece bedroom set—$28.50
1 rug pad 9x12—$1.50
2 bathroom rugs—$.50
1 9-piece dining room set—$35.00
1 occasional table—$5.00
1 electric sweeper—$8.50
3 bed springs—$9.00
3 mattresses—$15.00
1 table lamp—$3.75
2 night tables—$1.00
1 card table—$1.50
2 iron beds—$8.00
1 ironing board—$.50
1 makeup table—$2.50
2 night tables—$5.00
1 3-piece living set—$2.50
1 mirror—$9.00
1 day bed—$.50
1 smoker stand—$.50
1 lamp—$3.75
7 pictures—$1.25
1 rug pad 10x12—$3.50
2 rugs 9x12—$15.00 each
1 rug 9x12—$10.00
1 rug 27x54—$2.00
2 rugs—$4.00
1 trunk and contents—$10.00
1 grip—$.50
2 traveling bags—$5.00
2 steamer trunks—$14.00

1 box of clothes—$1.00

2 boxes of dishes—$12.50[4]

Listed under jewelry, separate from the above-mentioned items, the following pieces were listed:

1 three-stone diamond ring, white gold, center stone ⅜—$20.00

1 two-and-one-half-carat diamond white gold
 mounting—$175.00

1 yellow gold 14k plain ring, white gold—$3.50

1 seven-stone diamond wedding ring, white gold—$7.50[5]

Ma and Fred had joint accounts at the Woodlawn Safety Deposit Company in Chicago and the Commercial Bank and Trust Company in Ocala, Florida. The accounts in Chicago contained more than $6,000. The Florida accounts contained in excess of $20,000.[6]

The legal dispute over Ma and Fred's possessions was argued by attorneys for George Barker and representatives for the government for several months. While waiting for the matter to be settled, George was doing all he could to acquire the funds to bury his wife and son. He managed to get the money together by the latter part of September 1935.[7]

On October 1, 1935, nine months after the pair were killed, George arrived at the mortuary to claim the mummified bodies of his family. They were transported by ambulance to the Haines-Woodard Funeral Home in Webb City, Missouri. The October 1, 1935, edition of the *Sikeston Standard* reported that Ma and Fred were brought first to George's place of business when the hearse reached town. "John Woodward, a member of the Haines-Woodard Undertaking Company of Webb City, Missouri, stopped at the Ancell Brothers Service Station Friday morning with the bodies of Fred Barker, and his mother, Kate for George Barker to review."

The *Joplin News Herald* reported on the arrival of the remains and on the number of residents who visited the mortuary to view Ma and Fred's unopened caskets. "Brief funeral services were conducted at the graves Tuesday afternoon in a cemetery northwest of Miami, Missouri," the article in the *Joplin News Herald* noted. "The funeral procession, including two hearses, is expected to leave Webb City at 1 p.m. Tuesday for the cemetery."[8]

Approximately fifty people, a few of them relatives, including George Barker, attended the short ceremony at the cemetery near Welch, Oklahoma. According to the October 3, 1935, article in the *Miami News-Record*, "Government agents, a member of the Kansas State Highway Patrol, and a member of the Oklahoma Bureau of Investigation were present at the cemetery." They were there in the event Alvin Karpis or Harry Campbell, former gang associates of the Barkers, should attend the funeral.

"As two hearses rolled into the weed grown burial ground, an airplane roared overhead," the report continued. "Even in death the Barkers were still a menace, and the airplanes carried scouts who scanned side roads with powerful glasses for suspicious automobiles. None was seen. The usual custom of gangsters to popup at the last rites for their friends was evidently not followed out."

The FBI report noted that the minister who presided over the service invoked the blessings of the Deity upon surviving members of the family. The minister qualified the request for such blessings with the statement "If it be Thy will."[9]

The bodies were buried next to the grave of Herman Barker. Ma and Fred had been laid to rest, but the question of who would get a piece of their estate remained the source of much agitation among the banks and businesses they had robbed. On December 7, 1935, the *Joplin Globe* carried an article announcing that the Citizens National Bank of Fort Scott, Kansas, had filed suit against the probate judge and administration from distributing the estate until they had a chance to make a claim. The *Joplin Globe* article read:

> In the suit, filed for the January court term, the bank seeks an injunction to restrain Probate Judge Adolph McGee from issuing any more orders relative to the estate, and attack the legality of the

*Jasper county probate court's jurisdiction. Legality of the appoint-
ment of George Barker, father living in Webb City and acting as
administrators of the estates of Fred and Arizona Barker also is
assailed. Claude Kenney, attorney for the administrator, and S. L.
Wolfenbarger, bondman, also are named defendants.*

*It is contended in the petition that neither Fred Barker nor his
mother were legal residents of Marion County at the time of their
deaths at the hands of federal agents in Florida. Therefore it is contended that the appointment of George Barker and Frank Dixon
as administrators was illegal, and all acts of the probate court in
connection with disposing of the estate should be declared null and
void. Several thousand dollars already has been paid out to the
administrators and to Kenney, it is stated in the petition, and it
is contended that the entire estate is "threatened with dissipation."*

*In addition to seeking an injunction, the bank asks appoint-
ment of a receiver to take charge of the assets of the estate of Fred
Barker and Arizona Barker, and that the circuit court adjudge the
respective rights of creditors. It is also asked that the administrators
and Kenney be required to return to the estate such money as they
have been given and is now available.*

The disposition of Ma and Fred's personal belongings was decided
by the courts in early January 1936. Their estate, estimated at $20,000,
was awarded to Ma's long-suffering husband. After paying legal fees,
delinquent storage unit bills, court costs, and administration expenses,
George received $1,100. He was satisfied with the amount and told
friends and neighbors that he didn't require much to live on.[10] An
article about the outcome of the estate settlement and the notorious
Barkers, and Ma in particular, in the March 16, 1936, edition of the
Franklin Evening Star concluded with a comment by FBI director
Hoover on the matter. "The way of the transgressor is hard," Hoover
offered. "The average woman has a natural dread of any kind of violence, but once started on the road outside the law she becomes just
as desperate as a man. She accepted a life of crime by choice. The

Barkers killed for the fun and never learned what the word 'mercy' meant."

From his cell in Alcatraz, Arthur Barker had a considerable amount of time to reflect on the life that he, his mother, and his brothers lived. Registered as Prisoner #268-AZ, he was kept in isolation in a cell not far from "Birdman" Robert Stroud. Arthur was required by prison officials at the intake facility in Leavenworth, Kansas, to participate in a series of in-depth interviews with social workers, doctors, psychiatrists, and chaplains. He told the social worker about his father and how he admired him for the honest life he always led. He wanted George to have the $5,600 he'd stashed in a savings account in a bank in Chicago. Arthur explained he'd acquired the money gambling and that none of the funds were from the Bremer ransom. The US Penitentiary, Leavenworth, Kansas, Admission Summary #46928 noted that the social worker considered Arthur to be "rather slick and oily . . . and decidedly untrustworthy."[11]

Arthur was found to be in excellent health physically, but psychiatrists determined he had difficulties. He registered eighty-one on the Stanford-Binet Intelligence Quotient, giving him a mental age of thirteen. His SAT score declared his effective level of schooling to be equivalent to a fifth grader. He was deemed by prison inmate personnel to be someone who would work hard and not be a discipline problem. The same personnel decided that Alcatraz would be the appropriate facility for Arthur to serve his sentence.[12]

Alcatraz was one of eight major institutions that practiced the Pennsylvania System. The Pennsylvania System was the leading influence in penology for over a century and was the forerunner of modern corrections. The system encouraged solitary confinement for prisoners and was designed to keep prisoners separate even as they worked in order to keep them from being distracted and impeding their repentance.[13]

Alcatraz was designed to be a disciplinary fortress. Repeat offenders like Arthur Barker and Alvin Karpis were conditioned to believe there was no way off "the Rock," as it was called. Officially completed in 1912 the penitentiary resembled a stationary battleship. Inmates often referred to the prison as Hellcatraz.[14]

When Arthur arrived at Alcatraz, guards lined the balconies of buildings, and riot guns, Winchester .30-06 rifles, and machine guns followed his every move. Alvin Karpis received the same reception. Both men were ushered to Warden James A. Johnston's office for a brief interview and an explanation of what life would be like at Alcatraz. When the warden was finished with Arthur, he was led to the bathroom, where the guards removed his handcuffs and manacles. He was made to shower and then a medical officer performed a cavity search. Arthur was then taken to an area where he was issued heavy woolen socks and underwear, tan brogan shoes, gray overalls, and a flannel mechanics cap. Once dressed, he was escorted to his cell, seven and one half feet high, nine feet long, and six feet wide. The bed was a steel-frame bunk that folded down from the wall. Other furnishings included a little chair one could sit on while writing on a small table, a shelf, and a small, metal washbasin and toilet.[15]

As far as personal possessions, Arthur was issued the following: two aluminum drinking cups; a cake of shaving soap; a shaving brush; a metal mirror; a bar of regular soap; a toothbrush; toothpowder; a comb; nail clippers; a sack of low-grade tobacco; a corncob pipe; toilet paper; shoe polish; face and bath towels; a whisk broom for sweeping out the cell; a rule book; a razor blade; and a safety.[16]

Hot showers were allowed once a week. Prisoners were strictly regimented. They rose at precisely 6:30 a.m. At 6:50 they faced their doors and waited until 6:55, when a whistle signaled the moment when they were to leave their cells and form single lines, facing the mess hall. Prison rules laid down the order of entry into the mess hall in excruciating detail and also specified the exact rules to be followed when they ate.[17]

"Twenty minutes are allowed for eating," the rules noted. "When they finished eating, the prisoners placed their knives, forks, and spoons on their trays: the knife at the left, the fork in the center, and the spoon on the right side of the tray. They then sat erect with their hands down at their sides. After all of the men had finished eating, a guard walked to each table to see that all utensils were in their proper place. He then returned to his position."[18]

Prisoners were given specific jobs. Arthur was assigned to the mat shop, where convicts converted used tires into doormats. San Francisco newspapers reported that Arthur "used a combination of charisma and brutality to inspire both fear and loyalty among his peers." Arthur eventually bullied his way into controlling the mat shop, beating the shift supervisor into relinquishing his position. According to Alvin Karpis's memoirs, "Fellow cons said Arthur ran the shop like a little Hitler."[19]

Arthur vented his rage and frustration for being incarcerated primarily on former Barker-Karpis Gang member Volney Davis. When the federal agents apprehended Volney in June 1935, the criminal told authorities all they wanted to know about working with Ma and her boys. Arthur resented Volney for talking and threatened to kill him for his actions. Volney was eventually involved in a fist fight with Alvin Karpis. Alvin lost, and neither Arthur nor Alvin spoke to Volney again. With the exception of Volney, all the former members of the Barker-Karpis Gang interned at Alcatraz met in the prison yard to socialize with one another. The convicts reminisced about the old days and made plans for the days ahead. Their plans for the immediate future included escaping from the penitentiary.[20]

Arthur was the mastermind behind the idea to escape from Alcatraz. He knew attempts had been made before to break out of the institution but felt the inmates who were killed in the process were not mentally stable enough to do the job right. He recruited more than a dozen men to help him orchestrate an exit. Page 142 of the memorandum prepared by Director Hoover for the attorney general revealed that there were a number of tools available to inmates determined to get away.[21]

"To those of us who have found it necessary to proceed in the work area around the blacksmith shop, it is obvious that there is an unlimited source of material for escape tools," the memo, based on information given to the FBI agents by a guard at the penitentiary, noted. "With the number of men who work in that area with limited supervision it is easy to see how tools can be made by these men when unobserved. Tools of escape are brought into cellblocks through the kitchen or kitchen basement. There is likewise material in shops which can be secreted out."[22]

Arthur and his cohorts managed to acquire a mitre box saw, a spool (an instrument similar to a putty knife) used to spread printer's ink, a thin steel bar in which one side had been converted into a saw edge, two heavy pieces of wire thirty inches in length, and razor blades. Arthur and his fellow gangsters began laying out how they would eventually use the items to escape the penitentiary in early 1937. The convicts spent more than two years learning everything they could about the structure of the Rock, including passageways, windows, guard locations, and routines. For Arthur it was studying a bank to be robbed or the habits of a potential kidnap victim. He determined that the first floor of the Model Industries Building on the northwest point of the island presented the best opportunity for making a break. The tower guard could not see the factory's ocean side.[23]

The guards at Alcatraz did a regular head count of the inmates who had been sent to the facility. A head count was performed several times during the day and in each area, from the individual cells to the work stations. When the guards couldn't see all the prisoners assigned to the mat shop, they assumed the missing men were working out of sight in a back room. That noticeable assumption persuaded Arthur to believe at least two men could sneak out in daylight and hide. For a short window of time, the guards would think nothing of a couple of absent convicts.[24]

When all the planning on the ground was complete, Arthur tackled the escape on water. How to get from Alcatraz to the shore one and one-half miles away in rough ocean waters with strong currents was worrisome. The island was often blanketed with fog, particularly in winter. Arthur and the others who hoped to get away believed they'd be able to swim to land hidden by the fog.[25]

On December 16, 1937, two of Arthur's associates jumped out of the mat shop window and made their way toward a fence surrounding the prison walls. They climbed over it and fell into the water below. By the time the guards were alerted to the escape, the convicts had disappeared. Federal prison authorities believe the pair drowned in the swift tides of San Francisco Bay. According to the December 16, 1937, edition of the *Hammond Times*, "After an all-night search of the bay by five coast guard boats, a patrol of the mainland by state and city police, and a search of the caves on Alcatraz Island, Warden James A. Johnston declared: 'I believe they drowned and that their bodies were swept toward the Golden Gate by the strong ebb tides. They decided to take a desperate chance in the water.'"

Arthur and the other men who had been involved with the plot to get off the island were not deterred by what authorities claimed happened to their fellow inmates. The bodies of the two men were never found, and because of that the prisoners were convinced the convicts' escape was a success. Tales of how the outlaws hijacked a car after swimming to shore circulated throughout the prison population. Rumors that the men managed to make it to South America gave daring inmates hope that they too could be free.[26]

At 4 a.m. on January 13, 1939, Arthur and four of his cohorts decided it was time to leave Alcatraz. Five convicts sawed their way out of their individual cells and crossed the corridor of the cellblock to a window on the outside wall where a bar had been broken loose and a steel frame had been cut out. A memorandum written by Hoover for the attorney general explained in detail what occurred:

> *It was by this means that the prisoners escaped. Each of the five prisoners had worked on the bars in his respective cell and the window each night for years. The cell bars had been covered from time to time with floor wax instead of putty which is usual practice in such attempts as this.*
>
> *When the sawing of the bars was completed, the blades were thrown into the lavatories so that any search of the cells would not*

disclose the blades. The heavy bar on the inside of the outside wall window is made of steel and could not be cut. The prisoners pried it loose with an instrument they had made known as a screw-jack. The use of this screw-jack caused a tension which snapped the bars several times. It was determined that the saws and screw-jack were smuggled into the isolation ward many weeks ago. The saw blades went through prison inspection in view of the fact that they were glued into musical instruments believed to be mouth harps.

It was the plan of the five prisoners to get away on a raft which they crudely made from lumber and driftwood readily obtainable upon the shores of Alcatraz Island. The raft was tied together with sheets torn in strips.[27]

Being the first to be sighted, Arthur Barker and an inmate named Dale Stamphill refused orders by guards to halt. They were then immediately fired upon. Inmates Rufus McCain and William Martin were pulled out of the water at a point very near to the point of the island which is nearest to San Francisco.[28]

More shots were fired at Arthur and Stamphill. Henry Young, the fifth convict following closely behind Arthur, stopped when told and threw his hands in the air in surrender. Arthur continued running toward the raft and was shot in the head and leg. Stamphill was shot in both legs. As the guards moved in on the injured inmates, Arthur called out: "I'm crazy as hell! I should never have tried it!"[29]

Both Arthur and Stamphill were transported to the penitentiary hospital. The report prepared by chief medical officer and surgeon Dr. Romney M. Ritchey reported that when Arthur was first brought in, he was greatly confused but partly conscious. He complained of pain in his left leg, which was broken. Later on during the morning, he was restless in bed and would rally to look around him but made no statement or gave any indication that he understood the situation more than to realize at times his own precarious physical condition. Everything possible was done to improve his condition, and Dr. E. M. Townsend of the US Marine Hospital was called in to consult.[30]

"During the afternoon he became more restless and confused and was constantly rolling about in bed," Dr. Ritchey's report noted. "His circulation became weaker during the afternoon and his breathing more labored and it was realized that he probably would not survive the night. A spinal puncture revealed a large amount of blood in the spinal fluid showing that there was bleeding into the cranial cavity resulting from a skull fracture."[31]

Arthur died at 5:40 p.m. on Friday, January 13, 1939. The cause of death listed on the death certificate reads "Fracture of Skull." An inquest by the city and county of San Francisco and the state of California was conducted shortly after Arthur's passing. The coroner's report noted that Arthur Barker met his death attempting to escape from Alcatraz prison from gunshot wounds inflicted by guards unknown. "From the evidence at hand," the report continued, "we, the jury, believe this escape was made possible by the failure of the system for guarding prisoners now in use at Alcatraz Prison and we recommend a drastic improvement by those in authority."[32]

Arthur Barker was buried in an unmarked grave in San Francisco's Coloma Cemetery on January 16, 1939. The residents in the Northern California city breathed a collective sigh of relief with the announcement that the prisoner's escape was thwarted. Arthur's criminal background and violent end were blamed on Ma. Reports of the fiendish influence she had over her sons appeared again in newspapers across the country. The January 22, 1939, edition of the *Helena Independent Record* read:

America has lost its No. 1 homemade gangster. With the body of Arthur (Doc) Barker, bullet pierced in a vain attempt to escape from Alcatraz buried this week the nation's saddest reminder that criminals—as well as good and great men—can be reared at their mother's knee. For "Doc" Barker always followed his mother's teaching.

He believed implicitly what she told him from the time he was a headstrong, but innocent child—that he was right, whatever he did, and the rest of the world was wrong when it disagreed.

He followed her to Sunday school, and sang gospel hymns with gusto rivaled only by her own. He fled to sure protection in her arms whenever his father tried to correct him for some youthful wrong. And when at last the police came he relied on her glib, falsifying tongue to free him.

Had his home environment been different, "Doc" might never have been any more a serious menace than other mischievous boys. He might never have murdered a fellow man. He might not now be among the degraded dead, but happily living, leading sons of his own in fishing and hunting expeditions like those his father planned for him before his doting mother interfered.

But time cannot run backwards. "Doc" Barker did become a menace. Under his mother's wings, he and all his brothers and their pals became the most blood-thirsty, gun gang in the country. And now he is dead, killed—by the guns of the law.

Alvin Karpis, who had threatened to kill FBI director Hoover when Ma and Fred Barker were shot in January 1935, registered his displeasure with the officials at Alcatraz over the way Arthur died. He thought it was cowardly that the fellow outlaw was shot in the head.[33]

The public at large expressed their appreciation to the staff at the penitentiary for using "whatever method was at their disposal to stop the inmates from escaping."[34]

Director Hoover received numerous letters of support for making sure federal agents around the country did their jobs. "I thought it would take a generation before the federal prosecutors would be regarded with fear and respect which they formerly held," one grateful citizen in Sacramento wrote Hoover in February 1939, "but through your splendid work you have not only brought this about within a few years, but the campaign of the Department of Justice for the law enforcement has awakened the whole body of citizenry of the United States to the necessity of the enforcement of the criminal laws."[35]

An attorney in Memphis, Tennessee, wrote Hoover to review the accomplishments of the Department of Justice since he was made

Dotted line shows path of Arthur Barker and his four companions
in their unsuccessful attempt at escape COURTESY OF THE SAN FRANCISCO
HISTORY CENTER, SAN FRANCISCO LIBRARY

director and put an end to the Barker-Karpis Gang. The lawyer wrote:

> *Kidnapping doesn't pay, and now all of Ma Barker's band know that. It becomes interesting to check the record of the department over the last three plus years. A total of sixty-three kidnapping cases has been reported and one-hundred-seventy-three persons have been convicted. Some twenty-nine are serving life sentences and a total of 2,028 years has been imposed on other members of kidnap gangs. Four kidnappers died before they came to trial. It amounts to a job devastating in its thoroughness and supplies what seems to be entirely conclusive proof that kidnapping does not pay.*[36]

Hoover was pleased with the praise he and his G-Men received and reiterated to the press his thoughts about Ma Barker and her boys. "The Barker-Karpis Gang had ramifications that reached from the Pacific Coast to Chicago and from there south into Florida and Texas," Director Hoover told reporters in Washington, DC, after Arthur was killed. "We've reached the end of the bitter saga of Ma Barker."[37]

CHAPTER TWELVE

End of an Era

ON JANUARY 14, 1939, IMMEDIATELY FOLLOWING AN AUTOPSY OF THE slain convicted kidnapper Arthur Barker, a staff member at the San Francisco coroner's office made a death mask of the dead man's face.[1]

A memorandum written by a representative of the San Francisco division of the FBI noted that a plaster mold of Arthur's face had to be made as close to his death as possible. "Well before bloating and the elements distort the character of expression," the memo read. The process of making the mold was included in the note dated April 20, 1939. "Apply grease to the face and especially any facial hair, including eyebrows. Once the plaster dries layer plaster bandages mixed with water on the face. The first layer captures the details, even wrinkles, while the other layers reinforce the first. Then carefully remove the hardened mold, or negative, from the face. Finally, pour a substance like wax or a metal such as bronze into the negative to make a positive, three-dimensional death mask."[2]

The memo, outlining the dos and don'ts of making a death mask, was addressed to J. Edgar Hoover's office. "This is a good death mask," the note read. "I am arranging for a negative mold of the same to be made at once so that several copies can be made and used in the Director's office or wherever else it may be considered desired to exhibit."[3]

The mask made of Arthur's face was not the first FBI director Hoover requested to be made. He had one poured of gangster John Dillinger in July 1934. Four masks of Dillinger's face were made, and Hoover proudly had one on display in his office. The mask captured every detail of Dillinger's face: the bullet wound, the scrapes from where he had hit the pavement, the bloating and the swelling from the heat and pooling blood, and even the telltale signs of underground plastic surgery. Arthur's mask was just as telling. His original death mask was placed for safe keeping in the glass exhibit case on displaying moulage (the process of making molds) in the front exhibit room of the San Francisco coroner's laboratory.[4]

Hoover collected mementos from the FBI's war against violent criminals like the Barker-Karpis Gang. In addition to Arthur's death mask, he kept a photograph of Ma and Fred lying in state at the morgue in his files. It served as a reminder of the department's accomplishments under his leadership.[5]

Arthur Barker's attempt to escape from Alcatraz prompted FBI director Hoover to order

Death masks such as the one San Francisco's coroner's technician Paul Green is holding were regularly made of inmates who tried to escape Alcatraz. Arthur Barker's death mask was made less than twenty-four hours after he was shot and killed. COURTESY OF THE SAN FRANCISCO HISTORY CENTER, SAN FRANCISCO LIBRARY

drastic improvements of the guard system at the penitentiary. The January 25, 1935, edition of the *Washington Star* reported that eleven of America's most dangerous criminals had tried to break out of the facility in a thirteen-month period and something needed to be done to prevent future attempts.

A coroner's jury blamed "failure of the system" for what had occurred. "The citizens of San Francisco unite in an effort to have a more suitable location for the imprisonment of the type of desperados at present housed in Alcatraz," the *Washington Star* quoted the coroner T. B. W. Leland. "There appears to be only the matter of water between the prisoners and liberty."

Additional guards were hired at the facility and assigned to look over corners and dark areas of hallways and check exercise yards where inmates could disappear in the shadows. Extra surveillance equipment was installed in individual cells and showers, and metal detectors were added at several points in the main cellblock. The detectors would disclose any metal object, no matter how small, that a convict might try to take to his cell.[6]

Among the remaining inmates at Alcatraz who would have to endure the consequences of Arthur Barker's actions were former members of the Barker-Karpis Gang. Volney Davis, convicted in July 1935 for his part in the kidnapping of Edward Bremer, spent more than twenty-three years at the penitentiary. He was released in the late 1950s. He married Daisy Irene Graham on May 21, 1960, in Contra Costa County, California, and resided in Guerneville, California. He died on July 20, 1979, in Sonoma County, California.[7]

Harry "Dutch Sawyer" Sandlovich received a life sentence for his role in the Edward Bremer kidnapping. He was released at the end of his life, perhaps due to illness, and passed away from cancer in a Chicago hospital in 1957.[8]

After the Kansas City massacre in June 1933, Vernon Miller fled to the East Coast, staying with mobster Abner Zwillman in New Jersey until Miller killed a Zwillman gunman in an argument. Leaving for Chicago on October 23, 1933, Miller posed as a salesman for an optical supply house while living with girlfriend Vi Mathias until federal agents raided her apartment on the morning of November 1, 1933. Shooting his way out, however, Miller was able to escape from federal agents.[9]

On November 29, 1933, a motorist discovered Miller's body in a roadside ditch outside Detroit, Michigan. He appeared to have been tortured by strangulation with a clothesline and beaten to death with a claw hammer. Miller appeared to have been the victim of a gangland slaying.[10]

Russell "Slim Gray" Gibson spent much of his early criminal career with the Central Park Gang and participated in numerous bank robberies with them. He, like the rest of the gang, was tracked down by the FBI during early 1935. Federal agents managed to trace him and his wife to a Chicago hideout used by the Barkers and raided the apartment building on January 8, 1935. The raid was bungled from the start as the FBI set off tear gas in the wrong apartment, causing a panic among the tenants. When local police officers arrived on the scene, they nearly opened fire on federal agents, whom they believed were gangsters. Hoping to escape in the confusion, Gibson attempted to make it to the fire escape armed with a Browning automatic rifle and a .32 caliber pistol. FBI agents were waiting for Gibson, however, and opened fire. Despite wearing a bulletproof vest, Gibson was killed by the agents' high-powered rifles instantly. His wife was arrested on charges of harboring fugitives.[11]

William Weaver was sentenced to life in prison for the Bremer kidnapping as well. He arrived at Alcatraz on August 7, 1936. He died at the penitentiary of natural causes on June 20, 1944.[12]

Harry Campbell evaded authorities until May 7, 1936. Federal agents located the gangster in Toledo, Ohio. He was living a quiet life with his wife, Gertrude Miller. She denied knowing anything about him having a criminal past, as did Toledo police chief Ray Allen, who visited with the couple frequently. Five days after Harry was captured, he pled guilty to his involvement in the kidnapping of Edward Bremer and spent the remainder of his days as Inmate #322 at Alcatraz.[13]

Lawrence Devol, alias Larry "Chopper" O'Keefe, was arrested for a series of bank robberies while a member of the Barker-Karpis Gang. He was incarcerated in the Minnesota State Hospital for the Insane. He escaped and was involved in a gunfight that resulted in the death of three policemen and was killed in Enid, Oklahoma, on July 8, 1936.[14]

Alvin Karpis's story at Alcatraz lasted twenty-five years. His prison record was riddled with write-ups by the warden for fighting, refusing to work, possession of contraband, and insolence to officers. Alvin was in and out of solitary confinement and had his privileges revoked on numerous occasions. In 1969 he was paroled and deported to Canada. He relocated to Spain and rented an apartment on the Costa Del Sol. Alvin penned two books about his life as a public enemy before authorities found him and arrested him in 1936. He was seventy-one years old. Alvin was unrepentant for any of the crimes he committed. "There are no apologies, no regrets, no sorrows, and no animosity," he wrote in his autobiography. "What happened happened."[15]

Edward Bremer, the St. Paul, Minnesota, bank president who was kidnapped by the Barker-Karpis Gang in 1934, died on May 4, 1965, of a heart attack. He was sixty-seven years old.[16]

J. Edgar Hoover, whose first arrest was when he physically apprehended Alvin Karpis, was credited with putting behind bars the last of the major gangsters of the 1930s and helping to cement the reputation of the Federal Bureau of Investigation. He would go on to lead the bureau for thirty-six more years, dying in his sleep on May 2, 1972.[17]

The women involved with members of the Barker-Karpis Gang lived to tell the tale of life with a band of thieves, kidnappers, and murderers. Wynona Burdette, sweetheart of Harry Campbell, and Dolores Delaney, companion of Alvin Karpis, testified at their trials and gave detailed information about the crimes committed by Ma and her boys.[18]

The women were not shy about relaying what they knew, specifically of Ma Barker. According to Edna Murray, girlfriend of Volney Davis, in an article she wrote for the October 1936 edition of *Startling Detective Adventures* titled "I Was a Karpis-Barker Gang Moll," "Ma was a shrewd, overly protective, and overly familiar with her sons, particularly Fred."

Dolores, Wynona, and Edna were each sentenced to five years in prison for harboring fugitives. For more than eighty years, residents in Ocklawaha, Florida, have traded stories about the day fifteen G-Men gunned down Ma and Fred Barker at their lakefront hideout in the quiet fishing village on Lake Weir.[19]

Locals then believed that the mother and son who were killed on January 16, 1935, were part of a vacationing northern family known as the Blackburns. Word later swept through the small citrus-belt town of three hundred residents that the two were none other than sixty-three-year-old Ma Barker and her thirty-three-year-old son Fred, two of the most notorious members of the dreaded Barker-Karpis Gang.[20]

To this day historians and scholars argue over details about the siege at the Barker home, habits of the Barkers, and what led J. Edgar Hoover's FBI men to the rolling hills of southeastern Marion County.

The home where the well-known gangsters were shot and killed still stands. George Albright, caretaker of the house, hopes the home will be transformed into a museum. "The condition of the home is wonderful, the original furnishings to the time are still in it so from a biographical and historical stand point this is the perfect property to showcase the gun battle itself, the rise and fall of the gangster movement, and the rise of the FBI and the successes. It's still a defining event in American history and it deserves to be protected."[21]

George Barker died on February 28, 1941, in Joplin, Missouri, from natural causes. He had lived out his final days working at a filling station. Occasionally, a curious tourist who knew about Ma and his sons would stop and ask about his infamous family. According to historian and author John Koblas, George was always friendly and respectful. "They were good boys," he would say about his children, "and Ma, she loved them to death." Until his passing at the age of seventy-six, George contributed ten dollars a year to the upkeep of his family's graves.[22]

George's family lies isolated in an expanse of grass pasture at the crest of a hill off Oklahoma Highway 10, east of Welch, in a small, rural cemetery. A herd of cattle grazes peacefully in the pasture surrounding the neatly mowed, fenced graveyard that occupies two acres atop the hill.[23]

Rural farmsteads and two small country churches dot the landscape within a few miles of the spot. At the extreme north side of the Williams Timber Hill Cemetery, well away from the other graves and

Cemetery where Ma and her boys are buried in Welch, Oklahoma

family plots, lie five graves defined by one stone marker and four small metal markers. The four small, glass-fronted metal markers, which contain lines of typed verse, implore a merciful rest for a mother and sons who found no peace in life:[24]

Father, George Barker. February 1941.
Through clouds and storms, He gently clears the way.

The final resting place of Ma and her sons. Herman's body is on the far right, Ma's body is next to Herman's, and Fred's remains are on the other side of his mother. Markers for Arthur and Lloyd are on the far left.

Arthur Barker, died 1939.
Lord, I deserve justice, but mercy is what I plead.
Let me cling to thy hand, only thou knowest my need.

Fred Barker, January 16, 1935.
Let us not forget He who gives us life understands all the reasons.

Mother, Kate Barker, January 16, 1935.
The darkest night shall end in bright day.

The slips of verse in the small metal markers were written by newspaper columnist Frances Baker in 1970.

Excerpts from Thomas M. McDade's Journal
Special Agent Thomas M. McDade was one of more than a dozen
federal officers involved in a gun battle with Ma Barker and her son
Fred in Ocklawaha, Florida, on January 16, 1935. Agent McDade's
firsthand account of his experiences with various members of the

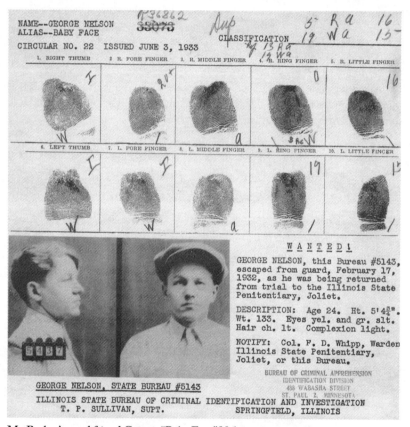

Ma Barker's good friend George "Baby Face" Nelson COURTESY OF THE MINNESOTA
HISTORICAL SOCIETY

Barker-Karpis Gang and fellow gangster Baby Face Nelson provides insight into the inner workings of the Justice Department and offers details about how Ma Barker met her violent end.

November 9, 1934
Spent day on wiretap for Monte Carter who is supposed to know Bremer [Edward Bremer] hideout. Nothing doing so tap removed after 10 days. Returned to office at 8:30 p.m. Played poker with Melvin Purvis, Samuel P. Cowley, and other agents. Won $2.25 game ended at 11:30 p.m.

November 10, 1934
Spent all day visiting hospitals trying to locate Edna Murray who is Volney Davis's paramour. Found plenty of Hanson's (Davis's Alias) but didn't find her. Returned to the office at 5 p.m. Then went to two taxi stands to try to locate driver who took Volney Davis to his girl's apartment. Received my .38 calibre [sic] super automatic which I took apart and had trouble assembling. To bed at 11:30 p.m.

November 12, 1934
Spent all day visiting city hospitals trying to locate Edna Murray without success.

November 13, 1934
Finished the remainder of the hospitals without avail. Listed 40 hospitals I visited looking for Edna Murray.

November 16, 1934
Volney Davis is supposed to contact a girl nearby the room we have and will call here if he comes in. Waiting on a spot like this and that of last night is like waiting for the start of a race; you get all excited inside. After returning to the office went to a saloon at 47th Street and Lake Park Avenue where Slim Gray is supposed to visit. Sat there drinking beer and looking the place over. One fellow tried to get me to play a

horse in a race in a bookies next door. Went to dinner, then found Clarence Hurt watching the place from a car. Sat in Hurt's car till 10 p.m. Hurt says that Gray (real name Russell Gibson) started as a bicycle thief and handling "hot" bikes! And now wanted for kidnapping, the boy who made good!! Hurt, one of the men who killed Dillinger (Charles Winstead Jr. was the other) arrested Gray in Oklahoma some time before.

November 19, 1934
Drove to Streator, Illinois. 101 miles from Chicago to check up on L. A. Hobson who is writing to Violet Grigg. Found he received mail general delivery, put mail cover on him. Very mild and rained much of the day, dispensed with topcoat it was so warm. Musing I thought of how it is said that Old Kate Barker worries so when her sons, Freddie and Doc, are pulling a job just as any mother might though they be kidnapping. Thence to 596 Hawthorne Street to watch Slim Gray's sister-in-law who moved there from Camellia Street.

November 22, 1934
Left at 9:15 a.m. and drove downtown. Stopped off to see the Navy Pier. Consulted with an officer of the Federal Reserve Bank concerning numbers on the Bremer ransom money. In the cellar saw girls counting piles and piles of bills. Was told there was about 20 million there and that 5 to 6 million passes through each day.

November 27, 1934
A day I will never forget. Up at 8 a.m. and hung about plant till noon when I went to lunch. While eating saw Mrs. Guymon's boyfriend's car pull up so rushed out and trailed in Ford with Ryan trailing in his car. They only went to the doctor's and returned. Ryan called the office at 2:45 and Cowley said for both of us to go to Lake Geneva on a tip on Baby Face Nelson and to watch for a Ford sedan. Outside Barrington, Illinois we both spotted a car coming towards us. We turned back and they had already turned. They turned again and running about 40–50 miles per hour they ran alongside and the driver yelled to us to pull

over. A man in the back seat had a rifle or tommy pointed in at us. I stepped on the gas and ran down the road and they opened fire. The plunk of the shots sounded on our rear. We bent low and Ryan started firing through the rear window with an automatic. I kept the accelerator to the floor and ran about 72–75 m.p.h. We drew away from them but they continued to follow. We looked for a road to turn off to phone or get to cover from their guns but had to run to Palatine. In trying to turn in I went too fast ran off the road into a field. We jumped from the car and Ryan borrowed an attendant's at a gas station to get to a phone. I watched the road but they didn't follow. Purvis advised us to come back and phone in half an hour. When we phoned from Park Ridge Zimmer told Ryan that Hollis and Cowley had met them, that Hollis was killed and Cowley badly hurt. We watched the road a while, then come into town. Hung about for almost an hour when four of us drove to Lake Bluff to raid a place where Nelson might stop. I took a shot gun and at Waukegan we got three officers who came with us. It poured all night and we went through a house and farm buildings without success. Thoroughly soaked we got back at 4:30 a.m. and at 5 I lay down in one of the prisoners rooms and slept till eight. Cowley died of his wounds.

December 1, 1934

Came in the office at 9 a.m. and Tillman and I were about to go out to the tap at Guymon's when a standby order was issued to wait for trouble. Learned today that Nelson spotted our car from the missing license plate in the rear and suspected us of being "hoods" of G-men. One of Ryan's bullets smashed the water jacket and kept them from catching us. All this came from Mrs. Nelson now in custody but unknown to anyone except the agents. We sat around till 5 p.m. when we were told to go home and report back at 1 a.m.

December 21, 1934

Brown and Madala dropped up to the plant we learned that there are nine plants now with no one in the office. From the tap learned that Mrs. G. [Mrs. G. K. Ryan, one of Ma Barker's aliases] leaves for

Kansas City at 10:30 p.m. for the holidays. Fred and I saw her off on the train. At the office learned that the Barker's, Karpis and Slim are all in town and things may be happening tomorrow. So to bed after reading G & S.

December 23, 1934
Went to the office at 10 a.m. and Madala and I went out to see about putting in a wiretap on some whores who may know the Barkers. Couldn't find the main box and Sunday being bad for reconnoitering we came back. At 3:30 Tillman and I went out with guns looking for the gang cars. We toured the southside haunts then came in at 6:30 p.m. Had to stay in the office till 9 p.m. when we were released so home and sat clipping and finally to bed.

December 25, 1934
Christmas—up at 7:30 and to a plant at 442 Arlington St. to watch 409. It is a home for prostitutes going out for business. Friends of Doc Barker's girlfriend live there. Sat in the window till midnight observing the persons entering and leaving their home and to bed about 2:30 a.m.

January 4, 1935
Downtown from the plant was held at the office by a standby order. Waited about till midnight and then were told to go home. Two cars of men have been seen and it is believed Karpis drove one and Willie Harrison the other.

January 8–9, 1935
Left plane and stayed in office all day waiting to crash two places for the gang. At 6 o'clock Gillespie, Larry and I went to 432 Surf St. to join the gang there to take anyone leaving the place while another group crashed 3912 Pine Grove Ave. Gillespie left us in the car around the corner from 432 to get the lay of the land. As he reached the house Doc Barker and Mildred came out. Campbell, Walsh, and Muzzey went for them. Walsh stuck a pistol at Doc and Jerry Campbell

pointed a tommy in his face. Doc raised his hands then dodged to run across the street. He got about 10 feet when he fell. The boys stood over him and Bob Jones coming up the alley from covering the rear of the house put handcuffs on him. He had no pistol on him but $300 in cash. Muzzey then came back for Larry and I and we learned what had happened. Jones and Campbell took Doc in to the office and with the key to their apartment Larry and I went in the front, letting Gillespie in the rear. We all had machine guns and were ordered to wait to see if Fred would show up. In the apartment we found a machine gun, two drums, a pistol and a bullet proof vest. I sat at the window from 1 a.m. to 8 a.m. watching and waiting for someone to come. About midnight Campbell came back to tell us that the Pine Grove apartment had been raided. After surrounding it Connelly called (on the house phone) Mrs. Gray, Slim's wife, to tell all to come out one at a time. Slim rushed out the back door with a Browning automatic rifle. He fired it three times when Doc White hit him with a bullet from a .351 rifle which ripped thru his bullet proof vest and tore thru his stomach. Slim died shortly thereafter. When hit, he pulled off the vest and ran a few steps with a pistol in hand but collapsed. Monte Carter, Mrs. Gray, and Ruth Heidt came out of the front of the apartment and were taken. The agents did put gas in the wrong apartment and had the whole neighborhood coughing and crying.

We did not leave our apartment until 4:30, I have no sleep in this time. We packed all of Barker's clothes and those of Mildred in their bags and cleaned out the apartment. There were about 10 suits there without there being as much as a button in any of the pockets. Brought it all to the office where I saw Carter (Byron Bolton) and Doc Barker in chains in the detention rooms.

January 16, 1935
Nine of us drove in two cars 120 miles to Ocklawaha on Lake Weir. Met five other agents near there and we proceeded to surround the building on the lake. Fred Barker and his mother Kate were the only ones in the house at the time. We arrived at the house at 5:30 a.m. and

took the positions assigned to us. I had a gas gun, a tommy and was wearing a bullet proof vest. We waited till 6:45–7:00 when it became light when Connelly yelled out for Fred and Kate to come out with their hands up. Kate said something but what it was no one seems to know. We waited almost 10 or 15 minutes but no one came out so Muzzey and I fired gas shells but they didn't go into the house. Immediately they began firing from the house and the boys A–D answered with a volley.

From then on there was sporadic firing but no shots came from the house after 9 a.m. We continued to shoot and put in gas but no one answered or came out. At 12:30, the worker for the Barkers went in and found both of them dead in the top front bedroom. Fred had 10 holes in his left shoulder 2 in his chest and one thru the head. Kate had three holes in her chest. She had been firing a tommy with a 100 drum clip. They had fired about 150 shots from 2 tommys, a 33 Winchester rifle and a .45 Colt automatic which had been shot out of her hand splitting the butt, jamming the gun and wounding her hand. The gas lingered in the house. I went in with my camera and took some photos. Took Freddie's knife as a souvenir. Harry Campbell and his girl had been at the house but had left almost a week before.

January 22, 1935
Arrived in Chicago at 7:35 a.m. In late morning drove to Bensenville with Ryan to see if we could locate people who might be able to identify some of the kidnappers. Neighbors around the hideout and stores were interviewed without success. On Sunday Jan 20, the Atlantic City police found the car Karpis and Campbell were driving from the number broadcast by the Division but they shot their way out of the hotel and escaped.

January 30, 1935
Up at 11 a.m. and finally to the tap at room where we sat till 6 p.m. Six hour shifts is the present plan and makes it very enjoyable. Hope to pick up a lead on Karpis and Campbell. 8 telephones being tapped

here. Had dinner at Zimmerman's then Dickstein and I saw "David Copperfield" a good picture, so home and to bed.

February 6, 1935

To River Grove again and got a man who lives across the street from our suspected harborer to keep his eyes open for Karpis. At four o'clock was told to go home and come in at midnight. It appeared that someone had been taken and we would guard him but his identity was a secret. At 7:30 p.m. was called to the office and learned that Volney Davis had been taken in Kansas City and was being brought by plane to Chicago. The plane was forced down at Yorkville, Ill. and the two agents bringing him in took him to town to phone the office. They took the shackles off him and one phoned the office. Volney knocked down the agent and escaped in a car he picked up on the street.

Squads were formed and we patolled [*sic*] the roads at Bensenville and Elmhurst and visited many of the gang contact taverns. Back in the office at 2:30 a.m. and finally home and to bed at 3:30.

February 7, 1935

Metcalfe and I were on a plant for Volney all day till 4:30 p.m. then to the office where we stood by for instructions. Went to sleep in a cell from 10 p.m. till 3:30 a.m. when Matt Gleason was brought in for questioning. Gleason was contacted by Volney Davis the night of his escape and Gleason gave him $5.00 and then sold a ring for Davis to get him $50. Gleason was to meet Davis the next night but he didn't show. Nichols, Metcalfe and I questioned Gleason from 4 a.m. to 11 a.m. Friday and when he lied on several questions he was pushed about a bit then finally admitted the truth.

February 19–27th

On plant at Waller St. for Volney Davis, Tillman and I covering it. On 20th went over ground of Barrington shooting with Ryan and the U.S. Attorney for purposes of trial. Did many accounting problems in plant. On 27th informed I was suspended for 15 days for the Matt

Gleason affair. Metcalfe and Nichols were asked to resign. McRae relieved me at Waller St. on 27th—back to hotel.

April 11, 1935 Thursday
Went to realty co. to get key for apartment opposite bookie place supposed to be frequented by Moran for purposes of observation. Couldn't get keys immediately so went to neighborhood but place is quiet and probably not open due to police raids. Yesterday Campbell and I trailed a man home because he resembled Volney Davis. Today I checked on the address at the Post Office and found it was a rooming house run by a German family, apparently reputable. While passing the house, I saw the man go out so I went in and talked to the landlady who seemed honest enough and who said she had no boarders who came in within the last two months (period Volney is at large). Person we thought was he was a boarder named Shenk, an unemployed German who was with her 7 years. Returned to office to work on files. Left at 5:15. Stayed in all evening fixing clippings and listening to the radio.

April 15, 1935
Worked on files in the office all day. To the movies early then left at 10:30 p.m. for St. Paul for trial of Doc Barker and other defendants in Bremer kidnapping.

April 16, 1935
Arrived in St. Paul at 8:20. Sat in court most of day listening to Bremer testify. In evening Larry, Cohen and I visited the State House and saw House in session. To bed at 11:30.

April 20, 1935
Larry and I went on leads on a motor vehicle theft case to River Falls, Wisc. Had a nice drive over and back. Subject had abandoned car after having it all winter. Stolen from Mass. Interviewed farmer he worked for and sheriff. Drove back to St. Paul in time for a party for the agents given by Eddie Bremer at his brewery. After much singing

and drinking of beer we bowled. Finally back to the hotel and to bed at 12.

April 23, 1935
Informed I will not have to testify as they have decided not to put Doc Barkers [*sic*] guns in evidence. Left St. Paul at 12:30 on the Burlington Zephyr, the new streamlined train and arrived in Chicago at 7 p.m. A fast comfortable ride. Met Margaret McGill and had a pleasant evening.

April 25, 1935
Finished Bremer auto report. Dinner with Hicks and at a movie in the evening.

September 28, 1935
Checked cases and reading files. Read how Hamilton was buried and found.

John Hamilton was wounded at South St. Paul, April 23, 1934 while fleeing from Little Bohemia with ["Nelson and" crossed out] Dillinger and Van Meter. Hamilton was taken (?) to the apartment of Volney Davis at 415 E Fox St Aurora where he lived for 10 days and was walking around ½ hour before he died at 3 p.m. Doc Barker and Davis went to Oswego to dig the grave and between 9 & 10 o'clock Willie Weaver, Doc Barker, Davis, Van Meter, Dillinger and Harry Campbell took the body to the grave. Davis bought 10 cans of lye which Dillinger poured on Hamilton's hands and face after saying in a low voice "Red, old pal, I hate to do this, but I know you'd do the same for me." Barker and Van Meter filled in the hole and Dillinger and Van Meter left the others at Aurora. Davis also states that Dr. Moran is supposed to have been murdered by Russell Gibson and Doc Barker who dumped his body in Lake Erie. Rumor also has it that Harrison was also murdered by the gang.

Barker Aliases and Addresses

Arizona Donnie Barker (neé Clark)
    Kate Barker
    Ma Barker
    Mrs. F. A. Hunter
    Mrs. G. K. Ryan
    Mrs. G. E. Lavender
    Mrs. Blackburn

Herman Barker
    J. H. Hamilton
    L. C. Whittier
    D. W. Bowers
    R. L. Douglas
    Al Ayers
    R. D. Snodgrass
    Clarence Sharp
    Bert Lavender
    Edgar Murphy

Arthur Barker
    Doc Barker
    Dock Barker
    Claude Dade
    Bob Barker
    Rob Dale

Lloyd Barker
    Lloyd Burke
    Lloyd Parker

Lloyd Anderson

Fred Barker

Mr. J. Stanley
F. G. Ward
Ted Murphy
J. Darrow
Edwin Bergstrom
J. Stanley Smith
Al Matterson
T. C. Blackburn
Frank Murphy
Fred Barton
Amos Rankin
F. R. Lang

Known Barker Addresses

Longfellow Apartments, Kansas City, Missouri
414 West 46th Terrace, Kansas City, Missouri
6612 Edgevale Rd., Kansas City, Missouri
4804 Jefferson St., Kansas City, Missouri
603 E. Main St., Carterville, Missouri
Twin Oaks Apartments, St. Paul, Minnesota
1031 South Roberts St. West, St. Paul, Minnesota
114 Home Avenue, Oak Park, Illinois
432 Serf St., Chicago, Illinois
401 Cincinnati St., Tulsa, Oklahoma

Known Barker Hangouts

Harvey Club, Cleveland, Ohio
Bill Graham's Rex Club, Reno, Nevada
Harry Sawyer's Green Lantern Saloon, St. Paul, Minnesota
Q. P. Inn, Maywood, Illinois
Roadhouse, Fox River Grove, Illinois

CRIMES COMMITTED BY THE BARKERS

Herman Barker
   1910: Highway robbery, Webb City, Missouri
   March 1915: Highway robbery, Joplin, Missouri
   March 1915: Attempted burglary, Joplin, Missouri
   July 1916: Burglary of Hawkins and Miller Jewelry Store,
      Springfield, Missouri
   October 1916–May 1920: Burglary, Minnesota, Iowa, Montana,
      Tennessee; and grand larceny, St. Paul, Minnesota
   December 1925: Armed bank robbery, Washington, Arkansas
   May 1926: Burglary of eight jewelry stores in Tulsa, McAlester,
      and Muskogee, Oklahoma
   June 1926: Auto theft, Fairfax, Oklahoma
   December 1926: Armed robbery of Oklahoma State Bank,
      Oklahoma City, Oklahoma
   January 1927: Armed robbery of the West Fork Bank, West Fork,
      Arkansas
   January 1927: Armed robbery of the First National Bank of
      Jasper, Jasper, Missouri
   August 1927: Cashing stolen bank bonds, Cheyenne, Wyoming
   August 1927: Burglary of Crystal Ice Plant, Newton, Kansas
   August 1927: Evading arrest and attempted homicide, Newton,
      Kansas

Lloyd Barker
   March 1915: Highway robbery, Joplin, Missouri
   1921: Vagrancy, Tulsa, Oklahoma
   1921: Robbery of US mail, Baxter Springs, Kansas

Arthur Barker

July 1918: Auto theft, Muskogee, Oklahoma

1919: Auto theft, Muskogee, Oklahoma

January 1920: Attempted robbery of Coweta Bank, Coweta, Oklahoma

February 1920: Escape from jail and evading arrest, Joplin, Missouri

January 1921: Attempted robbery, Muskogee, Oklahoma

August 1921: Armed robbery and homicide of night watchman Thomas J. Sherill, Tulsa, Oklahoma

December 1932: Armed robbery of Third Northwestern National Bank and homicide of police officer, Minneapolis, Minnesota

April 1933: Armed robbery of Fairbury Nebraska Bank, Fairbury, Nebraska

June 1933: Kidnapping of William J. Hamm Jr., St. Paul, Minnesota

August 1933: Armed robbery of payroll at Stockyards National Bank, St. Paul, Minnesota

September 1933: Armed robbery of bank messengers and homicide of police officer, Chicago, Illinois

September 1933: Armed robbery of the Union State Bank, Amery, Wisconsin

January 1934: Kidnapping of Edward G. Bremer, St. Paul, Minnesota

January 1934: Attempted homicide of police officer, St. Paul, Minnesota

March 1934: Homicide of George Ziegler aka Fred Goetz, Cicero, Illinois

April 1934: Homicide of William B. Harrison, Ontarioville, Illinois

Fred Barker

August 1922: Auto theft, Tulsa, Oklahoma

September 1922: Armed robbery of US mail truck, Miami, Oklahoma

January 1923: Grand larceny, Tulsa, Oklahoma

November 1925: Armed bank robbery, Washington, Arkansas

February 1926–May 1926: Burglary of eight jewelry stores, Tulsa, McAlester, and Muskogee, Oklahoma

1926: Armed bank robbery, Winfield, Kansas

January 1927: Armed robbery of First National Bank of Jasper, Jasper, Missouri

October 1931: Armed robbery of Mountain View Bank, Mountain View, Missouri

December 1931: Armed robbery and homicide of police officer, West Plains, Missouri

December 1931: Burglary, Tulsa, Oklahoma

April 1932: Homicide of A. W. Dunlop aka George Dunlop, Lake Franstead, Minnesota

June 1932: Armed robbery of Fort Scott Kansas Bank, Fort Scott, Kansas

July 1932: Armed robbery of Cloud County Bank, Concordia, Kansas

September 1932: Armed robbery of Citizens National Bank, Wahpeton, North Dakota

December 1932: Armed robbery of Third Northwestern National Bank and homicide of police officer, Minneapolis, Minnesota

April 1933: Armed robbery of Fairbury Nebraska Bank, Fairbury, Nebraska

June 1933: Kidnapping of William J. Hamm Jr., St. Paul, Minnesota

August 1933: Armed robbery of payroll at Stockyards National Bank, St. Paul, Minnesota

September 1933: Armed robbery of Union State Bank, Amery, Wisconsin

September 1933: Armed robbery of bank messengers and homicide of police officer, Chicago, Illinois

January 1934: Kidnapping of Edward G. Bremer, St. Paul, Minnesota

January 1934: Attempted homicide of police officer, St. Paul, Minnesota

July 1934: Homicide of Dr. Joseph P. Moran, Chicago, Illinois

NOTES

Chapter One: Brains of the Operation

1 *Pioneer Press*, January 20, 1934; FBI Files, RCS: TD I.C. #7-576, 1935–36, The Kidnapping of Edward George Bremer; Karpis and Trent, *Alvin Karpis Story*, 164–66; Koblas, "Ma,"195–96.

2 Karpis and Trent, *Alvin Karpis Story*, 164–66; FBI Files, RCS: TD I.C. #7-576, 1935–36, The Kidnapping of Edward George Bremer.

3 *Pioneer Press*, January 23, 1934; FBI Files, RCS: TD I.C. #7-576, 1935–36, The Kidnapping of Edward George Bremer; Karpis and Trent, *Alvin Karpis Story*, 164–166; Koblas, *"Ma,"* 195–96.

4 *Pioneer Press*, January 20, 1934; Koblas, *"Ma,"* 195–96; FBI Files, RCS: TD I.C. #7-576, 1935–36, The Kidnapping of Edward George Bremer.

5 *Pioneer Press*, January 20, 1934; Koblas, *"Ma,"* 195–96; FBI Files, RCS: TD I.C. #7-576, 1935–36, The Kidnapping of Edward George Bremer.

6 FBI Files, RCS: TD I.C. #7-576, 1935–36, The Kidnapping of Edward George Bremer; Koblas, *"Ma,"* 195–96.

7 FBI Files, RCS: TD I.C. #7-576, 1935–36, The Kidnapping of Edward George Bremer; Koblas, *"Ma,"* 195.

8 *News* (Frederick, MD), September 24, 29–34; *Biddeford Daily Journal*, May 4, 1937.

9 FBI Files, RCS: TD I.C. #7-576, 1935–36, The Kidnapping of Edward George Bremer.

10 Karpis and Trent, *Alvin Karpis Story*, 165–68; FBI Files, RCS: TD I.C. #7-576, 1935–36, The Kidnapping of Edward George Bremer.

11 *Albert Lea Evening Tribune*, January 19, 1934.

12 FBI Files, RCS: TD I.C. #7-576, 1935–36, The Kidnapping of Edward George Bremer.

13 Karpis and Trent, *Alvin Karpis Story*, 167–71.

14 Ibid.

15 FBI Files, RCS: TD I.C. #7-576, 1935–36, The Kidnapping of Edward George Bremer.

16 Karpis and Trent, *Alvin Karpis Story*, 161–66; Koblas, *"Ma,"* 194–95.

17 *San Antonio Light*, February 12, 1938.

18 FBI Files, RCS: TD I.C. #7-576, 1935–36, The Kidnapping of Edward George Bremer; St. Paul, Minnesota, History and Early Association of the Karpis-Barker Gang Prior to the Abduction of Mr. Bremer.

19 *San Antonio Light*, February 12, 1938.

20 FBI Files, RCS: TD I.C. #7-576, 1935–36, The Kidnapping of Edward George Bremer; Karpis and Trent, *Alvin Karpis Story*, 167–71.

21 Karpis and Trent, *Alvin Karpis Story*, 167–71.

22 Division of Investigation/FBI Files #7-30, January 20, 1934.

23 Ibid.

24 FBI Files, RCS: TD I.C. #7-576, 1935–36, The Kidnapping of Edward George Bremer; Division of Investigation/FBI Files #7-30, January 20, 1934.

25 Division of Investigation/FBI Files #7-30, January 20, 1934.

26 FBI Files, RCS: TD I.C. #7-576, 1935–36, The Kidnapping of Edward George Bremer; Division of Investigation/FBI Files #7-30, January 20, 1934.

27 Koblas, *"Ma,"* 196–98; FBI Files, RCS: TD I.C. #7-576, November 19, 1936, The Kidnapping of Edward George Bremer; Division of Investigation/FBI Files #7-30, January 20, 1934.

28 FBI Files, RCS: TD I.C. #7-576, 1935–36, The Kidnapping of Edward George Bremer; Division of Investigation/FBI Files #7-30, January 20, 1934; Koblas, *"Ma,"* 196–98.

29 Karpis and Trent, *Alvin Karpis Story*, 165–71.

30 Ibid.

31 Ibid.

32 FBI Files, RCS: TD I.C. #7-576, 1935–36. The Kidnapping of Edward George Bremer.

33 Swierczynski, *Encyclopedia of the FBI's Ten Most Wanted List*, 272–73.

34 FBI Files, RCS: TD I.C. #7-576, 1935–36, The Kidnapping of Edward George Bremer.

35 *Pioneer Press*, January 23, 1934; *El Paso Herald*, January 23, 1934; Murphysboro *Daily Independent*, January 23, 1934; Koblas, *"Ma,"* 199–207.

36 FBI Files, RCS: TD I.C. #7-576, 1935–36, The Kidnapping of Edward George Bremer; Division of Investigation/FBI Files #7-30, January 20, 1934.

37 FBI Files, RCS: TD I.C. #7-576, 1935–36, The Kidnapping of Edward George Bremer; Division of Investigation/FBI Files #7-30, January 20, 1934.

38 Koblas, *"Ma,"* 199-207; FBI Files, RCS: TD I.C. #7-576, 1935–36, The Kidnapping of Edward George Bremer; Division of Investigation/FBI Files #7-30, January 20, 1934.

39 Koblas, *"Ma,"* 199-207; FBI Files, RCS: TD I.C. #7-576, 1935–36, The Kidnapping of Edward George Bremer; Division of Investigation/FBI Files #7-30, January 20, 1934.

40 *San Antonio Light*, May 8, 1934.

41 *Gettysburg Times*, March 22, 1934; *San Antonio Light*, May 8, 1934.

42 FBI Files, RCS: TD I.C. #7-576, 1935–36, The Kidnapping of Edward George Bremer; Division of Investigation/FBI Files #7-30, January 20, 1934; *Beatrice Daily Sun*, March 22, 1934.

43 FBI Files, RCS: TD I.C. #7-576, 1935–36, The Kidnapping of Edward George Bremer; Division of Investigation/FBI Files #7-30, January 20, 1934.

44 FBI Files, RCS: TD I.C. #7-576, 1935–36, The Kidnapping of Edward George Bremer; Division of Investigation/FBI Files #7-30, January 20, 1934.

45 Karpis and Trent, *Alvin Karpis Story*, 54–56; FBI Files, RCS: TD I.C. #7-576, 1935–36, The Kidnapping of Edward George Bremer.

46 Karpis and Trent, *Alvin Karpis Story*, 54–56; FBI Files, RCS: TD I.C. #7-576, 1935–36, The Kidnapping of Edward George Bremer.

47 Koblas, *"Ma,"* 216–18; FBI Files, RCS: TD I.C. #7-576, 1935–36, The Kidnapping of Edward George Bremer.

48 FBI Files, RCS: TD I.C. #7-576, 1935–36, The Kidnapping of Edward George Bremer.

Chapter Two: Ruthless and Daring

1 *Kansas City Star*, March 29, 1936; *Joplin Globe*, July 22, 1939; Koblas, *"Ma,"* 12–15.

2 Winter, *Mean Men*, 4–9, *Kansas City Star*, March 29, 1936.

3 *Joplin Globe*, July 22, 1939; Koblas, *"Ma,"* 12–15; Winter, *Mean Men*, 4–9.

4 Koblas, *"Ma,"* 12–15.

5 Federal Bureau of Investigation Files/Report I. C. #7-576-3775 January 19, 1935, Barker-Karpis Gang.

6 *Kansas City Star*, March 29, 1936.

7 www.ancestry.com/Arizona Barker; *Lawrence County Historical Society Bulletin* 120, July 1991; Trekell, *A History of Tulsa Police Department*, 112–14.

8 *Lawrence County Historical Society Bulletin* 120, July 1991; Koblas, *"Ma,"* 12–15.

9 Federal Bureau of Investigation Files/Report I. C. #7-576-3775 January 19, 1935–36, Barker-Karpis Gang; Winter, *Mean Men*, 1–5; www.ancestry.com/George Barker; www.ancestry.com/Arizona Barker.

10 *Lawrence County Historical Society Bulletin* 120, July 1991; Koblas, "Ma," 12–15.

11 www.ancestry.com/Arizona Barker; *Lawrence County Historical Society Bulletin* 120, July 1991.

12 Koblas, *"Ma,"* 12–15; Winter, *Mean Men*, 1–5; www.ancestry.com/George Barker; www.ancestry.com/Arizona Barker.

13 *Kansas City Star*, March 29, 1936; *Lawrence County Historical Society Bulletin* 120, July 1991; Winter, *Mean Men*, 6–9.

14 Winter, *Mean Men*, 13–15.

15 *Lawrence County Historical Society Bulletin* 120, July 1991; Koblas, *"Ma,"* 17–21.

16 *Lawrence County Historical Society Bulletin* 120, July 1991; Winter, *Mean Men*, 18–22; Koblas, *"Ma,"* 12–15.

17 *Joplin Globe*, July 22, 1939; Federal Bureau of Investigation Files/Report I. C. #7-576-3775 January 19, 1935, Barker-Karpis Gang.

18 Federal Bureau of Investigation Files/Report I. C. #7-576-3775 January 19, 1935–36, Barker-Karpis Gang.

19 *Joplin Globe*, November 16, 1915; Federal Bureau of Investigation Files/Report I. C. #7-576-3775 January 19, 1935, Barker-Karpis Gang.

20 *Tulsa Tribune*, March 22, 1949; Winter, *Mean Men*, 5–7.

21 *Springfield Missouri Republican*, August 9, 1916; *Tulsa Tribune*, March 22, 1949

22 Federal Bureau of Investigation Files/Report I. C. #7-576-3775 January 19, 1935, Barker-Karpis Gang.

23 Federal Bureau of Investigation Files/Report I. C. #7-576-3775 January 19, 1935, Barker-Karpis Gang; Koblas, *"Ma,"* 29–32.

24 Winter, *Mean Men*, 17–18; Federal Bureau of Investigation Files/Report I. C. #7-576-3775 January 19, 1935, Barker-Karpis Gang; Koblas, *"Ma,"* 29–32.

25 Federal Bureau of Investigation Files/Report I. C. #7-576-3775 January 19, 1935, Barker-Karpis Gang; Koblas, *"Ma,"* 14–20.

26 Federal Bureau of Investigation Files/Report I. C. #7-576-3775 January 19, 1935, Barker-Karpis Gang; Koblas, *"Ma,"* 14–20.

27 Weiner, *Enemies*, 12–15; www.fbi.gov/about-us/history/directors/hoover.

28 *Marion Star*, March 11, 1916; Weiner, *Enemies*, 12–15; www.fbi.gov/about-us/history/directors/hoover.

29 *Saturday Spectator*, February 18, 1920; Federal Bureau of Investigation Files/Report I. C. #7-576-3775 January 19, 1935, Barker-Karpis Gang.

Chapter Three: The Firstborn

1 *Joplin Globe*, July 22, 1939; *Kansas City Star*, March 29, 1936; Federal Bureau of Investigation Files/Report 76-4175, 1939, Arthur Barker.

2 Federal Bureau of Investigation Files/Report RCS: TD I.C. #7-576, November 19, 1936 Barker-Karpis Gang; *Joplin Globe*, July 22, 1939; *Kansas City Star*, March 29, 1936.

3 Federal Bureau of Investigation Files/Report 76-4175, 1939, Arthur Barker; Federal Bureau of Investigation Files/Report RCS: TD I.C. #7-576, November 19, 1936 Barker-Karpis Gang.

4 *Master Detective*, May 1935.

5 Federal Bureau of Investigation Files/Report 76-4175, 1939, Arthur Barker.

6 US Department of Justice, Arthur Barker Arrest Record #37343, March 4, 1935; Federal Bureau of Investigation Files/Report RCS: TD I.C. #7-576, November 19, 1935, Barker-Karpis Gang; Winter, *Mean Men*, 7–8.

7 US Department of Justice, Arthur Barker Arrest Record #37343, March 4, 1935.

8 *Fayetteville Daily Democrat*, April 1, 1927; US Department of Justice, Arthur Barker Arrest Record #37343, March 4, 1935; Winter, *Mean Men*, 18–19.

9 Federal Bureau of Investigation Files/Report 76-4175, 1939, Arthur Barker; Winter, *Mean Men*, 21.

10 Federal Bureau of Investigation Files/Report RCS: TD I.C. #7-576, 1935–36, Barker-Karpis Gang; Koblas, *"Ma,"* 14–17.

11 *Master Detective*, May 1935; Federal Bureau of Investigation Files/Report RCS: TD I.C. #7-576, 1935–36, Barker-Karpis Gang.

12 *Brainerd Daily Dispatch*, November 8, 1920; Federal Bureau of Investigation Files/Report RCS: TD I.C. #7-576, 1935–36, Barker-Karpis Gang.

13 Federal Bureau of Investigation Files/Report RCS: TD I.C. #7-576, 1935–36, Barker-Karpis Gang; *Brainerd Daily Dispatch*, November 8, 1920.

14 Federal Bureau of Investigation Files/Report RCS: TD I.C. #7-576, 1935–36, Barker-Karpis Gang.

15 Ibid.

16 Winter, *Mean Men*, 18–19; Federal Bureau of Investigation Files/Report RCS: TD I.C. #7-576, 1935–36, Barker-Karpis Gang.

17 Federal Bureau of Investigation Files/Report RCS: TD I.C. #7-576, 1935–36, Barker-Karpis Gang; Newton, *Encyclopedia of Robberies, Heists and Capers*, 170–71.

18 *Master Detective*, May 1935; Koblas, *"Ma,"* 26–29.

19 Federal Bureau of Investigation Files/Report RCS: TD I.C. #7-576, 1935–36, Barker-Karpis Gang.

20 Ibid.

21 Winter, *Mean Men*, 50–51; Federal Bureau of Investigation Files/Report RCS: TD I.C. #7-576, 1935–36, Barker-Karpis Gang.

22 Winter, *Mean Men*, 48–53; Federal Bureau of Investigation Files/Report RCS: TD I.C. #7-576, 1935–36, Barker-Karpis Gang.

23 *Master Detective*, May 1935; Federal Bureau of Investigation Files/Report RCS: TD I.C. #7-576, 1935–36, Barker-Karpis Gang.

24 Winter, *Mean Men*, 48–53; Federal Bureau of Investigation Files/Report RCS: TD I.C. #7-576, 1935–36, Barker-Karpis Gang.

25 Federal Bureau of Investigation Files/Report RCS: TD I.C. #7-576, November 19, 1936 Barker-Karpis Gang.

26 Winter, *Mean Men*, 54–57; Federal Bureau of Investigation Files/Report RCS: TD I.C. #7-576, 1935–36, Barker-Karpis Gang.

27 Winter, *Mean Men*, 61–65; Federal Bureau of Investigation Files/Report RCS: TD I.C. #7-576, 1935–36, Barker-Karpis Gang; *Joplin Globe*, January 20, 1924.

28 *Master Detective*, May 1935; Winter, *Mean Men*, 48–53; Federal Bureau of Investigation Files/Report RCS: TD I.C. #7-576, 1935–36, Barker-Karpis Gang.

29 Winter, *Mean Men*, 48–53; Federal Bureau of Investigation Files/Report RCS: TD I.C. #7-576, 1935–36, Barker-Karpis Gang.

30 Winter, *Mean Men*, 64–66; Federal Bureau of Investigation Files/Report RCS: TD I.C. #7-576, 1935–36, Barker-Karpis Gang.

31 *Springfield Leader*, January 26, 1927; Winter, *Mean Men*, 73–75; Federal Bureau of Investigation Files/Report RCS: TD I.C. #7-576, 1935–36, Barker-Karpis Gang.

32 Winter, *Mean Men*, 75–76; *Joplin Globe*, January 18, 1927, and January 22, 1927; *Sequoyah County Democrat*, January 21, 1927.

33 *Amarillo Daily News*, April 1, 1927; *Joplin Globe*, April 29, 1927.

34 *Albuquerque Journal*, August 3, 1927.

35 Ibid.

36 Federal Bureau of Investigation Files/Report RCS: TD I.C. #7-576, 1935–36, Barker-Karpis Gang.

37 Ibid.

38 Ibid.; Winter, *Mean Men*, 95–98.

39 *Emporia Gazette*, August 29, 1927; Winter, *Mean Men*, 97–98.

40 *Billings Gazette*, September 1, 1927; *Emporia Gazette*, August 29, 1927; Winter, *Mean Men*, 97–98.

41 *Joplin Globe*, September 27, 1927.

42 *Tribune Republican*, October 7, 1927; Federal Bureau of Investigation Files/Report RCS: TD I.C. #7-576, 1935–36, Barker-Karpis Gang.

43 *Sedalia Capital*, September 20, 1927; *Lincoln Evening Journal*, September 27, 1927; Federal Bureau of Investigation Files/Report RCS: TD I.C. #7-576, 1935–36, Barker-Karpis Gang.

44 *Joplin Globe*, September 27, 1927; *Miami Daily News*, September 26, 1929.

Chapter Four: Losing Lloyd

1 *Master Detective*, May 1935; Koblas, *"Ma,"* 34–36.

2 *Amarillo Globe Times*, June 19, 1959; *Evening Star*, March 22, 1949.

3 Koblas, *"Ma,"* 33–35; Federal Bureau of Investigation, Freedom of Information Privacy Acts, Subject: Herman Barker (Death of), File #26-9961.

4 *Master Detective*, May 1935; Federal Bureau of Investigation Files/Report RCS: TD I.C. #7-576, 1935–36, Barker-Karpis Gang; Koblas, *"Ma,"* 2–4.

5 Federal Bureau of Investigation Files, RCS: TD I.C. #7-576, 1935–36 Barker-Karpis Gang; Fleury, *Public Enemy #1*, 38–39; *Tulsa Tribune*, March 22, 1949.

6 *Joplin Globe*, July 7, 1921.

7 *Master Detective*, May 1935.

8 *Fort Scott Daily Tribune*, July 16, 1921; *Fort Scott Daily Monitor*, July 16, 1921; *Joplin News Herald*, January 13, 1922, and January 17, 1922.

9 *Master Detective*, May 1935.

10 Ibid.

11 Federal Bureau of Investigation Files, RCS: TD I.C. #7-576, 1935–36 Barker-Karpis Gang.

12 *Charleston Daily Mail*, March 22, 1949; Federal Bureau of Investigation Files, RCS: TD I.C. #7-576, 1935–36 Barker-Karpis Gang.

13 Federal Bureau of Investigation Files, RCS: TD I.C. #7-576, 1935–36 Barker-Karpis Gang.

14 *Joplin Globe*, March 22, 1949.

15 Federal Bureau of Investigation Files, RCS: TD I.C. #7-576, 1935–36 Barker-Karpis Gang; Federal Bureau of Investigation Files/Report DN-62-723, Lloyd Barker aka "Red" Research May 12, 1949.

16 Federal Bureau of Investigation Files/Report DN-62-723, Lloyd Barker aka "Red" Research May 12, 1949.

17 Ibid.

18 Ibid.

19 Federal Bureau of Investigation Files/Report DN-62-723, Lloyd Barker aka "Red" Research May 12, 1949.

20 *Butte Montana Standard*, April 5, 1949; *Joplin News Herald*, January 13, 1922.

Chapter Five: Public Enemy

1 Fleury, *Public Enemy #1*, 44–47; Karpis and Trent, *Alvin Karpis Story*, 166–69; Koblas, *"Ma,"* 198–99; Federal Bureau of Investigation Files/Report RCS: TD I.C. #7-576, 1935–36 The Kidnapping of Edward George Bremer.

2 Koblas, *"Ma,"* 198–99; Federal Bureau of Investigation Files/Report RCS: TD I.C. #7-576, 1935–36 The Kidnapping of Edward George Bremer.

3 Koblas, *"Ma,"* 198–99; Federal Bureau of Investigation Files/Report RCS: TD I.C. #7-576, 1935–36 The Kidnapping of Edward George Bremer; *Pioneer Press*, January 23, 1934.

4 Koblas, *"Ma,"* 198–99; Federal Bureau of Investigation Files/Report RCS: TD I.C. #7-576, 1935–36 The Kidnapping of Edward George Bremer; *Pioneer Press,* January 23, 1934.

5 Associated Press, July 22, 1939; *Pageant,* December 1959; Federal Bureau of Investigation Files/Report RCS: TD I.C. #7-576, 1935–36 The Kidnapping of Edward George Bremer.

6 Koblas, *"Ma,"* 12–15; *Kansas City Star,* March 29, 1936; *Joplin Globe,* July 23, 1939.

7 *Muskogee Times-Democrat,* September 28, 1922; Federal Bureau of Investigation Files/Report 76-4175, 1939, Arthur Barker.

8 *Muskogee Times-Democrat,* January 20, 1921; Federal Bureau of Investigation Files/Report 76-4175, 1939, Arthur Barker.

9 *Muskogee Times-Democrat,* January 20, 1921; Federal Bureau of Investigation Files/Report 76-4175, 1939, Arthur Barker.

10 Federal Bureau of Investigation Files/Report 76-4175, 1939, Arthur Barker; *Muskogee Times-Democrat,* September 28, 1922.

11 *Sequoyah County Democrat,* January 21, 1927; *Amarillo Daily News,* May 7, 1927.

12 Koblas, *"Ma,"* 18–21; Federal Bureau of Investigation Files/Report 76-4175, 1939, Arthur Barker.

13 *Kansas City Star,* March 29, 1936; *Joplin Globe,* July 23, 1939.

14 Associated Press, July 22, 1939.

15 Federal Bureau of Investigation Files/Report 76-4175, 1939, Arthur Barker.

16 Winter, *Mean Men,* 31–34; *Ada Evening News,* August 26, 1921; Federal Bureau of Investigation Files/Report 76-4175, 1939, Arthur Barker.

17 *Ada Evening News,* January 16, 1923.

18 Federal Bureau of Investigation Files/Report 76-4175, 1939, Arthur Barker; *Daily Ardmoreite,* January 16, 1922; Winter, *Mean Men,* 27–29.

19 Federal Bureau of Investigation Files/Report 76-4175, 1939, Arthur Barker; *Daily Ardmoreite,* January 16, 1922; Winter, *Mean Men,* 27–29.

20 Federal Bureau of Investigation, Freedom of Information Privacy Acts, Subject: Herman Barker (Death of), File #26-9961.

21 *Morning Avalanche,* December 29, 1939; Karpis and Trent, *Alvin Karpis Story,* 118–19.

22 Koblas, *"Ma,"* 34–36; Karpis and Trent, *Alvin Karpis Story,* 115–16.

23 *Kansas City Kansan,* August 7, 1922.

24 Ibid.

25 *Morning Tulsa Daily World,* September 7, 1922.

26 Federal Bureau of Investigation Files/Report RCS: TD I.C. #7-576, 1935–36, Barker-Karpis Gang; *Daily Ardmoreite,* September 22, 1922; *Quanah Tribune Chief,* March 23, 1923; Winter, *Mean Men,* 35–37.

27 *Ada Evening News,* December 21, 1925.

28 *Taylor Daily Press,* October 14, 1923.

29 Federal Bureau of Investigation Files/Report RCS: TD I.C. #7-576, 1935–36, Barker-Karpis Gang; Winter, *Mean Men,* 35–37.

30 *Ada Evening News,* December 21, 1925.

31 Federal Bureau of Investigation Files/Report RCS: TD I.C. #7-576, 1935–36, Barker-Karpis Gang; Winter, *Mean Men*, 35–37.

32 Federal Bureau of Investigation Files/Report RCS: TD I.C. #7-576, 1935–36, Barker-Karpis Gang; Winter, *Mean Men*, 35–37.

33 Taylor, *American Hauntings*, 25–28; Federal Bureau of Investigation Files/Report RCS: TD I.C. #7-576, 1935–36, Barker-Karpis Gang; Winter, *Mean Men*, 35–37.

34 Federal Bureau of Investigation Files/Report RCS: TD I.C. #7-576, 1935–36, Barker-Karpis Gang.

35 Ibid.

36 Ibid.

37 Ibid.

38 *Ogden Standard-Examiner*, November 21, 1927.

39 Lansing Prisoner Files, Lansing, Kansas Inmate Fred Barker; Koblas, *"Ma,"* 30–32.

40 Koblas, *"Ma,"* 38–40; Federal Bureau of Investigation Files/Report RCS: TD I.C. #7-576, 1935–36 Barker-Karpis Gang.

41 *Miami Daily News-Record*, January 27, 1927.

42 *Miami Daily News-Record*, January 27, 1927, and April 12, 1927; *Chillicothe Constitution Tribune*, October 24, 1927.

43 *Lincoln Star*, October 9, 1927.

44 *Master Detective*, May 1935; www.fbi.gov/history.

45 Sifakis, *Mafia Encyclopedia*, 269; *Master Detective*, May 1935.

46 Federal Bureau of Investigation Files/Report RCS: TD I.C. #7-576, 1935–36, Barker-Karpis Gang; *Master Detective*, May 1935; www.fbi.gov/history.

Chapter Six: Murder in Wisconsin

1 Karpis and Trent, *Alvin Karpis Story*, 80–84.

2 Ibid.

3 Ibid.

4 Ibid.

5 Federal Bureau of Investigation Files/Report RCS: TD I.C. #7-576, 1935–36, Barker-Karpis Gang; Federal Bureau of Investigation Files/Report 62-43010, May 1936 Alvin Francis Karpis.

6 Federal Bureau of Investigation Files/Report RCS: TD I.C. #7-576, 1935–36, Barker-Karpis Gang; Federal Bureau of Investigation Files/Report 62-43010, May 1936 Alvin Francis Karpis.

7 Karpis and Trent, *Alvin Karpis Story*, 37; Federal Bureau of Investigation Files/Report RCS: TD I.C. #7-576, 1935–36, Barker-Karpis Gang; Federal Bureau of Investigation Files/Report 62-43010, May 1936 Alvin Francis Karpis, 29; Koblas, *"Ma,"* 37–38.

8 Federal Bureau of Investigation Files/Report RCS: TD I.C. #7-576, 1935–36, Barker-Karpis Gang; Federal Bureau of Investigation Files/Report 62-43010, May 1936 Alvin Francis Karpis.

9 Federal Bureau of Investigation Files/Report RCS: TD I.C. #7-576, 1935–36, Barker-Karpis Gang; Federal Bureau of Investigation Files/Report 62-43010, May 1936 Alvin Francis Karpis.

10 Federal Bureau of Investigation Files/Report RCS: TD I.C. #7-576, 1935–36, Barker-Karpis Gang; Federal Bureau of Investigation Files/Report 62-43010, May 1936 Alvin Francis Karpis.

11 *Miami Daily News-Record*, March 24, 1930.

12 Federal Bureau of Investigation Files/Report 62-43010, May 1936, Alvin Francis Karpis.

13 Karpis and Trent, *Alvin Karpis Story*, 83–84.

14 Koblas, *"Ma,"* 53–55; Karpis and Trent, *Alvin Karpis Story*, 40.

15 Winter, *Mean Men*, 107–8; Karpis and Trent, *Alvin Karpis Story*, 83–84.

16 Winter, *Mean Men*, 107–8; Karpis and Trent, *Alvin Karpis Story*, 83–84.

17 Federal Bureau of Investigation Files/Report 62-43010, May 1936 Alvin Francis Karpis; Winter, *Mean Men*, 107–8; Karpis and Trent, *Alvin Karpis Story*, 42–45.

18 Koblas, *"Ma,"* 38–40; Federal Bureau of Investigation Files/Report RCS: TD I.C. #7-576, 1935–36, Barker-Karpis Gang; Federal Bureau of Investigation Files/Report 62-43010, May 1936 Alvin Francis Karpis.

19 Winter, *Mean Men*, 113–14.

20 Ibid.

21 Federal Bureau of Investigation Files/Report RCS: TD I.C. #7-576, 1935–36, Barker-Karpis Gang; Karpis and Trent, *Alvin Karpis Story*, 88–90.

22 Koblas, *"Ma,"* 54–55; Karpis and Trent, *Alvin Karpis Story*, 88–90.

23 Federal Bureau of Investigation Files/Report RCS: TD I.C. #7-576, 1935–36, Barker-Karpis Gang; Karpis and Trent, *Alvin Karpis Story*, 88–90.

24 Federal Bureau of Investigation Files/Report RCS: TD I.C. #7-576, 1935–36, Barker-Karpis Gang.

25 *Joplin Globe*, December 22, 1931; *Macon Chronicle-Herald*, December 22, 1931.

26 *West Plains Daily Quill*, December 19, 1931.

27 Karpis and Trent, *Alvin Karpis Story*, 73–74; Federal Bureau of Investigation Files/ Report RCS: TD I.C. #7-576, 1935–36, Barker-Karpis Gang.

28 *Minnesota Police Journal*, August 1991; Maccabee, *John Dillinger Slept Here*, 67–68.

29 www.fbi.gov/history; Kunz, *St. Paul: Saga of an American City*, 126.

30 Koblas, *"Ma,"* 57–59; Karpis and Trent, *Alvin Karpis Story*, 73–74.

31 www.fbi.gov/history.

32 Karpis and Trent, *Alvin Karpis Story*, 102–4; Koblas, *"Ma,"* 61–62.

33 Karpis and Trent, *Alvin Karpis Story*, 87.

34 *Macon Chronicle-Herald*, January 14, 1932.

35 Federal Bureau of Investigation Files/Report RCS: TD I.C. #7-576, 1935–36, Barker-Karpis Gang; Karpis and Trent, *Alvin Karpis Story*, 89–90; *Jefferson City Post-Tribune*, July 18, 1932.

36 *Current Local*, May 5, 1932.

37 Karpis and Trent, *Alvin Karpis Story*, 87–89.

38 Ibid.

39 Ibid.

40 Ibid.

41 Federal Bureau of Investigation Files/Report RCS: TD I.C. #7-576, 1935–36, Barker-Karpis Gang.

42 Koblas, *"Ma,"* 68–69.

43 Karpis and Trent, *Alvin Karpis Story*, 89–90.

44 Ibid.

45 Federal Bureau of Investigation Files/Report RCS: TD I.C. #7-576, 1935–36, Barker-Karpis Gang.

46 Ibid.

47 Karpis and Trent, *Alvin Karpis Story*, 89–90.

48 Federal Bureau of Investigation Files/Report RCS: TD I.C. #7-576, 1935–36, Barker-Karpis Gang; Karpis and Trent, *Alvin Karpis Story*, 89–90.

Chapter Seven: Careless Crimes

1 *Evening Huronite,* September 30, 1932; Koblas, *"Ma,"* 99–101;Federal Bureau of Investigation Files/Report RCS: TD I.C. #7-576, 1935–36, Barker-Karpis Gang.

2 *Evening Huronite*, September 30, 1932; Koblas, *"Ma": The Life and Times of Ma Barker and Her Boys*, 99–101; Federal Bureau of Investigation Files/Report RCS: TD I.C. #7-576, 1935–36, Barker-Karpis Gang.

3 *Evening Huronite*, September 30, 1932; Koblas, *"Ma,"* 99–101; Federal Bureau of Investigation Files/Report RCS: TD I.C. #7-576, 1935–36, Barker-Karpis Gang.

4 *Evening Huronite*, September 30, 1932; Koblas, *"Ma,"* 99–101; Federal Bureau of Investigation Files/Report RCS: TD I.C. #7-576, 1935–36, Barker-Karpis Gang.

5 *Bismark Tribune*, October 1, 1932; Koblas, *"Ma,"* 103–4; Federal Bureau of Investigation Files/Report RCS: TD I.C. #7-576, 1935–36, Barker-Karpis Gang.

6 *Richland County Farmer Globe*, October 7, 1932; Karpis and Trent, *Alvin Karpis Story*, 45–50; Federal Bureau of Investigation Files/Report RCS: TD I.C. #7-576, 1935–36, Barker-Karpis Gang.

7 Karpis and Trent, *Alvin Karpis Story*, 45–50.

8 Federal Bureau of Investigation Files/Report RCS: TD I.C. #7-576, 1935–36, Barker-Karpis Gang.

9 *Master Detective*, May 1935; www.wplucey.com; Federal Bureau of Investigation Files/ Report RCS: TD I.C. #7-576, 1935–36, Barker-Karpis Gang.

10 *Leavenworth Times*, April 15, 1920; Koblas, *"Ma,"* 78; Skousen, *True Stories from the Files of the FBI*, 95.

11 Federal Bureau of Investigation Files/Report RCS: TD I.C. #7-576, 1935–36, Barker-Karpis Gang; Koblas, *"Ma,"* 95–96; Skousen, *True Stories from the Files of the FBI*, 95–96.

12 Federal Bureau of Investigation Files/Report RCS: TD I.C. #7-576, 1935–36, Barker-Karpis Gang; *Master Detective*, May 1935.

13 Federal Bureau of Investigation Files/Report RCS: TD I.C. #7-576, 1935–36, Barker-Karpis Gang; *Master Detective*, May 1935.

14 *Amarillo Globe*, June 19, 1959; *Joplin Globe*, July 22, 1939; *Master Detective*, May 1935.

15 *Amarillo Globe*, June 19, 1959; *Joplin Globe*, July 22, 1939; *Master Detective*, May 1935.

16 *Master Detective*, May 1935.

17 Karpis and Trent, *Alvin Karpis Story*, 64–65.

18 Ibid., 82–83, 106–7; Federal Bureau of Investigation Files/Report RCS: TD I.C. #7-576, 1935–36, Barker-Karpis Gang.

19 Karpis and Trent, *Alvin Karpis Story*, 106–7.

20 Federal Bureau of Investigation Files/Report 76-4175, 1939, Arthur Barker; Koblas, *"Ma,"* 106–8; *Chillicothe Constitution Tribune*, December 19, 1932.

21 *Chillicothe Constitution Tribune*, December 19, 1932.

22 Ibid.

23 Koblas, *"Ma,"* 108–9; Federal Bureau of Investigation Files/Report RCS: TD I.C. #7-576, 1935–36 Barker-Karpis Gang.

24 Federal Bureau of Investigation Files/Report RCS: TD I.C. #7-576, 1935–36, Barker-Karpis Gang.

25 Koblas, *"Ma,"* 108–9; Federal Bureau of Investigation Files/Report RCS: TD I.C. #7-576, 1935–36, Barker-Karpis Gang.

26 *Lincoln Evening Journal*, December 17, 1932; Karpis and Trent, *Alvin Karpis Story*, 127–29.

27 Koblas, *"Ma,"* 108–9; Federal Bureau of Investigation Files/Report RCS: TD I.C. #7-576, 1935–36, Barker-Karpis Gang.

28 Federal Bureau of Investigation Files/Report RCS: TD I.C. #7-576, 1935–36, Barker-Karpis Gang.

29 *Mankato Free Press*, December 22, 1932.

30 Koblas, *"Ma,"* 131; Federal Bureau of Investigation Files/Report RCS: TD I.C. #7-576, 1935–36, Barker-Karpis Gang.

31 Karpis and Trent, *Alvin Karpis Story*, 69.

32 *Time*, October 29, 1934; Federal Bureau of Investigation Files/Report RCS: TD I.C. #7-576, 1935–36, Barker-Karpis Gang; *Independent Record*, February 10, 1935.

33 *Time*, October 29, 1934; Federal Bureau of Investigation Files/Report RCS: TD I.C. #7-576, 1935–36, Barker-Karpis Gang; *Independent Record*, February 10, 1935.

34 Koblas, *"Ma,"* 134–35.

35 *Sunday World Herald*, March 3, 1969; Koblas, *"Ma,"* 134–35.

36 *Sunday World Herald*, March 3, 1969; Federal Bureau of Investigation Files/Report RCS: TD I.C. #7-576, 1935–36, Barker-Karpis Gang.

37 *Sunday World Herald*, March 3, 1969; Federal Bureau of Investigation Files/Report RCS: TD I.C. #7-576, 1935–36, Barker-Karpis Gang; Koblas, *"Ma": The Life and Times of Ma Barker and Her Boys*, 134–35.

38 *Sunday World Herald*, March 3, 1969; Federal Bureau of Investigation Files/Report RCS: TD I.C. #7-576, 1935–36, Barker-Karpis Gang.

39 *Sunday World Herald*, March 3, 1969; Federal Bureau of Investigation Files/Report RCS: TD I.C. #7-576, 1935–36, Barker-Karpis Gang.

40 Federal Bureau of Investigation Files/Report RCS: TD I.C. #7-576, 1935–36, Barker-Karpis Gang.

41 *Hutchinson News*, April 4, 1933; *Belleville Telescope*, April 6, 1933.

42 *Hutchinson News*, April 4, 1933; *Belleville Telescope*, April 6, 1933.

43 Koblas, *"Ma,"* 134–35; Federal Bureau of Investigation Files/Report RCS: TD I.C. #7-576, 1935–36, Barker-Karpis Gang.

44 *Belleville Telescope*, April 6, 1933.
45 Koblas, *"Ma,"* 142–43; Federal Bureau of Investigation Files/Report RCS: TD I.C. #7-576, 1935–36, Barker-Karpis Gang.
46 Karpis and Trent, *Alvin Karpis Story*, 153–54.
47 Federal Bureau of Investigation Files/Report RCS: TD I.C. #7-576, 1935–36, Barker-Karpis Gang.
48 Ibid.
49 Ibid.; Federal Bureau of Investigation Files/Report 76-4175, 1939, Arthur Barker.
50 Federal Bureau of Investigation Files/Report 76-4175, 1939, Arthur Barker; Federal Bureau of Investigation Files/Report RCS: TD I.C. #7-576, 1935–36, Barker-Karpis Gang.
51 Federal Bureau of Investigation Files/Report 76-4175, 1939, Arthur Barker; Federal Bureau of Investigation Files/Report RCS: TD I.C. #7-576, 1935–36, Barker-Karpis Gang.
52 Karpis and Trent, *Alvin Karpis Story*, 157–60.

Chapter Eight: Pleasing Ma

1 *Master Detective*, May 1935; Poulsen, *Don't Call Us Molls*, 190, 248; Karpis and Trent, *Alvin Karpis Story*, 59–60.
2 *Master Detective*, May 1935; Poulsen, *Don't Call Us Molls*, 190, 248; Karpis and Trent, *Alvin Karpis Story*, 59–60.
3 Karpis and Trent, *Alvin Karpis Story*, 59–60.
4 Poulsen, *Don't Call Us Molls*, 190, 248; Lynch and Russell, *Where the Wild Rice Grows*, 56–58.
5 Karpis and Trent, *Alvin Karpis Story*, 59–60, 86–87.
6 Ibid.
7 Karpis and Trent, *Alvin Karpis Story*, 105–7.
8 *Master Detective*, May 1935; Karpis and Trent, *Alvin Karpis Story*, 107–8.
9 Federal Bureau of Investigation Files/Report RCS: TD I.C. #7-576, 1935–36, Barker-Karpis Gang; *Master Detective*, May 1935; Karpis and Trent, *Alvin Karpis Story*, 90–91.
10 Koblas, *"Ma,"* 273–76; *Master Detective*, May 1935.
11 Karpis and Trent, *Alvin Karpis Story*, 90–91.
12 Federal Bureau of Investigation Files/Report RCS: TD I.C. #7-576, 1935–36, Barker-Karpis Gang.
13 *Manitowoc Herald-Times*, June 23, 1932; *Shamokin News-Dispatch*, June 17, 1933.
14 Karpis and Trent, *Alvin Karpis Story*, 127–29; Federal Bureau of Investigation Files/Report RCS: TD I.C. #7-576, 1935–36, Barker-Karpis Gang.
15 Federal Bureau of Investigation Files/Report RCS: TD I.C. #7-576, 1935–36, Barker-Karpis Gang; *Shamokin News-Dispatch*, June 17, 1933.
16 *Evening Independent*, June 19, 1933; *Hope Star*, June 17, 1933; Koblas, *"Ma,"* 167–68.
17 *Gambling*, November 1999; *Master Detective*, May 1935; Federal Bureau of Investigation Files/Report RCS: TD I.C. #7-576, 1935–36, Barker-Karpis Gang.
18 *Master Detective*, May 1935; Federal Bureau of Investigation Files/Report RCS: TD I.C. #7-576, 1935–36, Barker-Karpis Gang.

19 Mahoney, *Secret Partners*, 58–62; *Evening Independent*, June 19, 1933; *Hope Star*, June 17, 1933.

20 *Oshkosh Daily Northwestern*, June 17, 1933.

21 *Pioneer Press*, August 6, 1972.

22 Ibid.

23 *Decatur Herald*, June 30, 1933.

24 Ibid.; *Daily Times*, June 13, 1933; Federal Bureau of Investigation Files/Report RCS: TD I.C. #7-576, 1935–36, Barker-Karpis Gang.

25 Karpis and Trent, *Alvin Karpis Story*, 145–46.

26 Federal Bureau of Investigation Files/Report RCS: TD I.C. #7-576, 1935–36, Barker-Karpis Gang.

27 www.fbi.gov/news/stories/2003/september/hamm090803.

28 Ibid.

29 *Gettysburg Times*, November 29, 1933; *News* (Frederick, MD), December 1, 1933.

30 *Amarillo Globe Times*, June 19, 1959; Federal Bureau of Investigation Files/Report RCS: TD I.C. #7-576, 1935–36, Barker-Karpis Gang.

31 Karpis and Trent, *Alvin Karpis Story*, 144–46; Federal Bureau of Investigation Files/Report RCS: TD I.C. #7-576, 1935–36, Barker-Karpis Gang; *Brainerd Daily Dispatch*, July 31, 1933.

32 Karpis and Trent, *Alvin Karpis Story*, 144–46; Federal Bureau of Investigation Files/Report RCS: TD I.C. #7-576, 1935–36, Barker-Karpis Gang; *Brainerd Daily Dispatch*, July 31, 1933.

33 www.fbi.gov/history; *Oshkosh Daily Northwestern*, July 26, 1933.

34 Federal Bureau of Investigation Files/Report RCS: TD I.C. #7-576, 1935–36 Barker-Karpis Gang.

35 Ibid.

36 Karpis and Trent, *Alvin Karpis Story*, 157–59.

37 *Logansport Pharos-Tribune*, September 22, 1933.

38 Ibid.

39 Ibid.

40 Ibid.

41 Federal Bureau of Investigation Files/Report RCS: TD I.C. #7-576, 1935–36 The Kidnapping of Edward George Bremer.

42 Ibid.

43 Ibid.

44 Ibid.

45 Ibid.

46 Ibid.

47 Ibid.

48 Ibid.

49 *Waco News-Tribune*, March 23, 1934.

50 *Master Detective*, May 1935; Karpis and Trent, *Alvin Karpis Story*, 169–71.

51 Federal Bureau of Investigation Files/Report RCS: TD I.C. #7-576, 1935–36, Barker-Karpis Gang.

52 Ibid.

Chapter Nine: Dangerous Criminals

1 Karpis and Trent, *Alvin Karpis Story*, 176–78; *Master Detective*, May 1935.

2 https://archives.org/details/universal_newsreels/gangsters.

3 Ibid.

4 Karpis and Trent, *Alvin Karpis Story*, 176-78.

5 Federal Bureau of Investigation Files/Report RCS: TD I.C. #7-576, 1935–36, Barker-Karpis Gang; Koblas, *"Ma,"* 273–76.

6 *Moorhead Daily News*, June 1, 1934.

7 Ibid.

8 *Register*, May 16, 1935; Federal Bureau of Investigation Files/Report RCS: TD I.C. #7-576, 1935–36, Barker-Karpis Gang.

9 Federal Bureau of Investigation Files/Report 76-4175, 1939, Arthur Barker; Federal Bureau of Investigation Files/Report RCS: TD I.C. #7-576, 1935–36, Barker-Karpis Gang.

10 Karpis and Trent, *Alvin Karpis Story*, 178–79; Poulsen, *Don't Call Us Molls*, 258–59.

11 Poulsen, *Don't Call Us Molls*, 258–59; Morton, *Mammoth Book of Gangs*, 127.

12 Koblas, *"Ma,"* 275–77; Federal Bureau of Investigation Files/Report 76-4175, 1939, Arthur Barker.

13 Federal Bureau of Investigation Files/Report 76-4175, 1939, Arthur Barker; *Master Detective*, May 1935.

14 Federal Bureau of Investigation Files/Report 76-4175, 1939, Arthur Barker; *Master Detective*, May 1935.

15 Federal Bureau of Investigation Files/Report 76-4175, 1939, Arthur Barker; *Master Detective*, May 1935.

16 Federal Bureau of Investigation Files/Report 76-4175, 1939, Arthur Barker; *Master Detective*, May 1935.

17 Federal Bureau of Investigation Files/Report 76-4175, 1939, Arthur Barker; *Master Detective*, May 1935.

18 Federal Bureau of Investigation Files/Report 76-4175, 1939, Arthur Barker; *Master Detective*, May 1935.

19 Federal Bureau of Investigation Files/Report 76-4175, 1939, Arthur Barker; *Master Detective*, May 1935.

20 Federal Bureau of Investigation Files/Report 76-4175, 1939, Arthur Barker; *Master Detective*, May 1935.

21 Morton, *Mammoth Book of Gangs*, 132–33; Skousen, *True Stories from the Files of the FBI*, 149.

22 Federal Bureau of Investigation Files/Report RCS: TD I.C. #7-576, 1935–36, Barker-Karpis Gang.

23 Ibid.

24 Ibid.

25 Karpis and Trent, *Alvin Karpis Story*, 182–83.

26 *Master Detective*, May 1935; Karpis and Trent, *Alvin Karpis Story*, 183–84; Koblas, *"Ma,"* 278–79.

27 Federal Bureau of Investigation Files/Report RCS: TD I.C. #7-576, 1935–36, Barker-Karpis Gang; *Edge Magazine*, July 25, 1965; *Master Detective*, May 1935.

28 Koblas, *"Ma,"* 278–79; Karpis and Trent, *Alvin Karpis Story*, 185–86.

29 Koblas, *"Ma,"* 278–79; Karpis and Trent, *Alvin Karpis Story*, 185–86.

30 Karpis and Trent, *Alvin Karpis Story*, 185–86.

31 Federal Bureau of Investigation Files/Report RCS: TD I.C. #7-576, 1935–36, Barker-Karpis Gang.

32 Ibid.

33 *Belvidere Daily Republican*, January 9, 1935.

34 *Florida Times Union*, January 17, 1935; *New York Times*, January 17, 1935; Federal Bureau of Investigation Files/Report RCS: TD I.C. #7-576, 1935–36, Barker-Karpis Gang.

35 *Master Detective*, May 1935.

36 Federal Bureau of Investigation Files/Report RCS: TD I.C. #7-576, 1935–36, Barker-Karpis Gang; *Springfield Daily News*, January 18, 1935.

37 Federal Bureau of Investigation Files/Report RCS: TD I.C. #7-576, 1935–36, Barker-Karpis Gang; *Springfield Daily News*, January 18, 1935.

38 *Master Detective,* May 1935; Federal Bureau of Investigation Files/Report RCS: TD I.C. #7-576, 1935–36, Barker-Karpis Gang; *Springfield Daily News*, January 18, 1935.

39 Lamme, *Florida Lore Not Found in History Books*, 82–84.

40 Ibid.; Federal Bureau of Investigation Files/Report RCS: TD I.C. #7-576, 1935–36, Barker-Karpis Gang.

41 Lamme, *Florida Lore Not Found in History Books*, 82–84; Federal Bureau of Investigation Files/Report RCS: TD I.C. #7-576, 1935–36, Barker-Karpis Gang.

42 Lamme, *Florida Lore Not Found in History Books*, 82–84.

43 Federal Bureau of Investigation Files/Report RCS: TD I.C. #7-576, 1935–36, Barker-Karpis Gang.

Chapter Ten: Gunfight at Lake Weir

1 *Reading Times*, January 17, 1935; *Moberly Monitor Index*, January 17, 1935.

2 Federal Bureau of Investigation Files/Report RCS: TD I.C. #7-576, 1935–36, Barker-Karpis Gang; *Springfield Leader*, January 16, 1935; *Atlanta Georgian*, January 17, 1935.

3 *Dallas Morning News*, January 17, 1935; Federal Bureau of Investigation Files/Report RCS: TD I.C. #7-576, 1935–36, Barker-Karpis Gang.

4 *Washington Star*, January 25, 1939; *San Francisco Chronicle*, January 18, 1939; Federal Bureau of Investigation Files/Report RCS: TD I.C. #7-576, 1935–36, Barker-Karpis Gang.

5 *Master Detective*, May 1935; Koblas, *"Ma,"* 282–84.

6 Ibid.; Quimby, *Devil's Emissaries*, 143.

7 Federal Bureau of Investigation Files/Report RCS: TD I.C. #7-576, 1935–36, Barker-Karpis Gang.

8 Ibid.

9 Ibid.

10 Ibid.

11 Ibid.

12 *Chicago Tribune*, October 20, 1935; Federal Bureau of Investigation Files/Report RCS: TD I.C. #7-576, 1935–36, Barker-Karpis Gang.

13 *Moberly Monitor Index*, January 17, 1935; *Springfield Leader*, January 17, 1935.

14 Karpis and Trent, *Alvin Karpis Story*, 189–91.

15 Federal Bureau of Investigation Files/Report RCS: TD I.C. #7-576, 1935–36, Barker-Karpis Gang.

16 Ibid.

17 *Moberly Monitor Index*, January 21, 1935.

18 Federal Bureau of Investigation Files/Report RCS: TD I.C. #7-576, 1935–36, Barker-Karpis Gang.

19 Karpis and Trent, *Alvin Karpis Story*, 196–99; Federal Bureau of Investigation Files/Report RCS: TD I.C. #7-576, 1935–36, Barker-Karpis Gang.

20 Karpis and Trent, *Alvin Karpis Story*, 196–99; Federal Bureau of Investigation Files/Report RCS: TD I.C. #7-576, 1935–36, Barker-Karpis Gang.

21 *Logansport Pharos-Tribune*, February 8, 1935.

22 *Denton Record-Chronicle*, February 1, 1935.

23 Karpis and Trent, *Alvin Karpis Story*, 199–200.

24 *Daily Messenger*, August 29, 1935.

25 *Dayton Daily News*, July 21, 1935.

26 *Pottstown Mercury*, August 21, 1935.

27 *Ames Daily Tribune-Times*, April 19, 1935.

28 Federal Bureau of Investigation Files/Report RCS: TD I.C. #7-576, 1935–36, Barker-Karpis Gang; *Ames Daily Tribune-Times*, April 19, 1935.

29 *Ironwood Daily Globe*, April 22, 1935; Federal Bureau of Investigation Files/Report RCS: TD I.C. #7-576, 1935–36, Barker-Karpis Gang.

30 *Ironwood Daily Globe*, April 22, 1935; Federal Bureau of Investigation Files/Report RCS: TD I.C. #7-576, 1935–36, Barker-Karpis Gang.

31 *Marshall Evening Chronicle*, April 18, 1935.

32 *Sandusky Register*, January 22, 1936.

33 Federal Bureau of Investigation Files/Report RCS: TD I.C. #7-576, 1935–36, Barker-Karpis Gang.

34 Ibid.

35 *Muscatine Journal and News Tribune*, May 17, 1935.

36 *Pottstown Mercury*, May 18, 1935.

37 *Jacksonville Daily Journal*, May 26, 1935.

38 Karpis and Trent, *Alvin Karpis Story*, 249–50; *Daily Messenger*, July 13, 1936.

39 *Reading Times*, July 13, 1936; Karpis and Trent, *Alvin Karpis Story*, 249–50.

40 *Reading Times*, July 13, 1936.

41 *Daily Capital News*, July 28, 1936.

42 *Salt Lake Tribune*, August 6, 1936.

43 Federal Bureau of Investigation Files/Report RCS: TD I.C. #7-576, 1935–36, Barker-Karpis Gang.

Chapter Eleven: Waiting for a Grave

1 *Bradford Era*, January 17, 1935; *Miami Daily News-Record*, January 18, 1935.

2 Federal Bureau of Investigation Files/Report RCS: TD I.C. #7-576, 1935–36, Barker-Karpis Gang; *Miami Daily News-Record*, January 18, 1935; McIver, *Touched by the Sun*, 72–77.

3 Federal Bureau of Investigation Files/Report RCS: TD I.C. #7-576, 1935–36, Barker-Karpis Gang; *Joplin News Herald*, October 1, 1935.

4 Jasper County Records, Inventory and Appraisement Documents, October 10, 1935.

5 Ibid.

6 Ibid.

7 Federal Bureau of Investigation Files/Report RCS: TD I.C. #7-576, 1935–36, Barker-Karpis Gang; *Joplin News Herald*, October 1, 1935.

8 *Joplin News Herald*, October 1, 1935.

9 Federal Bureau of Investigation Files/Report RCS: TD I.C. #7-576, 1935–36, Barker-Karpis Gang; *Joplin News Herald*, October 1, 1935.

10 Jasper County Records, Inventory and Appraisement Documents, October 10, 1935; *Joplin Globe*, December 7, 1935.

11 US Department of Justice, Arthur Barker Arrest Record #37343, March 4, 1935; Federal Bureau of Investigation Files/Report 76-4175, 1939, Arthur Barker; US Penitentiary Leavenworth, Admission Summary.

12 Federal Bureau of Investigation Files/Report 76-4175, 1939, Arthur Barker; US Penitentiary Leavenworth, Admission Summary.

13 Federal Bureau of Investigation Files/Report 76-4175, 1939, Arthur Barker.

14 Ibid.

15 Ibid.

16 Ibid.

17 Ibid.

18 Madigan and Miller, *Alcatraz: Rules, Regulations and a Brief History*, 15–22; Federal Bureau of Investigation Files/Report 76-4175, 1939, Arthur Barker.

19 Karpis and Trent, *Alvin Karpis Story*, 251–53; Madigan and Miller, *Alcatraz: Rules, Regulations and a Brief History*, 15–22.

20 Karpis and Trent, *Alvin Karpis Story*, 251–53; Livesay, *On the Rock: Twenty-Five Years in Alcatraz*, 35–37.

21 Federal Bureau of Investigation Files/Report 76-4175, 1939, Arthur Barker.

22 Ibid.

23 Ibid.

24 Ibid.

25 Ibid.

26 *Hammond Times*, December 16, 1937.

27 Federal Bureau of Investigation Files/Report 76-4175, 1939, Arthur Barker.

28 Ibid.

29 Ibid.

30 Ibid.

31 Ibid.

32 *Valley Morning Star*, January 14, 1939; Federal Bureau of Investigation Files/Report 76-4175 Arthur Barker 1939.

33 Federal Bureau of Investigation Files/Report 62-43010, May 1936 Alvin Francis Karpis.

34 Federal Bureau of Investigation Files/Report 76-4175, 1939, Arthur Barker.

35 Ibid.

36 Ibid.

37 *Master Detective*, May 1935; Federal Bureau of Investigation Files/Report 76-4175, 1939, Arthur Barker.

Chapter Twelve: End of an Era

1 Federal Bureau of Investigation Files/Report 76-4175, 1939, Arthur Barker.

2 Ibid.

3 Ibid.

4 Ibid.

5 Ibid.

6 *San Francisco News*, January 14, 1939.

7 *Greenville Evening Banner*, June 3, 1935; *Austin Daily News*, December 17, 1964.

8 *Bismarck Tribune*, April 19, 1935.

9 *Somerset Daily American*, March 29, 1951.

10 Newton, *Encyclopedia of Robberies, Heists, and Capers*, 258–59.

11 *Butte Montana Standard*, January 10, 1935.

12 Newton, *Encyclopedia of Robberies, Heists, and Capers*, 258–59.

13 *Toledo News Bee*, May 8, 1936.

14 *Moorhead Daily News*, July 9, 1936; *Bismarck Tribune*, April 1, 1935.

15 *Salina Journal*, August 29, 1979; United States Penitentiary, Conduct Report, Alcatraz, California, Re: Alvin Karpis No. 325-AZ.

16 *News Journal*, May 6, 1965.

17 *Emporia Gazette*, January 3, 1939.

18 *Anniston Star*, January 5, 1936; *Southwest Times*, June 9, 1937.

19 *Startling Detective Adventures*, October 1936.

20 *Master Detective*, May 1935.

21 Koblas, *"Ma,"* 420; *Master Detective*, May 1935.

22 *Joplin Globe*, June 24, 1982.

23 Ibid.

24 Ibid.

BIBLIOGRAPHY

General Sources

Fleury, John. *Public Enemy #1: The Biography of Alvin Karpis—America's First Public Enemy.* New York: Absolute Crime Books, 2013.

Karpis, Alvin, and Bill Trent. *The Alvin Karpis Story.* New York: Ishi Press, 1971.

Koblas, John. *"Ma": The Life and Times of Ma Barker and Her Boys.* St. Cloud, MN: North Star of St. Cloud, 2008.

Kunz, Virginia. *St. Paul: Saga of an American City.* Staunton, VA: American Historical Press, 1980.

Lamme, Vernon. *Florida Lore Not Found in History Books.* Port St. Joe, FL: Star Publishing, 1978.

Livesay, Robert. *On the Rock: Twenty-Five Years in Alcatraz: The Prison Story of Alvin Karpis.* Rev. special ed. Oakville, ON: Little Brick Schoolhouse Publishing, 2008.

Lynch, Larry, and John Russell. *Where the Wild Rice Grows: A Sesquicentennial Portrait of Menomie.* Menomie: Wisconsin Menomie Sesquicentennial Commission, 1996.

Maccabee, Paul. *John Dillinger Slept Here: A Crooks' Tour of Crime and Corruption in St. Paul 1920–1936.* St. Paul: Minnesota Historical Society Press, 1995.

Madigan, Paul J., and E. J. Miller. *Alcatraz: Rules, Regulations and a Brief History.* Longboat Key, FL: Ocean View Publishing, 2008.

Mahoney, Tim. *Secret Partners: Big Tom and the Barker Gang.* St. Paul: Minnesota Historical Press, 2013.

McCord, Monty. *The 1931 Hastings Bank Job and the Bloody Bandit Trail,* South Carolina: The History Press, 2013.

McIver, Stuart B. *Touched by the Sun. Vol. 3 of Florida Chronicles,* Sarasota, FL: Pineapple Press, 2008.

Morton, James. *The Mammoth Book of Gangs: The Fascinating Inside Story of Over 30 Notorious Gangs.* London: Running Press, 2012.

Newton, Michael. *The Encyclopedia of Robberies, Heists, and Capers.* New York: Checkmark Books, 2002.

Poulsen, Ellen. *Don't Call Us Molls: Women of the John Dillinger Gang.* Little Neck, NY: Clinton Cook Publishing, 2002.

Quimby, Myron. *The Devil's Emissaries.* Brooklyn, NY: A. S. Barnes Publishing, 1969.

Sifakis, Carl. *The Mafia Encyclopedia: From Accardo to Zwillman.* New York: Checkmark Books, 2005.

Skousen, Cleon. *True Stories from the Files of the FBI.* Salt Lake City, UT: Izzard Ink, 2014.

Swierczynski, Duane. *The Encyclopedia of the FBI's Ten Most Wanted List: Convicts, Robbers, Terrorists and Other Rogues.* New York: Skyhorse Publishing, 2014.

Taylor, Troy. *American Hauntings: The Roadside Guide to American Hauntings.* Cambridge, MA: Whitechapel Press, 2004.

Trekell, Ronald. *History of Tulsa Police Department 1882–1990.* Tulsa, OK: The Department, 1989.

Weiner, Tim. *Enemies: A History of the FBI.* New York: Random House, 2013.

Winter, Robert. *Mean Men: The Sons of Ma Barker.* Danbury, CT: Rutledge Books, 2000.

Newspapers

Abilene Morning News, Abilene, Kansas, October 3, 1935.

Ada Evening News, Ada, Oklahoma, August 26, 1921; January 16, 1923; July 13, 1924; December 12, 1925; December 21, 1925; and May 26, 1927.

Albert Lea Evening Tribune, Albert Lea, Minnesota, June 17, 1933, and January 19, 1934.

Albuquerque Journal, Albuquerque, New Mexico, August 23, 1927.

Alton Evening Telegram, Alton, Illinois, July 16, 1936.

Amarillo Daily News, Amarillo, Texas, April 1, 1927, and May 7, 1927.

Amarillo Globe-Times, Amarillo, Texas, June 19, 1959.

Ames Daily Tribune-Times, Ames, Iowa, January 22, 1934, and April 19, 1935.

Anaconda Standard, Anaconda, Montana, August 10, 1927, and October 24, 1927.

Anniston Star, Anniston, Alabama, January 5, 1936.

Appleton Post-Crescent, Appleton, Wisconsin, December 19, 1932.

Atlanta Georgian, Atlanta, Georgia, January 17, 1935.

Austin Daily News, Austin, Minnesota, December 17, 1964.

Belleville Telescope, Belleville, Kansas, April 6, 1933.

Belvidere Daily Republican, Belvidere, Illinois, January 9, 1935.

Berkeley Daily Gazette, Berkeley, California, February 8, 1934.

Biddeford Daily Journal, Biddeford, Massachusetts, May 4, 1937.

Billings Gazette, Billings, Montana, September 1, 1927, and October 5, 1929.

Bismarck Tribune, Bismarck, North Dakota, September 30, 1932; October 1, 1932; April 1, 1935; April 19, 1935; and April 26, 1935.

Bradford Era, Bradford, Pennsylvania, January 17, 1935.

Brainerd Daily Dispatch, Brainerd, Minnesota, November 8, 1920; June 27, 1932; and July 31, 1933.

Brownsville Herald, Brownsville, Texas, February 8, 1934.

Butte Montana Standard, Butte, Montana, January 10, 1935, and April 5, 1949.

Call-Leader, Elwood, Indiana, August 12, 1933.

Charleston Daily Mail, Charleston, West Virginia, March 22, 1949.

Chicago Tribune, Chicago, Illinois, October 20, 1935.

Chillicothe Constitution-Tribune, Chillicothe, Missouri, October 24, 1927; December 19, 1932; and August 14, 1936.

Current Local, Van Buren, Missouri, May 5, 1932.

Daily Ardmoreite, Ardmore, Oklahoma, January 16, 1922; September 7, 1922; September 22, 1922; and July 13, 1924.

Daily Capital Journal, Salem, Oregon, January 17, 1935.

Daily Capital News, Jefferson City, Missouri, July 28, 1936.

Daily Messenger, Canandaigua, New York, August 29, 1935, and July 13, 1936.
Daily Times, New Philadelphia, Ohio, June 13, 1933, and June 19, 1933.
Dallas Morning News, Dallas, Texas, January 17, 1935.
Dayton Daily News, Dayton, Ohio, July 21, 1935.
Decatur Herald, Decatur, Illinois, June 20, 1933, and June 30, 1933.
Denton Record-Chronicle, Denton, Texas, February 1, 1935.
Denver Post, Denver, Colorado, January 16, 1935; January 17, 1935; and
    September 18, 1935.
Dothan Eagle, Dothan, Alabama, January 8, 1935.
El Paso Herald, El Paso, Texas, January 23, 1934.
Emporia Gazette, Emporia, Kansas, August 29, 1927, and January 3, 1939.
Evening Huronite, Huron, South Dakota, September 30, 1932.
Evening Independent, Massillon, Ohio, June 19, 1933.
Evening News, Harrisburg, Pennsylvania, July 11, 1936.
Evening Star, Washington, DC, March 22, 1949.
Evening Tribune, Albert Lea, Minnesota, January 25, 1936.
Fayetteville Daily Democrat, Fayetteville, Arkansas, April 1, 1927.
Florida Times Union, Jacksonville, Florida, January 17, 1935.
Fort Scott Daily Monitor, Fort Scott, Kansas, July 16, 1921, and July 22, 1921.
Fort Scott Daily Times, Fort Scott, Kansas, July 16, 1921, and July 22, 1921.
Franklin Evening Star, Franklin, Indiana, March 16, 1936.
Gettysburg Times, Gettysburg, Pennsylvania, November 29, 1933, and March 22, 1934.
Greenfield Daily Reporter, Greenfield, Indiana, May 15, 1935.
Greenville Evening Banner, Greenville, Texas, June 3, 1935.
Hammond Times, Munster, Indiana, December 16, 1937.
Harrisonburg Daily News, Harrisonburg, Virginia, January 23, 1934.
Havre Daily News-Promoter, Havre, Montana, September 30, 1937.
Helena Daily Independent, Helena, Montana, August 4, 1927.
Helena Independent Record, Helena, Montana, January 22, 1939.
Hope Star, Hope, Arkansas, June 17, 1933.
Hutchinson News, Hutchinson, Kansas, April 4, 1933 and August 14, 1938.
Independent Record, Helena, Montana, February 10, 1935.
Index-Journal, Greenwood, South Carolina, December 8, 1927.
Ironwood Daily Globe, Ironwood, Michigan, September 13, 1933; February 7, 1935;
    April 22, 1935; and July 18, 1936.
Jacksonville Daily Journal, Jacksonville, Illinois, May 26, 1935.
Jefferson City Post-Tribune, Jefferson City, Missouri, July 18, 1932.
Joplin Globe, Joplin, Missouri, November 16, 1915; July 7, 1921; January 13, 1922;
    April 6, 1923; January 20, 1924; January 18, 1927; January 19, 1927; January 22,
    1927; April 29, 1927; August 30, 1927; September 27, 1927; December 22, 1931;
    December 18, 1932; July 9, 1933; January 3, 1935; December 7, 1935; May 2, 1936;
    October 13, 1938; March 8, 1939; July 22, 1939; March 22, 1949; and June 24, 1982.
Joplin News Herald, Joplin, Missouri, January 13, 1922; January 17, 1922; and
    October 1, 1935.

Kane Republican, Kane, Pennsylvania, May 11, 1935.
Kansas City Kansan, Kansas City, Kansas, August 7, 1922.
Kansas City Star, Kansas City, Missouri, March 29, 1936.
Kingston Daily, Freeman Kingston, New York, May 5, 1965.
Leavenworth Times, Leavenworth, Kansas, April 15, 1920.
Lincoln Evening Journal, Lincoln, Nebraska, September 27, 1927, and
    December 17, 1932.
Lincoln Star, Lincoln, Nebraska, October 9, 1927; April 5, 1933; and May 8, 1933.
Logansport Pharos-Tribune, Logansport, Indiana, September 22, 1933; February 8, 1935;
    and January 13, 1939.
Macon Chronicle-Herald, Macon, Missouri, January 14, 1932, and December 22, 1932.
Manitowoc Herald-Times, Manitowoc, Wisconsin, April 20, 1931, and June 23, 1932.
Mankato Free Press, Mankato, Minnesota, December 22, 1932.
Marion Star, Marion, Ohio, March 11, 1916.
Marshall Evening Chronicle, Marshall, Michigan, April 18, 1935.
Marysville Daily Forum, Marysville, Missouri, December 21, 1931.
Miami Daily News-Record, Miami, Oklahoma, September 26, 1929; January 27, 1927;
    April 12, 1927; March 24, 1930; January 18, 1935; October 3, 1935; and
    July 14, 1936.
Miami News-Record, Miami, Oklahoma, January 27, 1927.
Moberly Monitor-Index, Moberly, Missouri, January 17, 1935, and January 21, 1935.
Monroe News-Star, Monroe, Louisiana, September 11, 1933.
Moorhead Daily News, Moorhead, Minnesota, July 22, 1932; June 27, 1933; June 1, 1934;
    May 1, 1934; and July 9, 1936.
Morning Avalanche, Lubbock, Texas, December 29, 1939.
Morning Tulsa Daily World, Tulsa, Oklahoma, December 6, 1921, and September 7, 1922.
Murphysboro Daily Independent, Murphysboro, Illinois, January 23, 1934.
Muscatine Journal and News Tribune, Muscatine, Iowa, May 13, 1935, and May 17, 1935.
Muskogee Times-Democrat, Muskogee, Oklahoma, January 20, 1921, and September 28,
    1922.
New York Times, New York, New York, January 17, 1935.
News, Frederick, Maryland, December 1, 1933, and September 24, 1934.
News, Russellville, Indiana, December 12, 1934.
News Journal, Mansfield, Ohio, May 6, 1965.
North Adams Transcript, North Adams, Massachusetts, February 14, 1935.
Ogden Standard-Examiner, Ogden, Utah, November 21, 1927.
Oregon Statesman, Salem, Oregon, June 17, 1933.
Oshkosh Daily Northwestern, Oshkosh, Wisconsin, June 17, 1933; July 26, 1933; and
    May 2, 1936.
Pioneer Press, St. Paul, Minnesota, January 20, 1934; January 23, 1934; and August 6, 1972.
Pottstown Mercury, Pottstown, Pennsylvania, May 18, 1935, and August 21, 1935.
Pulaski Southwest Times, Pulaski, Virginia, October 14, 1935.
Quanah Tribune Chief, St. Quanah, Texas, March 23, 1923.
Racine Journal-Times, Racine, Wisconsin, May 2, 1936.

Reading Times, Reading, Pennsylvania, January 17, 1935, and July 13, 1936.

Register, Sandusky, Ohio, May 16, 1935.

Reno Evening Gazette, Reno, Nevada, April 24, 1920; September 23, 1920; and May 2, 1935.

Richland County Farmer Globe, Wahpeton, North Dakota, October 7, 1932.

Salina Journal, Salina, Kansas, August 29, 1979.

Salt Lake Tribune, Salt Lake, Utah, December 17, 1932; September 11, 1933; June 30, 1935; August 6, 1936; and August 7, 1936.

Sandusky Register, Sandusky, Ohio, May 10, 1933; January 22, 1935; and January 22, 1936.

San Antonio Light, San Antonio, Texas, May 8, 1934; February 12, 1938; and May 8, 1938.

San Bernardino Country, San Bernardino, California, May 2, 1936, and August 29, 1979.

San Francisco Chronicle, San Francisco, California, January 18, 1939.

San Francisco News, San Francisco, California, January 14, 1939.

Saturday Spectator, Terre Haute, Indiana, February 18, 1920.

Sedalia Capital, Sedalia, Missouri, September 20, 1927.

Sedalia Democrat, Sedalia, Missouri, January 18, 1935, and March 23, 1949.

Sequoyah County Democrat, Sallisaw, Oklahoma, January 21, 1927.

Shamokin News-Dispatch, Shamokin, Pennsylvania, June 17, 1933.

Sikeston Standard, Sikeston, Missouri, October 1, 1935.

Somerset Daily American, Somerset, Pennsylvania, March 29, 1951.

Southwest Times, Pulaski, Virginia, October 14, 1935, and June 9, 1937.

Springfield Daily News, Springfield, Massachusetts, January 17, 1935, and January 18, 1935.

Springfield Leader, Springfield, Missouri, January 26, 1927; January 16, 1935; and January 17, 1935.

Springfield Missouri Republican, Springfield, Missouri, August 9, 1916; August 13, 1916; and August 22, 1916.

Sunday World Herald, Omaha, Nebraska, March 3, 1969.

Taylor Daily Press, Taylor, Texas, October 14, 1923, and October 28, 1925.

Toledo News Bee, Toledo, Ohio, May 8, 1936.

Tribune-Republican, Greeley, Colorado, October 7, 1927.

Tulsa Daily News, Tulsa, Oklahoma, January 13, 1922.

Tulsa Daily World, Tulsa, Oklahoma, December 28, 1922.

Tulsa Tribune, Tulsa, Oklahoma, March 22, 1949.

Valley Morning Star, Harlingen, Texas, January 14, 1939.

Waco News-Tribune, Waco, Texas, March 23, 1934.

Washington Star, Washington, DC, January 25, 1939.

West Plains Daily Quill, West Plains, Missouri, December 19, 1931.

Magazines/Newsletters

Edge, Chicago, Illinois, July 25, 1965.

Gambling, St. Paul, Minnesota, November 1999.

Lawrence County Historical Society Bulletin, Lawrence County, Arkansas, #120, July 1991.

Master Detective, New York, New York, Vol. 12, No. 3, May 1935.
Minnesota Police Journal, St. Paul, Minnesota, August 1991.
Pageant, Chicago, Illinois, Vol. 14, No. 19, December 1959.
Startling Detective Adventure, Peoria, Illinois, August 1939 and October 1936.
Time, New York, New York, October 29, 1934.

Legal Documents/Department of Justice Correspondence
Coroner Inquest, Re: Arthur Barker, by Coroner Thos. B. W. Leland, MD. Coroner,
    January 24, 1939.
Division of Investigations/FBI Files #7-30 January 20, 1934.
Federal Bureau of Investigation Files/Report DN-62-89785, April 15, 1949, Lloyd
    Barker (Death Of).
Federal Bureau of Investigation Files/Report DN-62-723, May 12, 1949, Lloyd Barker
    aka "Red" Research.
Federal Bureau of Investigation Files/Report I. C. #7-576-3775 January 19, 1935,
    Barker-Karpis Gang.
Federal Bureau of Investigation Files/Report RCS: TD I.C. #7-576, 1935–36, The
    Kidnapping of Edward George Bremer.
Federal Bureau of Investigation Files/Report RCS: TD I.C. #7-576, 1935–36, Barker-
    Karpis Gang.
Federal Bureau of Investigation Files/Report 62-43010, May 1936, Alvin Francis Karpis.
Federal Bureau of Investigation Files/Report 76-4175, 1939, Arthur Barker.
Federal Bureau of Investigation, Freedom of Information Privacy Acts, Subject: Herman
    Barker (Death of), File #26-9961.
Jasper County Records, Inventory and Appraisement Documents, October 10, 1935.
Lansing Prisoner Files, Lansing, Kansas, Inmate Fred Barker.
Memorandum to the Warden of Alcatraz Re: Arthur Barker, 268-AZ January 24, 1939.
Oklahoma Law Report, Volume 36-10, Supreme Court of Oklahoma McGhee vs.
    Atterberry No. 2055 November 7, 1912.
St. Paul, Minnesota, History and Early Association of the Karpis-Barker Gang Prior to
    the Abduction of Mr. Bremer.
State of Minnesota, Bureau of Criminal Apprehension Arrest Record/Intake Form for
    Fred Barker.
State of Minnesota, Bureau of Criminal Apprehension Investigation Record/Homicide
    Report for George E. Anderson/Dunlop.
State of Missouri, County of Jasper Inventory and Appraisement Documents in the
    Matter of the Estate of Arizona Barker, October 10, 1935.
State of Missouri, County of Jasper Probate Court Documents in the Matter of the
    Estate of Arizona Barker, December 28, 1935.
United States Government Memorandum, Lloyd Barker-Research/Crime Records,
    September 11, 1957.
United States Penitentiary, Conduct Report, Alcatraz, California, Re: Alvin Karpis No.
    325-AZ.
US Department of Justice, Arthur Barker Arrest Record #37343, March 4, 1935.

US Department of Justice, Letter to Special FBI Agent N. J. L. Pieper Re: Arthur E. Barker, January 20, 1939.
US Penitentiary Leavenworth, Kansas, Admission Summary #46928, Arthur Barker.

Websites

"Arizona Donnie 'Kate' Clark," www.ancestry.com.
"Arthur W. Dunlop," www.ancestry.com.
"Dead in Necropolis: Arthur 'Doc' Barker," *What's on the 6th Floor?* (blog), http://sfhcbasc.blogspot.com/2009/10/dead-in-necropolis-arthur-doc-barker.html.
"'Doc' on the Rock: Ripples from the Fall of Arthur Barker," by Joel GAzis-Sax, Tales from Colma, www.notfrisco.com/colmatales/barker.
"The FBI and the American Gangster, 1924–1938," www.fbi.gov/history.
"FBI-Latent Prints in the 1933 Hamm Kidnapping," www.fbi.gov/news/stories/2003/september/hamm090803.
"FBI Shooting of Fred & Kate Baker," Faded Glory: Dusty Roads of an FBI Era, http://historicalgmen.squarespace.com.
"The First National of Fairbury Gets Hit," *Home Brewed Mojo* (blog), http://homebrewedmojo.blogspot.com.
"George Barker," www.geni.com/people/GeorgeBarker.
"George Ellis Barker," www.ancestry.com.
"Herbert Allen Farmer," www.ancestry.com.
"The History of the FBI and J. Edgar Hoover," www.fbi.gov/history.
J. Edgar Hoover: A Primer—The Morning Delivery, www.wplucey.com/2011/11/j-edgar-hoover.
"Jenny Barker," www.ancestry.com.
"John William Farley," www.geneology.com/ftm/f/a/r/John-William-Farley.
"The Last Great Outlaw Gang," *American Hauntings* (blog), www.troytaylorbooks.blogspot.com.
"Lloyd Barker," www.ancestry.com
National Archives—Pretty Boy Floyd, John Dillinger, https://archives.gov/details/universal_newsreels/gangsters.
"Out of the Past: Tattoo Helped Lead to Barker Gang's Capture," *Panama City News Herald*, www.newsherald.com.
The Records and Legend of Ma Barker Shootout, George Albright Marion County Tax Collector website, www.mariontax.com.
The Streets of Saint Paul, www.streetsofsaintpaul.com.
"The Third Northwestern Bank Robbery in Minneapolis," Most Notorious! www.mostnotorious.com.
"Town Where Ma Barker Died Sure That Alligator Did Her In," *Chicago Tribune* https://articles.chicagotribune.com/1986-10-19.
Wynona Burdette and the FBI File: Barker-Karpis Gang, www.angelfire.com/mo3/mullenfamily/wynona2.html.

INDEX

About the Authors

Howard Kazanjian is an author and award-winning producer and entertainment executive who has been producing feature films and television programs for more than twenty-five years. While vice president of production for Lucasfilm Ltd., he produced two of the highest-grossing films of all time: *Raiders of the Lost Ark* and *Star Wars: Return of the Jedi.* He also managed production of another top-ten box office hit, *The Empire Strikes Back.* Some of his other notable credits include *The Rookies, Demolition Man,* and the two-hour pilot and first season of *JAG.*

Chris Enss is a *New York Times* best-selling author who has been writing about women of the Old West for more than a dozen years. She has penned more than thirty published books on the subject. Her book titled *Object Matrimony: The Risky Business of Mail-Order Matchmaking on the Western Frontier* won the Elmer Kelton Award for best nonfiction book of 2013. Enss's book *Sam Sixkiller: Cherokee Frontier Lawman* was named Outstanding Book on Oklahoma History by the Oklahoma Historical Society. She received the Spirit of the West Alive award, cosponsored by the *Wild West Gazette*, celebrating her efforts to keep the spirit of the Old West alive for future generations.